THE CITIES

A Methodist Report

The Methodist Church and
NCH Action For Children

NCH Action For Children
85 Highbury Park
London N5 IUD

Tel: 0171-226 2033
Fax: 0171-226 2537

The Cities. A Methodist Report
© NCH Action For Children 1997
Published by NCH Action For Children

ISBN 0 900984 56 2

20027587

Design: Michael Kaufmann
Cover Design: Maria Bengtsson
Produced by: NCH Action For Children
Printed by: Chapel Press

PREFACE

Membership of the Working Group

Joint chairs

Rev. Dr. John Vincent   Urban Theology Unit

Ms. Helen Dent   NCH Action For Children

Members

Ms. Caroline Abrahams   NCH Action For Children

Rev. Inderjit Bhogal   Urban Theology Unit

Mr. Paul Goggins   Church Action on Poverty

Mrs. Elizabeth Hartley   Methodist Division of Social Responsibility

Rev. Tony Holden   Urban Officer, Methodist Church

Rev. John Kennedy   Public Issues, Methodist Church

Rev. Garth Rogers   London Mission Committee, Methodist Church

Ms. Clare Sparks   NCH Action For Children

The Working Group presents what follows as its unanimous findings. We met together for fourteen day-long meetings between July 1995 and September 1996. Until July 1996 the Group was serviced by Clare Sparks as Researcher, Administrator and Writer. The final version of our Report was edited and written by Caroline Abrahams, except Part 1, Section 7 on Methodism which was written by Tony Holden and Part 6, Theological reflections on city life, which was produced by John Kennedy. John Vincent contributed substantially to all aspects of the Report. We do however, accept responsibility for it, together.

CONTENTS

CONTENTS

CONTENTS

INTRODUCTION

This is the Report of the Methodist Working Group on the Cities. The Working Group was established by the Methodist Conference in 1995, under Terms of Reference set out in Appendix 1. The four bodies involved in this project were the Home Mission and the Social Responsibility Divisions of the Methodist Church; NCH Action For Children, the child care arm of the Methodist Church; and the Urban Theology Unit. In addition, the Director of Church Action on Poverty, Paul Goggins, was an active member of this group.

Methodism has a long-established and continuing presence in our cities. The members of the Working Group brought with them a wide range of experience of ministering and living within our cities. NCH Action For Children, one of Britain's largest childcare charities, was established by a Methodist Minister, the Reverend Thomas Stephenson in 1869, in order to provide shelter and care to destitute children in London. It now runs many community-based projects in cities across Britain, most aimed at supporting children at risk and in need and their families. Some of these projects work with vulnerable young people – today's counterparts of the first homeless children who benefited from the charity's services. NCH Action For Children remains accountable to Methodist Conference. The Urban Theology Unit is an ecumenical educational charity, founded in 1969 to train and support urban community workers and ministers. It has a particularly strong relationship with Methodism through the founder, the Reverend Dr. John Vincent, who was joint Chair of the Working Group.

The Report is about the cities of Britain today. More specifically, it is about:
- the views and concerns of the ordinary people who live and work in our cities;
- the problems currently facing many of our cities;
- how these challenges may be best met and the quality of city life enhanced for everyone;

- the role which ought to be played in this process by individuals (be they Methodist, of other faiths or none); the Methodist Church and the State; and the principles which should underpin their action.

The Working Group members have no pretensions of expertise on urban policy. This Report does not purport to provide a definitive analysis of urban problems and their solutions, and is not aimed at academics. The Working Group does however, intend that it should be a useful contribution to a debate in which policy makers and academics are taking part, as well as the wider public. The Report is primarily written for the many ordinary people in Britain who are interested and concerned about our cities. The Report aims to reflect the complexities and paradoxes of city life, and to acknowledge the pleasures as well as the problems. The Working Group hopes to encourage everyone to feel part of the whole city, wherever they happen to live or work within its boundaries.

This Report now takes its place within a tradition firmly established by *Faith in the City* which was produced by the Archbishop of Canterbury's Commission on Urban Priority Areas, in 1985. That very important book focused national attention on the condition of Britain's urban priority areas, and proposed recommendations for the Church of England and the Nation. Many Church initiatives resulted, perhaps the best known of which was the creation of the Church Urban Fund, which has helped the Church of England to strengthen its presence in many of the most disadvantaged areas of our cities, sometimes with ecumenical co-operation. Last year, the same Group produced *Staying in the City*, which evaluated progress ten years on.

One of the major achievements of *Faith in the City*, as *Staying in the City* rightly points out, is that over the intervening ten years since its publication there has been a growing consensus concerning the twin themes put forward in the book, namely:

1 the need for an integrated approach to the problems of multiple deprivation;
2 the need in seeking solutions to listen to the voices of the local community.[1]

Ten years later, we are all acutely aware of the challenges faced by local and central Government, business, the Church and the voluntary sector in trying to put these principles into practical effect. In addition, our Report emphasises the dynamic context within which our cities are continuing to change.

The Working Party did its work within a period of about twelve months. This inevitably imposed very tight constraints on what we were able to achieve. We are extremely grateful for all the help and support received from very many people, within the Methodist Church and beyond, throughout the country.

A survey of views of city dwellers about city life was one of the main foundations of this Report. The Working Group would especially like to thank the more than one thousand people who completed a questionnaire, and the hundreds of Methodist ministers who helped with the task of organising the survey. As part of the process of developing this Report the Working Group also convened Consultation meetings in four cities: Newcastle, Cardiff, Glasgow and Salford. These events generated a great deal of invaluable material which has been incorporated into this Report, and the Group is particularly grateful to the people in these cities who organised and attended the meetings. A number of individuals and groups submitted written material for the Working Group to consider, and/or commented on drafts. We are very grateful for their contributions, which have also helped to shape the Group's thinking. The Report is further informed by a debate which took place at the Methodist Conference in June 1996. However, the Working Party must take final responsibility for the Report's content.

The Structure of this Report is as follows:

Part One is introductory and sets the context against in which our cities currently exist, including an overview of the role which Methodism has played in city life.

Part Two investigates what ordinary people think about living in our cities now, based on the findings from a national survey carried out as part of this project.

Part Three looks in greater detail at some of the most serious problems facing our cities today, drawing especially on what was learned from the consultation meetings in Newcastle, Cardiff and Glasgow.

Part Four is a largely descriptive case study of city regeneration in action, based on the experience of the city of Salford.

Part Five, drawing on all this evidence, examines where the future may lie for our cities; focusing on the necessity of balancing the imperative of encouraging wealth creation alongside the pursuit of broader social objectives embracing all city dwellers.

Part Six makes some theological reflections on our cities, drawn both from the Christian theological tradition and from the experience of Christians living and working in our cities today.

Part Seven makes recommendations for future action.

Part 1

THE CONTEXT IN WHICH OUR CITIES EXIST

1. The idea of 'the city'

This Report is about life in our cities, but the first challenge facing the Working Group was to decide which issues to include and which to omit. Many of the forces which impact on city life are part of the wider picture of life in Britain, such as the relative strength or weakness of the British economy. Part of the task in writing this Report has therefore been to try to distil the features which are distinctive about life in the city.

A further difficulty is that city life is quite clearly a product of the interrelationship of many forces. For example, in disadvantaged city areas the inhabitants often suffer from the impact of a combination of adverse factors: the lack of employment leads to poverty; this may force local businesses to move away in pursuit of economic survival and the more mobile residents to depart in search of better job prospects and improved quality of life; empty shops and homes become dilapidated and an invitation to vandalism; as the quality of the built environment decays incomers are further discouraged, and community vitality and self-esteem erodes. All these factors therefore impact on each other, in a variety of ways. This makes analysis difficult. In this Report the Working Group has separated out some of the components which affect city life because there appeared to be no other way of approaching the task, but it has tried to do so without losing sight of the fact that life in the city is the product of the interaction of many different things.

It is also important to recognise that the cities of Britain are very different, although this is masked by the increasing homogeneity of the rows of chain store facades in city high streets. A city's characteristics result from many factors, prominent among which are its regional links and distinctive history and culture.

Compared with cities in some other parts of the world most British cities are relatively old and often have an incredibly rich and individual heritage, and this is part of their fascination. The cities of Scotland and Wales can be expected to have their own national identities which differ in some respects from those of English cities. There is also 'the London factor' to take into account. For very many centuries London has been the dominant city within Great Britain and one of the major cities in the world. Some of the reasons for this are explored below. This Report acknowledges the distinctive position occupied by London, but also notes that many of the problems facing other cities in Britain are currently being experienced in London too.

Districts within our cities vary widely in terms of appearance, racial composition and cultural feel. This internal diversity contributes to city appeal and vitality. In *The Politics* the philosopher Aristotle wrote that, "*a city is composed of different kinds of men; similar men cannot bring a city into existence.*" Similarly, cities are essentially dynamic, and are constantly changing in response to the impact of local, regional, national and increasingly, international factors.

Dynamism and cultural diversity are therefore two of the most important and welcome features of cities. Together, they often generate the 'buzz' which is so attractive to many city dwellers, perhaps especially to the younger and more affluent. However, this is one of the many paradoxes of city life. The features which make living in the city so attractive to some are equally unwelcome to others. People experience cities in very different ways. The dynamism and complexity of city life which many enjoy may make the city seem unfriendly or even threatening to those who feel left behind and unlikely to benefit from the changes. Older people and those who are vulnerable, in particular, may feel this way. Some city dwellers make a conscious choice to live in the city centre, perhaps because of the ease of access to jobs, restaurants and theatres. Others prefer to live in the less congested suburbs where there is more space – perhaps enough for a garden of reasonable size – and can't wait to escape back home after a hard day in the city centre. Some feel they really belong to their local neighbourhood and expect to stay for quite a long time; others are just passing through.

On a more abstract theme, the city has traditionally been seen as necessary for the development of a civilisation. It has been suggested that *'vigour, energy, vitality: all the great civilisations – or civilising epochs – have had a weight of energy behind them.'*[2]

If so, this may explain why cities are so important, because they alone with their large and diverse populations can generate the new ideas which carry a culture forward. Although the earliest fixed settlements are found around 2,500 BC in the fertile valleys of the Nile, the Euphrates, Tigris, Indus and Yellow rivers, notions of the city reached their early peak in the Greek city state of Athens in about the 5th century BC. What was originally an association of clans became a small self-governing community in which all eligible citizens took part. For many citizens, the city and its laws constituted a moral order which was symbolised in buildings and public assemblies. The Romans then transplanted the city into previously uncharted, 'uncivilised' areas, including Britain.

It has been suggested that British – perhaps especially English – attitudes to the city have been a mixture of admiration and loathing since Roman times, and that more recently this is linked to an English tendency to romanticise life in the country.[3] Towns and cities were places for making money, country houses were places to live in. Man made the town, God the country. In this respect English attitudes have been perceived as being quite different from those of other Europeans and of Americans. In the nineteenth century it was said that *'the best society of Philadelphia was trying to improve and glorify Philadelphia, the best society of Manchester was trying to get out of it.'*[4]

An extreme manifestation of this anti-urban feeling was the Back to the Land movement, which flourished during the fifty years before the First World War. Under its auspices, about thirty rural communities were set up by groups of disenchanted urban intellectuals. Most of these settlements were relatively short-lived. Behind the Back to the Land movement was a much broader strand of opinion which was ill at ease with modern city life, as articulated by writers such as John Ruskin and William Morris. In the inter-war and post-war period these sentiments helped influence the building of the Garden Cities. Contemporary British ambivalence towards the city is symbolised by the conception of 'the Village in the City', and by the existence of glossy magazines like *Country Living*, the highest sales of which are in towns and cities.

Today, our larger cities in particular offer endless 'lifestyle choices' and leisure pursuits for those who are able to afford them. Part of the attractiveness of city life for some is the relative anonymity of living within such a large population. No one need feel that they do not fit in, that they are not catered for, that they are an oddity. People can come to the city and reinvent themselves, if that is what they want to do.

In contrast, there is a significant minority within most city populations who have very few if any choices and who are effectively excluded from enjoying most of the good things which cities offer. Some of these city dwellers are literally cut off from city facilities, particularly those who live on peripheral estates lacking sufficient public transport. Others are physically much nearer the centre of things but appear just as marginalised. This is the case for people living in disadvantaged inner city areas. One of the most damaging features of poverty is that it prevents people from taking a full part in the activities which other citizens take for granted. Poverty has been defined as a situation where resources are so seriously below those commanded by the average individual or family that the poor are, in effect, excluded from ordinary living patterns and customs.[5]

Research shows that socially excluded people within cities tend to be found in particularly disadvantaged localities and that poverty within cities is 'spatially distributed'[6]. It is also clear that certain groups within the population are over represented within these areas, including lone parents, the old and very old, economically marginalised young people, the long-term unemployed and the 'prematurely retired'.[7] Black people and those from other minority ethnic groups are also concentrated in disadvantaged city areas. For these city dwellers, the experience of racism often compounds the problem of social exclusion. Similarly, research clearly shows the increasing inequality within Britain in recent years, so that the gap between those who are socially excluded and the rest of the population has grown.[8]

The phenomenon of social exclusion does not only affect the cities but it is almost certainly at its most visible here, with the proliferation of pawnbrokers and charity shops, and the now far from uncommon sight of young people begging. Research also demonstrates that the most socially excluded areas of Britain are certain particularly disadvantaged city neighbourhoods.[9] The depth of the problems faced by these localities and the challenge this poses to policy makers are examined in much more detail later in the Report.

2. What makes a city a city?

Perhaps surprisingly, there is no agreed national definition of what makes a city a city, although most people probably think they know what a city is. Possible criteria include population density, land use and political and administrative arrangements. In England a city is often still viewed as an urban area with a cathedral. However, this ceased to be the official definition at the end of the nineteenth century, on the basis that otherwise there would be anomalous cities such as Wells and Ely, with populations of no more than about 10,000 each. Cities are therefore generally regarded as major population areas. In this sense the 'City of London' is an anomalous term, referring as it does to a district of London in which few people actually live.

An economic definition of a city is *'a settlement that consistently generates its economic growth from its own local economy.'*[10] The City of London fits much better with this kind of city definition. A conurbation (or 'Metropolitan area' in the United States) is a city which has physically expanded beyond its formal boundaries, the process engulfing former towns, and in some instances coalescing with other, formerly separate cities.

Today a city is created by Royal Charter or letter patent. Sunderland is the most recent addition to the list of British cities. It was declared a city in 1992, when it outbid 20 other competitors to become a city, to celebrate the 40th anniversary of the Queen's accession to the throne.

For the purposes of this Report, the Working Group decided to take a fairly pragmatic approach to the issue of city definition. The Report seeks to discuss the concerns of major urban populations, based particularly on the findings of a survey of Methodists living in cities, using the Methodist Church definition of a city; and on the content of the Consultation Meetings held in Newcastle, Cardiff, Glasgow and Salford.

3. Why do cities come into existence and grow?

The necessary condition for urban development is an agricultural surplus. If this exists then a town or city may develop for other reasons, for example, economies of scale of production, the uneven distribution of resources (eg. the 'Gold Rush' cities of the Western United States), or the needs of government (eg. Brasilia and Washington DC).

Although economics are the most important force behind the rise of cities other factors also often play a role, especially in explaining why towns grow at particular times and in specific places, eventually to become cities. These factors include security considerations (the greater safety which comes from clustering together), and the nature of existing political and social arrangements.

Economies of scale are the major economic reason for the growth of towns into cities, especially external economies of scale. The grouping together of firms allows them to use common services and suppliers, to create a market and to share the costs of training. Economies of scale are especially pronounced in large, diversified cities. In major cities, the various reasons for urban location and growth tend to be self-reinforcing. For example, a favourable site in terms of trade tends to generate wealth and encourage population growth, which in turn stimulates more trade.

The interaction of these principles lies behind the historical development of cities in Britain.

4. A brief history of British cities

The Romans occupied Britain in the first century BC and superimposed on the existing Celtic tribal structure their own model of urbanisation. Some of their towns may have been quite large: Roman London is estimated to have had a population of about 50,000. By the end of the third century some towns had regular street plans (eg. Exeter) while others had piped water (eg. Bath). However, it has been suggested that few Romano-British towns were characterised by vigorous commercial activity; most were simply centres of regional administration or garrison towns.[11] London was the exception. Its development and importance were due to its unusually favourable geographical position at the estuary of the River Thames, and on the shortest lines of communication between southern England and the continent. London became the administrative focus for the entire country.

After the Romans left Britain in 410 AD most of the towns declined and some disappeared altogether. Some urban life was handed down to the Anglo-Saxons from the Romano-British era but until the last century of Anglo-Saxon rule the towns were few and their role in economic life was small.

British towns really multiplied and grew between the eleventh and early thirteenth centuries. It has been suggested that their development at this time is explained by the fact that they were *'non-feudal islands in a feudal sea'*, immune from the constraints impeding trade and commerce elsewhere.[12] The medieval city reflected both the necessity of defence and the urge to profit, but over the next few hundred years greater political and military stability permitted increased concentration on wealth creation.

By the end of the 15th Century however, still only about 1 in 10 of the population lived in a town; and the only sizeable towns in England, apart from London, were Bristol, York, Coventry, Chester, Norwich and Exeter. London was by far the biggest and most important urban area, with a population of about 75,000 in 1500, surging to 225,000 by 1600.[13] London's growth as a commercial centre had been helped by the natural advantages of its site but also assisted by the location of Government at Westminster. The presence of a court and the existence of a port encouraged the growth of trades specialising in the manufacture of imported goods, particularly luxuries for the court. This in turn led to the development of banks and later of the maritime insurance market.

It has been suggested that it was at this time in London that a metropolitan elite first came into existence, based on the merchants and industrialists, reinforced by lawyers and professional men. Their new economic power was symbolised by the rise of the Livery company. However, such was the growth of London's population that the city devoured an enormous proportion of the agricultural resources of Southern England, causing local resentment, and there were growing social problems in the city. The city continued to grow, despite royal edicts in 1580 and 1593 seeking to prevent further encroachment into the surrounding countryside. Charities such as St Thomas's and St Bartholomew's (the origins of the present day hospitals) were set up in London to care for the sick. The Poor Law of 1597 gave the town councils of London, Coventry, Norwich and York, new machinery for responding to the needs of the urban poor.[14]

By the end of the 17th century the volume of trade passing through the legal quays of the Port of London accounted for nearly 80% of all British imports and exports. By 1770 this trade had doubled and by 1794 it had redoubled. The congestion was fantastic; there were often more than 1,400 ships between London Bridge and Deptford, leading to the expansion of the Docks beyond the Pool of London to St. Katherine's, West India Docks and the Isle of Dogs. Other cities also benefited from this great commercial prosperity. [15]

The arrival of free trade, the construction of large canals, and the invention of the steamship and of trains, put paid to London's shipping pre-eminence by the middle of the 19th century, because they eroded the Port of London's competitive advantages. However, these new developments led directly to the exponential growth of Britain's industrial cities, of which Manchester is perhaps the best example. The fact that town manufactures could be traded nationally and internationally encouraged increased economies of scale and the specialisation of cities in particular products, thus leading to the development of a steel city like Sheffield. A further element was that in the 19th century, while goods could be shipped long distances by sea, canal or rail, they could go short distances only slowly by horse and cart. This meant there was a considerable incentive to minimise short distance transfers, thus leading to the concentration of industry in towns and cities, particularly in ports, on the sites of the raw materials like coalfields, or at major markets like London.

When Queen Victoria ascended the throne in 1837, there were only five places in England and Wales other than London with a population of more than 100,000. By 1891 there were 23, and almost a third of the population lived in cities. Nearly a fifth of Scotland's entire population lived in Glasgow by this date, a fourfold increase over less than a century. London's population reached 5.6 million, making it the largest city in Europe. People flocked to the cities in search of work and money. However squalid and uncertain life in Victorian cities may have been, it was usually considered preferable to the miserable poverty and lack of prospects in the countryside. [16]

The rapid, largely unplanned growth of Britain's Victorian cities had profound social consequences. Gradually, as the 19th century advanced, steps were taken first to measure the social conditions within cities; and then to improve the quality of city life through, for example, sanitary reform and new house building. Urban policy and planning have their roots in this era, and were originally a response to the problems of our overcrowded Victorian cities. Conditions slowly improved, but infant mortality did not significantly fall in the cities until the early decades of the twentieth century. These reforms were spurred by several factors, including genuine philanthropy; concern about public disorder in turbulent cities, caused by the creation of 'two nations'; and the need to ensure that Britain had a reserve army of men fit enough to fight for their country.

For all their problems, Victorian cities were often the object of affection. Provincial cities nurtured a sense of loyalty through rivalry with each other and solidarity against London. They used their status as regional capitals to challenge the claims of the national capital, culturally and politically. The functions and finances of local government were reformed in response to previously endemic corruption, and the late Victorian era was a golden age for local government in the cities. Birmingham, for example, acquired the reputation of being the best governed city in the world in the 1870s and 1880s under the radical Liberalism of Joseph Chamberlain.[17]

As the 20th century has progressed, Western nations have gradually lost their previous monopoly in manufacturing, and the functions of cities in America and Europe have changed from trading goods to trading rights to goods, from shifting goods to shifting paper. While cities like Manchester and Sheffield grew through the Victorian era as centres for manufacturing wealth, the places where workforces were assembled and things were made, technological change means that it has often become economically more efficient for manufacturing to be concentrated in non-urban areas, or even in non-urban countries, where capital and human resources are cheaper than in British cities. All this has been made possible by improvements in communications and transport.

The growth of the world's major cities has progressively come to depend on the transfer of information over large distances via postal services, the telegraph, wireless and telephone, rather than on manufacturing. As transport costs reduced and with the growth of cheaper, faster road haulage, the need for proximity of manufacturing at major markets or on sites of raw materials diminished; and containerisation reduced the advantages of manufacturing at ports, thus leading to a dispersal of manufacturing away from conurbations and large cities. The transition from the industrial to the post-industrial age was made possible by progress in data processing and information transfer. For the first time industrial companies could work efficiently with plants spread over wide areas. Increasing mechanisation simplified industrial labour and made it possible to transfer technologies to developing countries.

The invention of mass transit transportation systems and the car have had an enormous impact on the physical appearance of our cities, as well as on their economic fortunes. In the early part of the 20th century the development of public transport, coupled with the availability of cheap mortgages, stimulated suburbanisation. Structural changes in the British economy led to the development of a new white-collar class, their numbers rising from 20% to 30% of the workforce between 1911 and 1951. Real wages also rose sharply for this population group and stimulated the demand for speculative building. Planning controls gradually came into force to ensure adequate standards of space and building quality. Although suburban houses were often derided by architects they were (and continue to be) very popular with many of their owners. They were also designed to express individuality through the variation of minor detail. Above all, these houses were meant to be as unlike council housing as possible.[18]

An important contribution to the urban scene in Britain in the first half of the twentieth century was the Garden City movement. The inspiration behind this was a book by Ebenezer Howard, *Garden Cities of Tomorrow*, published in 1902. In developing his ideas for decentralising industry and populations away from the congested cities, Howard drew on many influences, including the Back to the Land movement (referred to above), and pioneer industrial villages in the countryside such as Lever's Port Sunlight near Liverpool, and Cadbury's Bournville outside Birmingham.

The Garden City aimed to combine the best elements of town and country. Howard's original conception was that a group of people should establish a limited dividend company and borrow money to establish a Garden City in the countryside, far enough from the city to ensure that the land was cheap. They would persuade industrialists to relocate their factories there, and workers would move and build their own homes. The Garden City would have a fixed limit of about 32,000 people, and be surrounded in turn by its own green belt. It would be a self-sustaining and self-governing community, with its own mini-welfare state. Never was this vision to be fully realised.

In 1899 Howard set up the Garden City Association to try to put his ideas into practice, and gathered a group of like-minded people around him. In 1903, Letchworth, 34 miles from London was chosen as the site for the first Garden City. Progress in establishing a viable community there was slow however, mainly because of the reluctance of industry and workers to relocate. Other developments which began soon after were not so much Garden Cities, but Garden Suburbs, whose economies depended on commuting to the nearby city, not on local industries. They included Ealing (1906) and Hampstead (1907). Both of these owed their distinctive appearance (more open space, traffic largely 'designed out', variety of building styles but usually cottages) to the work of two architects and planners, Raymond Unwin and Barry Parker. The popular image of the Garden Suburb today owes more to their architecture than to Ebenezer Howard's original Garden City idea.

Welwyn Garden City was the second genuine Garden City (1919) and Wythenshawe arguably the third (although like many built in the inter-war years, it also had aspects of a satellite town). Wythenshawe was designed by Barry Parker in 1930 and described by him in 1945 as "now the most perfect example of a garden city."[19] It was built on land owned by the City of Manchester and financed by the local authority, not by private investors, and was only half a mile from the City's boundaries. Some of Wythenshawe's 1960s housing is less attractive but the vision of a Garden City remains, largely because of Parker's original design, with housing built around small greens and the very large open space, Wythenshawe Park, at its heart.

In 1946 the Government effectively nationalised the Garden City movement in the New Town Acts 1946, and decided that new towns should be built by public corporations, one for each town, financed directly by the Exchequer. Between then and 1950 the Labour Government designated 13 new towns, 8 of them in the London area, four of them quite close to each other in Hertfordshire. This centralist mechanism was quite controversial at the time, especially in Stevenage, and encouraged the Conservative Government, which took office in 1955, to announce a temporary moratorium on the creation of new towns. Although new towns are often regarded as a success, there has been a constant battle between the advocates of Garden Cities and those who would prefer a clearer differentiation between urban and country life.

After the Second World War, increasing car ownership encouraged suburban sprawl, especially in many cities in the United States. In Britain, this phenomenon has been checked by strict planning controls designed to sustain a 'green belt' around the city, and to mark a clear boundary between town and country. The Town and Country Planning Act of 1947 was the first major legislation of this type in Britain. A review of the effectiveness of these planning controls has concluded however, that, on the whole, affluent suburbanites have benefited the most from them, through the preservation of their comfortable lifestyle.[20] Less affluent residents in outer city areas have done much less well because of the relatively cramped space and high cost of their housing.

This review of British land use planning found however, that the people who lost out the most from the creation of the Green Belt were those left living in the inner city. People who had moved into public sector housing generally acquired good quality homes, better equipped certainly than the poorer owner-occupiers, but they were often forced to live at high densities and in high-rise blocks of flats, which many liked much less than their previous low-rise homes. The low-income private tenant, living in substandard, poorly maintained accommodation, did worst of all. The report concludes that: "*It was certainly not the intention of the founders* (of the planning system) *that people should lead cramped lives in homes destined for premature slumdom, far from urban services or jobs; or that city dwellers should live in blank cliffs of flats, far from the ground, without access to playspace for their children. Somewhere along the way a great ideal was lost, a system distorted and the great mass of the people betrayed.*"

In retrospect it seems extraordinary that anyone ever thought tower blocks were an appropriate response to the housing needs of the majority of the population, including families with children. At the end of the Second World War there was an enormous demand for housing, largely due to the destruction of many inner city areas by bombing. Most of these neighbourhoods were slums anyway, so there was an additional incentive to rebuild. Some politicians and planners always recognised that there was a general preference for private houses with gardens, but the problem was fitting everyone into the available space. If there was an overspill of housing this could not be matched by an equivalent out-movement of jobs, and the result would be localised unemployment. Moreover, the 'green belt' made indefinite outward expansion impossible.

The proportion of high-rise in the total public housing programme rose from 7% of the total in the late 1950s to 26% in the mid-1960s. The system of central government regulations and subsidies which developed at this time strongly favoured high-rise over other forms of construction. Many architects were keen to build tower blocks, in pursuance of the ideas of the Swiss architect Le Corbusier, who had envisaged a *Radiant City* of mass housing. However, Le Corbusier had designed his tower blocks for affluent people who could afford to pay for services, a world in which, it has been suggested, *"Mum isn't isolated at home with the babies, she is out shopping at Harrods. The children, when small, are taken to Kensington Gardens by Nanny. At the age of eight they go to prep school and at thirteen to public school, both residential. And during the holidays they are either away in the country or winter-sporting, sailing and so on: golden and brown in the playful wind and summer sun. At any rate they are not hanging around on the landing or playing with the dustbin lids."* [21]

It gradually became obvious that high rise flats were particularly unsuitable for families on low incomes with children, although the architectural fashion which followed, 'high density medium and low rise' also proved to be a design failure in Glasgow and on the Hulme Estate in Manchester, among other places. All too often the problem with these estates was that tenants were uprooted into *"hurriedly constructed system-built flats lacking amenities, environment, community; lacking in fact, almost anything except a roof and four walls."* [22] Some local authorities had bought estates 'off the peg', giving no thought to the planning of local services. The death knell for high rise came in 1968 when Ronan Point, a system built tower block in East London, collapsed after a gas explosion.

It is doubly unfortunate that the years during which 'high-rise' was most popular, were also those in which there was a great surge in building. Because many of the more desirable council homes have been sold under the 'Right to Buy', the result is that flats in tower blocks still comprise a significant proportion of public sector housing in most of our major cities. Many people still have no realistic choice but to live in them, including families with children. One consequence is that the architectural profession is still held in low public esteem, and there is a widespread popular distrust of modern buildings. This is despite the fact that most of the worst high-rise blocks were created without the input of architects or planners at all. The social, economic and housing problems in our cities produced by the disastrous foray into poorly planned high-rise building are part of the legacy with which urban policy makers are still grappling today.

5. Recent urban policy reviewed

As has already been noted, urban planning has its roots in the early responses of reformers to the social problems created by the rapid expansion of our Victorian cities. However, 'urban policy' is a term which only came into use in the 1960s, and which denotes the mix of policies (covering for example, transport, planning, housing and education) devised to address the perceived problems of modern cities. At this time, these problems were considered to be essentially those of the decaying inner cities.

Growing concern on the part of policy makers about the concentration of disadvantaged, ethnic minority communities within the inner city, and the resultant potential for public disorder, was one of the principal factors motivating the development of urban policy in the 1960s. It has been said that, *"Race has always been at the heart of urban policy"*, although equally, it has also been argued that the benefits accruing from urban policy programmes to black communities have usually been incidental rather than intrinsic.[23]

Although black people had been living in Britain for several centuries their number significantly increased during the 1940s and 1950s, when British governments encouraged immigration from the colonies and ex-colonies in order to augment the British labour force engaged in post-war reconstruction. People arrived first from the Caribbean and then later from India and Pakistan. In 1931 the black population was 100,000, rising to 400,000 in 1961 and 1.5 million in 1971. Many immigrants encountered racism. The desire of black people for mutual support in the face of this reaction was one of the factors leading to their concentration within certain British cities, a response which in turn has often generated further hostility from local white populations. Legislation aimed at curbing the immigration of black people was enacted in 1962, 68, 71 and now 1996, if the recent *Asylum Act* which concerns the rights of refugees is included. The links between race and inequality in inner city areas, and the impact of current urban policy on black communities are examined in greater detail later.

A further factor which lay behind the development of urban policy in the 1960s was new awareness of the continued presence of poverty in our cities. A series of reports, Milner Holland (1965) on London housing, Plowden (1967) on primary schools and Seebohm (1968) on social services, marked the official rediscovery of poverty in Britain. Enoch Powell's notorious speech of April 1968 on the problem of racial tension in cities, in which he recalled the River Tiber flowing with blood, produced an immediate panic political response from the Labour Government, then under the leadership of Harold Wilson. An urban programme was initiated to give special help to areas with high concentrations of black city dwellers. This mirrored a trend which was already evident in the United States, where the government under President Johnson developed new urban anti-poverty programmes after riots in American cities in 1964-7. The British *Community Development Programme* of 1969 was very similar to the *Model Cities Program* already in place in the United States.

Under the *Community Development Programme*, approaching £25 million was made available over five years to fund the establishment of twelve Community Development Projects (CDPs) in different British cities. It became clear to the CDP teams that the problems in the areas in which they were working were not susceptible to a 'quick fix', and that the causes of inner city poverty were complex and structural. This message was unwelcome both to the political leadership of the cities and to the Conservative government of the day, and in 1976 the CDP experiment was wound up.

However, three reports which were published by the Department of the Environment in 1977[24], focusing on Birmingham, Liverpool and Lambeth in south London, came to very similar conclusions to the CDP teams and ascribed inner city decay to the failure of entire urban economies, rather than simply to the fact of individuals and families falling below the poverty line.

This time the Government (by now Labour) responded and in a White Paper of 1977, later to become the *Inner Urban Areas Act* of 1978, it switched the emphasis of inner-city policy massively to economic renewal. From now on, inner city areas would be a high priority for new industrial development, the Urban Programme would be hugely expanded, and central-local government partnerships would be developed in response to the problems of some of the most severely disadvantaged neighbourhoods. Responsibility for administering the Urban Programme was shifted from the Home Office to the Department of the Environment and funding was increased to, for example, £125 million for the financial year 1979-80. The guidance and control of growth, the central concern of the British planning system since 1947, was replaced by the prioritisation of growth, at almost any cost. This shift in priorities was symbolised by the creation of new jobs in local authorities for 'economic development officers' at this time. [25]

The Conservative government which took office in 1979 reasserted its commitment to regenerating the inner city through the measures put in place by the *Urban Areas Act* of 1978, but with greater emphasis on centralist mechanisms such as the Development Corporation. This device had been used by the Labour government of 1945 for the construction of British new towns. It was chosen in 1979 for the same reasons as before, namely that it offered the possibility of by-passing local government bureaucracy and of being effective and quick. The Docklands and Merseyside Development Corporations were established in 1981 with eight others following over the next seven years. By 1990, the by then 10 Development Corporations absorbed approaching two thirds of the £550 million worth of government funding dedicated to urban regeneration in England. Conversely, the Urban Programme money which was administered by local authorities, was cut. [26]

Under the Development Corporations the primary task of planning became to facilitate the most feasible recycling of derelict urban industrial or commercial land to more viable uses. The strategy was consciously short term. The Chief Executive of the London Docklands Development Corporation (LDDC) explained, *"The sheer scale of dereliction which the LDDC was charged with addressing was of such an order that the only way to tackle the problem without an enormous influx of public funds... was to generate a kind of critical momentum, a development 'snowball' that would create a real credibility for Docklands early on amongst potential commercial and residential developers. Thus it was necessary to be opportunist with regard to proposals from developers."*[27]

A further element of Conservative urban regeneration policies was the use of relatively modest public funds to attract (or 'leverage', in the jargon) much higher private sector moneys. The designation of certain inner city areas as economic Enterprise Zones has been one of the ways in which this policy objective has been pursued. During 1980-1, eleven Enterprise Zones were created, including the Isle of Dogs in the heart of the London Docklands. Twenty seven Enterprise Zones were created in all. They were characterised by their exemption from the usual planning controls. In the Isle of Dogs for example, firms were offered the chance to build an industrial or commercial building of their choice, free from planning regulations, exempt from rates and with 100% tax relief on capital expenditure for the next ten years. Some small firms took the chance to move in and larger ones consolidated their operations. Then Olympia and York, Manhattan's biggest landlords, decided to build Canary Wharf and turned the Enterprise Zone into a property developer's goldmine. By 1990 a second, cheap building boom had swept away almost all of the multi-coloured sheds built less than five years earlier by small firms.

The fascination of Docklands is that it is quite clearly *"urban history in the making"*[28], and the Development Corporation's achievements there, thanks largely to Canary Wharf, have been considerable, producing many thousands of new jobs. However, the Corporation's actions have also been much criticised, most seriously on the basis that the indigenous population of the area has benefited very little, if at all, from the boom. A further criticism is that the Development Corporations' purview ends at their boundaries, so that they have been unable to integrate the local economic development they have sometimes stimulated into the wider regional economy. In Docklands for example, this has meant that there has been a failure of transport planning, for despite the efforts of the LDDC to ease traffic within its own boundaries north of the River Thames, all east-west traffic must feed into the A13, which is already massively congested and under the separate control of the Department of the Environment.

Various urban policy initiatives came and went during the 1980s, including City Action Teams, Task Forces, and the Action For Cities programme, launched in 1988. Responsibilities shifted from one Government department to another. It is scarcely surprising that in 1989 an Audit Commission report criticised urban support programmes as *"a patchwork quilt of complexity and idiosyncracy"*.[29]

Throughout the 1980s the issue of regenerating the cities was highly politicised. There was little common ground between a Conservative government with strong centralising tendencies, and local authorities in inner city areas run mainly by Labour administrations. Bitter battles were fought over issues such as rate-support grant, rate-capping and the control of local schools. Various measures, including the Local Government Finance Act 1982, the Rates Act 1984, and the creation of the Audit Commission in 1982 increased central control over local authority spending. The result was that by 1994 central government controlled 85% of local authority spending.[30]

It has been argued that this shift began under the Labour government in 1976, and is symptomatic of broader trends in the development of modern states and not simply the result of Conservative ideology; and that these measures served not to cut local authorities' share of public spending but rather to curb its otherwise apparently uncontrollable growth.[31] In 1986, the Greater London Council was abolished and a range of non-government organisations established to take over some of its London-wide functions. Since then quasi-autonomous non-governmental organisations (commonly known as 'quangos') have proliferated.

The need to regenerate Britain's most desolate inner city areas was given added urgency by riots or disturbances in, for example, Brixton (south London), Toxteth (Liverpool) and Moss Side (Manchester) in 1981; and in Handsworth (Birmingham) and Broadwater Farm (north London) in 1985. An official enquiry was set up into the Brixton riot under the chairmanship of Lord Justice Scarman. His report concluded that the disturbances did not constitute a 'race riot', but were due to a clash of cultures, exacerbated by the fact that the local black youth subculture was built on foundations of deprivation, racism and structural disadvantage[32]. *The Scarman Report* emphasised in particular:

1 the need for a concerted, better co-ordinated attack on the problems of the inner cities;
2 recognition and action to meet the special problems and needs of the ethnic minorities, based on an acceptance of them as full and equal members of a culturally diverse society;
3 the need to involve not just black people, but all the community, both nationally and locally, in a better directed response to these problems.

"It is essential that people are encouraged to secure a stake in, feel a pride in, and have a sense of responsibility for their own area." (para 6.42)

For much of the 1980s urban policy was moving away from these values, towards a preoccupation with the renewal of the physical fabric of inner city areas, rather than adopting the more holistic approach advocated in *The Scarman Report*. However, the *City Challenge* programme, which was launched in 1991, marked an important cultural shift in urban policy in several ways, not least because it took greater account of the need to address the social conditions in disadvantaged city areas, in addition to economic issues. Other features of *City Challenge* which have been widely praised are the fact that it gave a potential leadership role to the local authority; it demanded public, private and voluntary interests worked together in partnership; it had an area-based focus; and it consolidated a number of initiatives into a single programme.

More controversial were the fact that *City Challenge* was funded at a lower level than the Urban Development Corporations. Eleven areas were awarded *City Challenge* status, and £82.5 million was allocated each year for five years, compared with the £300 million plus, granted each year between 1991 to 1994 for the ten Urban Development Corporations in England and Wales. Moreover, the funding for *City Challenge* was not new but was redistributed ('top-sliced' in the jargon) from existing urban regeneration budgets.

A further feature which attracted adverse comment is that the *City Challenge* funding process was one of competitive bidding. In some ways this may seem an efficient way of distributing limited resources, but in areas which were 'losers', the expectations of local communities were raised, only to be dashed again. As *City Challenge* has been implemented it has proved to suffer from some of the failings of earlier schemes, such as short-termism and underfunding. The *City Challenge* focus on tightly defined geographical areas, while popular in some quarters has also been criticised because it makes linkages to the wider regional economy difficult. While its advocacy of a partnership approach was widely welcomed, the voluntary sector in particular often found that it was a very unequal partner alongside local authorities and quangos such as TECs (Training and Enterprise Councils).[33] Moreover, some local authorities appear to have been much more successful than others in involving the local community in the process of designing and implementing *City Challenge* schemes.[34]

The effectiveness of these urban policy initiatives was evaluated in a major study carried out by a team led by Professor Brian Robson of Manchester University, commissioned by the Department of the Environment.[35] The study found that the real value of government expenditure in a national sample of 123 city districts, including all the original 57 Urban Programme area, fell by about half in real terms in the 10 years between 1979 and 1989. The report's general conclusions were, *"The pattern that emerges, both for employment opportunities and residential attractiveness, is very mixed. There has been beneficial change – some of it relative, some absolute... But in the most deprived areas...policy has not been able to make significant inroads. The biggest and most deprived urban areas have generally experienced a continuing deterioration."*

The report recommended that future urban policy funding mechanisms should:
- encourage the establishment of long term partnerships in local areas
- provide local authorities with a more significant role
- foster the participation of the local community, and place more stress on community capacity-building in deprived areas
- improve the coherence of programmes across and within Government departments
- be administered at regional level.

Current urban policy: the Single Regeneration Budget

This brings the story of the development of British urban policy almost up to date. The latest urban policy initiative is the Single Regeneration Budget (SRB), which was developed in the light of Professor Robson's report and incorporates some of the changes he proposed.

The SRB was launched in November 1993. SRB merged 20 separate programmes previously administered by five different Government departments, totalling some £1.4 billion. Due to existing commitments such as *City Challenge*, only £125 million was available for 1995-6. SRB was therefore introduced at a time when urban and regeneration expenditure was being substantially reduced.[36]

SRB retains some important features of *City Challenge*, but also differs significantly in certain respects. The greatest similarity is that it is also allocated through a process of competitive bidding. Like *City Challenge*, it also encouraged the formation of multi-agency partnerships within bids in order to plan a strategic approach to local needs and priorities, and which might (for the first time) be led by TECs. It was expected that bids supported by the SRB would have to 'maximise the leverage' of the private sector (ie. attract a lot of complementary funding from business).

One of the differences between SRB and *City Challenge* however, is that bids for SRB are accepted from anywhere in England. The advantage is that this greater flexibility gives opportunities for areas with pockets of deprivation or other problems, such as Wakefield or Gloucester, to benefit from government regeneration funding.[37] However, in practice, this means that resources have been taken away from disadvantaged city areas, since there has been a reduction in the money allocated to Urban Programme areas. Before the advent of SRB these districts received 86% of government regeneration funding. However, they received only 69% of the £1.2 billion allocation of SRB money distributed in the first bidding round. This has provoked the criticism that the introduction of SRB *"provides evidence of the dilution of the Government's commitment to inner-city regeneration."*[38]

A significant innovation linked to the SRB was the creation of ten Integrated Government Offices (IGOs) for the Regions. The SRB is, in many ways, highly decentralised, since bids for SRB go to the IGOs, and decisions about allocating funding are also made there.

One task of the IGOs which is likely to become much more important in the next few years is their role as distribution points of regeneration funding from the European Union. In recognition of the growing importance of European Union regeneration funding, many urban local authorities have recently appointed 'European Officers', to help them bid for European money. European funding comes primarily from two sources, the European Regional Development Fund (ERDF) and the European Social Fund. There is also a special Community initiative called URBAN from which some cities may be able to benefit. ERDF grants are paid for projects concerned with economic regeneration and development, and which meet specific objectives set out by the Union. An ERDF grant normally pays up to 50% of the eligible costs of a project. The remainder, 'matching funding', has to be found by the prospective ERDF recipient, either from within its own resources or from other organisations, both private and public. Matching funding can also come from Government, through domestic grant regimes such as those covered by the SRB.

The guidance notes which were issued for SRB in April 1994 contained a wide ranging list of eight strategic objectives which potential bidders should pursue, namely, to:

1 Enhance the employment prospects, education, skills of local people, particularly the young and those at a disadvantage, and promote equality of opportunity
2 Encourage sustainable economic growth and wealth creation by improving the competitiveness of the local economy, including business support
3 Improve housing, through physical improvement, greater choice and better management and maintenance
4 Promote initiatives of benefit to ethnic minorities
5 Tackle crime and improve community safety
6 Protect and improve the local environment and infrastructure and promote good design
7 Enhance the quality of life of local people, including health, cultural and sports facilities
8 Harness the talents and resources of the voluntary sector and the community.

A number of evaluations have been carried out on the dispersal of funds under the first round of SRB, leading to the following criticisms:

1 It has been suggested that deprivation has been down-graded within the SRB criteria compared with those of some previous regeneration schemes, and economic development and the need to achieve leverage of private sector resources, over-emphasised. Prioritising

leverage may at first glance appear to be an efficient way of using scarce resources, but it also means that there is a risk that the most disadvantaged city districts are less likely to be allocated funding, because they will generally be less able to promote projects which appeal to the private sector. [39]

2 Some have complained that insufficient money is available to fund major housing renovation schemes, a vital component of urban renewal in some of the most disadvantaged city areas. This is partly because the money which was previously available to refurbish housing under the Estates Action programme before SRB is no longer available for this purpose. [40]

3 It has been suggested that black communities have been discriminated against by the introduction of the SRB, since less money appears to have been invested in schemes directly aimed at their benefit, compared with the position before the SRB. When SRB was introduced, all the grants which were traditionally targeted at black communities were put into the SRB. These included most of the moneys from *Section 11 Local Government Act 1966*, the *Ethnic Minority Grant*, and the *Ethnic Minority Business Initiative*. This funding was not, however, 'ring-fenced' (ie. safeguarded to benefit black communities) and the result is that in the first bidding round, only 8% of expenditure will be on schemes aimed specifically at the objective of benefiting black communities. [41]

4 Even setting aside the controversy about whether competition is the best way to allocate regeneration money, some bidders have suggested that the bidding process for SRB was flawed in several important respects. For example, the SRB timescales dovetailed poorly with those for other bids, such as European Union moneys. Secondly, too much variation in the responses of the various IGOs to bids was alleged, and too little transparency in the bidding process. [42]

5 Many have suggested that the SRB is underfunded, pointing to the fact that round one of the SRB was hugely oversubscribed. There were 256 'losing' bids, constituting a waste of resources in terms of the time and money spent in preparing bids. [43] However, it has also been suggested that the time spent in forming 'losing' partnerships will not have been wasted, and will benefit many areas in other ways. [44]

6 Voluntary sector agencies are widely perceived to have been marginalised in the SRB process, just as they often were under City Challenge;

in round one, voluntary sector led bids accounted for only 3% of the SRB funds allocated and most of this money went to one large scheme.[45]

When SRB was launched the Government invited three cities, London, Birmingham and Manchester, to produce a City Pride prospectus which set out a regeneration strategy and a ten year vision of the whole urban area. However, the SRB bidding guidance made it clear that there was no presumption that City Pride status gave SRB bids from these areas an advantage, and indeed, evidence from the first round suggested that Manchester and Birmingham were not particularly successful in their applications for funding.

Originally, it was widely thought that SRB would be discontinued after round one, but central Government responded to the large number of bids received by announcing that £40 million would be available in 1996/7 (round two); and £200 million in 1997/8 (round three). The Environment Select Committee conducted a review of SRB during the Summer of 1995 and concluded:

"We believe that the SRB has already demonstrated its potential to achieve excellent value for taxpayers' money. It is supporting not only the regeneration of cities, towns and smaller communities across England, but increasingly, genuine community and private sector involvement, integration of different government programmes and a new sense of partnership between local authorities, TECs and others....We therefore have no hesitation in recommending that the SRB should continue into a third and subsequent rounds...."[46]

In its Report, the Committee recommended some fairly minor changes to the SRB process, in response to criticisms of the kind reported above. For example, it called for greater consistency in the decision-making of the IGOs; more concentration on funding to help voluntary and community organisations take an active part in the formulation and implementation of SRB bids; and clear assessments by the Department of the Environment on the extent to which successful bids in round two allocated funding to ethnic minority groups, and for housing-related objectives. However, the Committee rejected calls for funding within SRB to be 'ring-fenced' for these purposes. A recent report analysing the contribution of the voluntary sector in successful second round bids for SRB (ie. for 1996/7) found that although there was a significant increase in the proportion of successful partnerships involving the voluntary sector, the quality of partnership varied greatly, and the involvement of the community sector had not been addressed by many local authorities and TECs.[47]

Conclusion

This review of the development of urban policy shows that government led interventions aimed at regenerating our cities have become much more sophisticated and strategic over the last thirty five years. Criticisms have continued to be voiced however, about many of the elements of these schemes, including the relative lack of involvement of and benefit to the black community; the marginalisation of the voluntary sector; the balance of objectives within schemes; and the conflicts between partnership and competition. Above all, there is the fear that despite all the money and effort which have been targeted at disadvantaged city areas, the benefits accruing to the people who live there have been relatively limited.[48]

A recent analysis of current trends in urban regeneration has been based on the projected budgets of government led schemes. It concludes that the expenditure invested at distressed urban areas is being progressively reduced, at the same time as all authorities are being affected by other large reductions in mainstream programmes which underpin urban regeneration initiatives. The analysis further suggests that the emphasis on 'leverage' within SRB shows that central Government may be trying to rely on an injection of private capital, to compensate for the withdrawal of public sector investment in inner cities. While this may benefit some neighbourhoods, it appears that many urban problems originate in decisions to withdraw private sector investment from distressed areas. This trend has persisted throughout the 20th century and has often been redressed only through substantial public sector investment. [49]

6. The Church and the city

It has already been noted that ambivalence often characterises secular attitudes towards the city. This is all the more true of the Church. Indeed, the former may be in no small part a result of the latter. Biblically and traditionally, Christians have often viewed the city as an evil and wicked place. Some of this understanding is derived from the experience of Israel as a nomad people, some from early Christians' experience as a minority within the Roman Empire. Some of it possibly arose from the mistaken belief that the world was soon to end.

In Britain, Christian distaste for city life reached a peak in the Victorian era when John Ruskin wrote, for example "...*the great cities of the earth...have become...loathsome centres of fornication and covetousness, the smoke of their sin going up into the face of heaven like the furnace of Sodom; and the pollution of it rotting and raging the bones and souls of the peasant people around them...*"[50] Then, as now, the struggle for Christians concerned the need to balance the two spheres of the religious and the secular, God's and Caesar's, the Church and the world, the Kingdom of God now and not yet.[51]

Yet in practice, the histories of the Church and our cities are inextricably linked. For several centuries from medieval times, the Church was in many ways a more influential institution than the State. It was truly international and provided many of the diplomats of the age. It had a monopoly on the delivery of education, and provided a route to power and riches for able men and women, regardless of birth, unlike the tightly regulated secular society. The Gothic Cathedrals which still adorn many of our cities today must have dominated the ramshackle towns and cities of the twelfth and thirteenth centuries to an extraordinary extent, and epitomise the power of the Church at that time.

The Act of Supremacy in 1543 made Henry VIII Supreme Head of the Church of England. The Church was never to be such an independent institution again, but it retained an important role within the life of the nation, particularly in the upper echelons of society. This was certainly true of the eighteenth century, when bishops were first and foremost politicians. Below the bishoprics there was a ladder of preferment, the value of which rose steadily as the nation's wealth grew. Non-residence was tolerated and plurality encouraged. In the North of England, the Midlands and much of London, urban growth bore no relation to the old pattern of parishes and there was little attempt to engage with the new industrial populations. These were some of the places where Methodism was later to flourish.[52] It was only in the late 1830s that a programme of church building was initiated by the Church of England in response to these changes in demography.

In the eighteenth century, city churches met many needs which had little to do with the spiritual. People walked their dogs in them, conducted business, children played; in short, churches functioned as more or less public, covered meeting places. Churches had the advantage of being accessible, centrally located and roofed, thus offering protection from the climate. Gradually however, the role of churches as urban meeting places was gradually assumed by secular buildings, such as, for example, the Pump Room in Bath.[53]

By the middle of the 19th century, religion appeared to be largely peripheral to the lives of the mass of city dwellers. The religious census of 1851 concluded that fewer than one in ten attended church or chapel on census day in London, Birmingham, Liverpool, Manchester, Sheffield and Newcastle, and attendances were generally lowest in working class districts.[54] However, Nonconformism played an important role in Victorian cities by providing a radical theological underpinning to the movement of urban reform, especially in Birmingham; and in publicising the conditions of the urban poor. A pamphlet published by Andrew Mearns, a Congregationalist minister in London in 1883, called *The Bitter Cry of Outcast London*, was a sensation and provoked calls for an official enquiry, eventually from Queen Victoria herself, and led directly to the appointment of the Royal Commission on the Housing of the Working Classes in 1884. These Nonconformists were above all practical Christians. Robert William Dale, an influential Congregationalist minister in Birmingham in the late 19th century, wrote *"the eleventh commandment is that thou shalt keep a balance sheet."* He called on Birmingham's Christians to work on the committees of hospitals and to become councillors and aldermen.[55]

Towards the end of the 19th century, attendances in Church of England city churches among working class people slightly increased, largely, it appears, through greater Church involvement in charity and social services. However, it has been suggested that the growth of the welfare state and the leisure industry in the 20th century eclipsed the role of churches as social centres, and led to the serious subsequent decline in membership and attendance. *"There never really was a 'golden age' for the Church of England in the city ... although most cities had a few conspicuously flourishing working class parishes, the hundreds who attended these churches were few if set beside the thousands who stayed away."* [56] Since 1945 secularisation has accelerated, in cities and elsewhere, and now affects all sections of society.

7. Methodism and the cities

Methodism has a value system which is shaped by a historic meeting of the Wesleyan form of Protestantism, together with lesser strands of Nonconformism, Dissent and Puritanism. Methodism is a Protestant, evangelical renewal movement, founded in the 18th century, by John Wesley. Methodism's characteristics are: a church organisation using itinerant, ordained and lay preachers; a fellowship which shares in worship around the Word and sacraments; and believers who accept the saving grace of Jesus Christ, which is available for all and who enter, through baptism and membership, into a process of growth towards Scriptural holiness in the Holy Spirit, involving prayer and discipline. Learning and devotion are stimulated by Bible centred class groups and house-groups, and at a personal and church level, there is an ethical and political life which expresses itself both in restraint, and in serving the materially and socially underprivileged.

From 1738, Wesley spent the next 53 years travelling and

preaching (at an average of 15 sermons a week). At first he was an Anglican and tried to preach within churches, but the Church became hostile and closed its doors. In fact, this brought him vaster audiences outside and took him to places lacking in religion. As has been explained above, these were often the villages, towns and outskirts of cities which were growing rapidly as a result of the Industrial Revolution, and where the Church of England was almost entirely absent. By 1784, 356 Methodist chapels had been built in these areas. It has been suggested that by 1760 Methodism was by far the most coordinated body of opinion in the country, the most fervent and dynamic, and that it particularly appealed to men and women with a social conscience whose families had only comparatively recently escaped from poverty. Early Methodism was not politically radical, however.[57] Methodism finally broke away from the Church of England in 1784.

The religious census of 1851 (see above) made the Wesleyans aware that they were failing to reach the mass of people living in cities. During the 19th century, many rich city churches had moved to the new affluent suburbs. The Methodist Conference of 1854 expressed a concern to *"penetrate the neglected masses of the heathenish population of our large cities"* and decided upon *"reviving the Home Missionary spirit of Methodism."* Then, in 1883, *The Bitter Cry of Outcast London* was published and galvanised Wesleyans, along with other denominations, into action. In 1885 the decision to convert declining city churches into Mission Chapels was taken. More practical interest was to be shown in the domestic and social well-being of the people in the neighbourhood of such chapels. Ministers were encouraged to concentrate on these chapels and to recruit lay helpers. One of the first Missions to be set up was the South London Mission in 1889, one of the districts which *The Bitter Cry of Outcast London* had described.

Like other Christian faith communities in Britain, modern Methodism has been affected by secularisation. However, alongside some serious decline in membership there has also been evidence of some enterprising and imaginative Christian mission. In 1996, out of some 6,678 Methodist churches in Britain, 2,291 (34%) are self-defined as city centre, inner city, urban estate or suburban. However, it is important to note that Methodist membership in the suburbs significantly exceeds that from the other city neighbourhoods.

As cities and large towns developed, so city centre churches were established. At the time of the Forward Movement and later in the Central Hall movement, some of these churches made a special effort to engage people for whom Church style buildings and worship were alien. By 1988, the national Methodist City Centre Churches Group was reviewing the mostly 19th century legacy of more than 360 city centre churches. Many of these were large, costly, inappropriate buildings with elderly, declining and commuting congregations. The stark option for many was to close or to adapt and change.[58]

In the inner city, churches have struggled to find ways of sharing their faith in ways that are in tune with the local culture. By the mid 1960s, the number of inner city churches was significantly decreasing. The trend became so stark that some Christians and Christian agencies chose to move into the inner city in an attempt to check the decline. To this factor was added the growing contribution of black Christians who had come to Britain as immigrants, and who either joined the denomination of their birthplace or formed new Pentecostal churches.

After its foundation in 1969, the ecumenical, but Methodist based Urban Theology Unit in Sheffield provided a focus for urban ministry, mission and theology. From 1973, the national Methodist Inner Cities Committee focused work at national level. During the 1980s, ministers and workers in the inner cities highlighted their concerns in three reports: *Two nations one gospel* (1981); *What churches can do* (1983); and *Gospel from the poor* (1984). This work in turn contributed to the Methodist Conference setting up the *Mission Alongside the Poor Programme* (1983-1996) and *MAPP Guide* (1995) and to specific actions and debates such as *A Petition of Distress in the Cities* (1993), endorsed by the Methodist Conference in 1992[59]. The national Methodist Urban Mission Committee, since 1992 has brought focus to Methodism's urban concerns.

On the outer urban estates, the Church struggled to make an impact. New, small churches were built and in some places ecumenical churches and partnerships were devised, but the dilemma persisted: how to be the Christian Church in a way that communicated with the local culture. The Urban Estates Group with their consultations at Luton Industrial College sought to support this work. They too became part of the emerging national Methodist Urban Mission Committee.[60] The suburban church has also struggled to adapt to urban development and change. The emergence of a multi-racial and multi-cultural society, and the continuing decline of the membership base has however, gradually led many suburban churches to find common cause with churches in other parts of the city.

In parallel to this activity the Industrial Mission movement, which linked historically with the worker priest movement, has sought to engage industry, commerce and business. It has done so largely through placing chaplains, often in ecumenical teams, as representatives of the churches in industrial companies.

A final strand has been the emergence of groups within Denominations which have focused on Christian life and witness in cities. These have ranged from Methodism's Mission Alongside the Poor Programme, to the Anglican Bishops' Advisory Group on Urban Priority Areas; from Church Action on Poverty to the Christians in Public Life Programme – Human City Initiative; from the Alliance of Radical Methodists, through to the evangelical Ixthus and City Cries. At the Liverpool Congress, *Jesus in the city* in November 1995, the single most striking reality was the sheer range of Christians and Christian groups present. Within the crucible of the city such co-operation must be the appropriate response.

In 1995 the Methodist Urban Mission Committee, after wide consultation with practitioners, set out its commitment to:

- The development of British cities and urban areas as good places in which to live.

- An understanding and analysis of cities, so that contexts are taken seriously: city centre, inner city, urban estate, suburban, city-wide, large towns, conurbations, and even the effect upon rural society.

- The presence and activity of the Methodist Church within the ecumenical Church alongside other faiths, including the concern for evangelism, discipleship and Church growth.

- The involvement of the Church in the city, in ways that take seriously: population, issues, structures, needs, power, wealth, creativity, the environment.

- The outreach of the Church to the city in ways that use many models of mission and ministry in word and deed, including specialised work, alongside the poor and disadvantaged and in partnership with all people of good will.

- Taking the poor and disadvantaged seriously, working for justice and wholeness, recognising all people as of equal worth.

- Hearing the good news of Christ from urban disciples and developing theology, mission, worship and spirituality from that witness.[61]

Such a commitment has not been easily won, or sustained without enormous cost. It has been extremely difficult for many city centre churches to adapt. Many inner city and outer estate churches have had to persevere to find appropriate ways of working. Others have been transformed by the contribution of Afro Caribbean and Asian Christians. For all of them the task has been the same: deciding how to be Christian people and churches in the modern British city.

8. Conclusion:
the context within which our cities and the Church exist today

The reviews earlier in this Section of the recent history of the Church in Britain show that for at least the last century and a half and probably for much longer, only a minority of city dwellers have regularly attended Church. However, it also demonstrates that the Church, both as an institution and through the contributions of many individual Christians, has been a powerful force for positive change in city life. The Church has often been, and continues to be, exceptionally well placed to bring people together and help stimulate constructive dialogue and change within city communities. For it is, among other things, by far the largest voluntary association in Britain, whose major impact on the city is through the diverse activities of its members.

Today, in contemporary Britain, many Christians working at grass roots level have a view of the city which is visionary. They see within it the possibility of the city of God. They struggle to develop humane values within a human city. They are among those who seek the common good. They pursue faithful, imaginative and prophetic goals. The Ecumenical Urban Forum (a group of urban practitioners) defines 'urban mission' as follows: "...*outreach by the Church, (through evangelism, social caring, political justice and concern for the environment) in our cities. This understanding contains within it a commitment to the poor and disadvantaged, and to the hope that cities can be good places in which to live and places in which God is found.*"[62] It is crucial that the action of Christians and the Church in the cities is underpinned by theology, drawn from tradition and from contemporary experience. Some reflections on how this task might be approached will be found later in this Report.

Britain is now a predominantly urban society. Only about 1 in 20 of the population live in the country rather than in a town or city. Most of the population is tightly concentrated in a city; 60% of the population (about 33 million people) live on 6% of the land. London remains as dominant in population and political terms as it has been for at least 1500 years: One in seven of the population (7.8 million people) live in London.[63]

However, there has been a perceptible trend across Britain in recent years suggesting that our cities are in decline. This is demonstrated by population loss, for example of 6% from inner London boroughs and of 9% from Liverpool throughout the 1980s. This haemorrhage away from cities, or 'counter-urbanisation' has been in terms not only of people but also of wealth, and arguably, rationale. Although there is some evidence to suggest that the population losses from Britain's cities are abating, these demographic trends are in stark contrast to the explosive urban growth being experienced in some other parts of the world. Nearly half the world's population now lives in a city. This proportion is projected to increase significantly over the next twenty years, largely as a result of increasing urbanisation in the developing world. By the year 2015, 12 of the world's largest cities are projected to be in Asia; only one, New York, will be in North America and none will be in Europe. By 2015, London's population is expected to stabilise at around 7.3 million, but Britain's biggest city will be dwarfed by Bombay (27.4 million) and Shanghai (23.4 million).[64] The quality of life in a city of such a scale is questionable, but the fact remains that these comparisons suggest that British (and European) cities are increasingly being left behind in a race for power and wealth, and reinforce a perception of relative decline.

As local and central Government, business, the Church and the voluntary sector work to try to regenerate our cities they do so in an environment which is increasingly competitive in inter-national terms. Much of this Report is concerned with how their efforts measure up to this huge challenge, and on the resulting impact on the ordinary men, women and children living in our cities today.

Part 2

PEOPLE'S VIEWS ABOUT LIVING IN OUR CITIES TODAY

The Methodist Conference and the Working Group thought it vital to find out what city dwellers, 'the silent majority', think about living in cities today. There are many institutions, official bodies and campaigning groups currently trying to influence the future direction of city development. But what are the priorities of those who are often at the receiving end of these interventions? Their views should be one of the most important factors determining policy in the cities.

1. The methodology of the Working Group's survey of the views of city Methodists

The main mechanism devised by the Working Group for consulting city dwellers was a very simple written questionnaire which was sent to a sample of Methodists living in cities. The Methodist Church membership in cities was therefore used as a 'proxy' for the city population as a whole. In certain respects, this group differs significantly from the general city population. In particular, it is older and less multi-cultural. Most Methodist Church members who live in cities come from the suburbs, but in this sense they mirror the wider population in most cities which is also concentrated beyond the inner city[65]. From the Working Group's point of view, one of the principal advantages of this approach was that it gave a voice to people whose views are often not heard in debates about city life.

The questionnaire which was sent out will be found in Appendix 2. The questionnaire was successfully piloted. Then, for administrative convenience, the questionnaires were sent out via Methodist churches in cities.[66] Ministers were asked to distribute them to members of their congregations. The churches were selected to reflect accurately their distribution by type within our cities, according to Methodist criteria, and across Britain as a whole; in research terms, the sample was 'stratified by region and type'. In October 1995, 4,800 question-naires were sent out. By the closing date, 1,154 had been returned. These formed the basis of the survey.

When the questionnaires were analysed, it was found that the people who had completed them were an accurate reflection of the Methodist membership in British cities, in terms of the type of church which they attended.

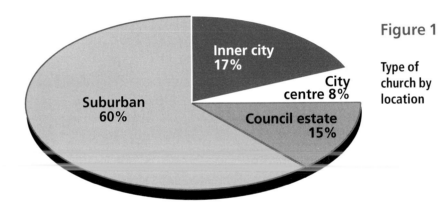

Figure 1

Type of church by location

The churches from which questionnaires were returned were also an accurate geographical representation of Methodism in cities across Britain, except that Scottish cities were seriously under represented and Greater Manchester slightly over represented.

Almost two thirds (62%) of the questionnaires were returned by women. About two thirds (64%) of respondents were aged 50 and over (equal proportions being aged between 50 and 64, and 65 plus); a quarter (26%) were aged between 20 and 49; and the remaining one in ten (11%) were aged under 30. Over 94% of the sample described themselves as white.

These characteristics reflect the composition of Methodist

congregations within cities. The consultation meetings subsequently held in a number of cities helped the Working Group to redress the imbalance of views within the questionnaire survey, from citizens and groups living and working in inner city areas, and on outlying estates. Further steps were also taken to seek a black perspective; and the views of people living in Scottish cities, both of which groups were under-represented in the survey. The information gained as a result will be found later in the Report.

2. The survey findings

Please note that not all percentages add to 100%, because some respondents gave more than one answer to some questions.

a) What people like best about city life

The first question gave people a list of 34 positive features of city life from which they were asked to select three of their choice. An 'other' box was also made available for respondents to select their own feature, should they wish to do so. The list was based closely on one recently used by the Department of the Environment for a survey of Londoners' attitudes to their city.

Figure 2 shows the ten most popular features of city life in the survey.

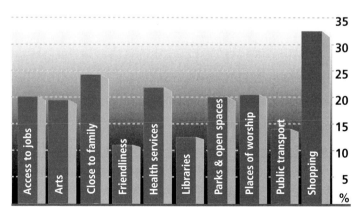

Figure 2

Ten most popular features of city life

Shopping was the single most popular attribute of city life in this survey and was chosen by about a third (32%) of people. The next two most popular features were chosen by between a fifth and a quarter of respondents, and were **being close to the family** (24%) and **health services** (22%).

There was then a grouping of four features, all of which were chosen by about a fifth of respondents. These were: **access to jobs; the arts; parks and open spaces;** and **places of worship.** Six other attributes were each selected by between one in eight and one in ten of the people who took part in the survey. These were (in descending order of popularity): **public transport; libraries; friendliness; leisure facilities; people;** and **eating out.**

There were relatively few differences in the responses of men and women. The only significant difference is that proportionately more women (27%) than men (19%) chose being close to the family as something they particularly liked about city life.

The variations in answers given according to age were more marked. Figure 3 demonstrates, not surprisingly, that access to jobs is of more importance to younger than older people. Another significant difference is that more than two in five (42%) of those aged under 30 chose shopping, as opposed to only about a quarter (27%) of those aged over 65. Conversely, access to health services, libraries, places of worship, and parks and open spaces were attributes which were selected more often by older respondents, especially by the 65 plus age group.

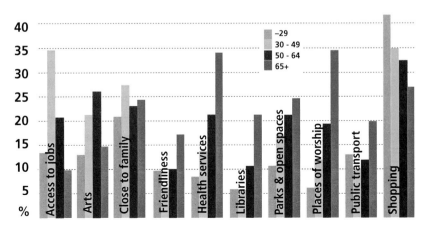

Figure

Ten most popular features by age

b) What people like least about city life

The second question in the questionnaire asked people to specify the three features of city life they liked least, this time without prompting them by means of a multiple choice list.

The least pleasant aspect of city life for most people was crime, which was selected by more than half (58%) of the respondents. This was closely followed by pollution (56%) and traffic (50%).

Some of the comments people made about crime included the following:

> *"I hate not being able to move freely and safely after dark."*

> *"There's a feeling that it is unsafe to walk in the streets alone and the thought that you might be attacked is more prevalent than it was 4 or 5 years ago."*

> *"Some areas tend to be a desert once the shops shut...the general public need to be able to go out at night to pursue their leisure and community activities feeling safe."*

Many respondents linked the issues of pollution and traffic. One such comment was:

> *"There should be less emphasis on facilities for private car users. A big push is needed towards subsidised public transport that is punctual, clean and pollution free."*

More than a fifth (22%) of people gave answers which were grouped together under a broad heading of lack of community. These include responses such as 'lack of neighbourliness' and 'uncaring cities'. About a fifth (20%) particularly disliked a number of attributes which have been grouped together as features of inequality. These include homelessness, poor housing conditions and racism. The only other negative attribute which a significant proportion of respondents chose was, the poor quality of the physical environment of the city, including bad planning; poorly maintained parks and public spaces; and ugly buildings. This was selected by one in eight (12%) of people surveyed.

There were no significant differences in the ways in which men and women answered this question. There was some variation however, according to age. Older people were more concerned about crime than other groups. Younger people were more worried than others about pollution. Those aged between 30 and 50 were more likely to mention lack of community than others in the survey. There were also some differences according to the type of church which people attended (presumably, this generally reflecting the places where people live). Members of council estate churches were the most likely to cite crime as their major dislike of city life, while those attending city centre churches were the most worried about traffic.

c) What people think would most improve the quality of city life

This question asked people for their ideas about what would do most to improve the quality of life in their city. The range of answers they gave are shown in Figure 4 below. Many of the answers which were given mirrored those to the

Figure 4

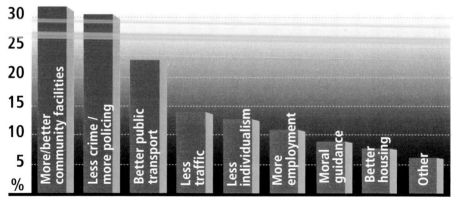

What would most improve life in the cities

question about what was most disliked about city life, and called for 'less' of whatever people had mentioned. However, some positive suggestions were also made. Almost a third (32%) of respondents recommended an increase and improvement in the provision of community facilities. More than a fifth (23%) called for improved public transport. One in ten (10%) thought that more employment opportunities would make the biggest difference to city life; and approaching this number of people

(8%) thought more and better housing was what was most needed. A slightly different type of answer was provided by about one in ten (9%) of respondents, who specified the importance of better moral guidance.

d) Helping specific groups in the community

People were asked to give their views about what would improve the quality of life for four selected groups of city dwellers.

1. Children

More than half of the respondents (58%) thought that better play facilities would be of greatest benefit to children living in the city. Specific comments included the following:

> *"Children should have access to safe play areas...which are kept secure from vandalism at night."*

> *"There should be scope for the creative use of unused/derelict land for development of play space, for example adventure playgrounds."*

About one in six (17%) gave examples of other types of community resources for children (including leisure centres and sports clubs). More than one in eight (13%) selected better educational provision. About one in ten (11%) gave answers related to the need for improvements to family life, including increasing the provision of mediation services, family support services and parenting skills.

2. Young people

Almost two thirds of respondents (64%) thought that better general community provision would do most to improve life for young people in cities, with an additional one in ten (9%) mentioning specifically the need for affordable leisure and community facilities. The enhanced availability of alcohol free activities was often recommended, as was greater provision of sports clubs. Two of the comments made were:

> *"They need somewhere to meet in the evening other than the local street corner – affordable leisure facilities that are not*

beyond the means of unemployed school leavers."

"Interesting, affordable activities where the emphasis is on participation as an alternative to drink/drugs and aimlessness."

3. Elderly people

A third (34%) of the people who answered this question said that measures to help older city dwellers to gain access to city facilities was what would do most to improve their quality of life, including better public transport, and easier physical access to shops. Slightly fewer respondents (31%) thought that the emphasis should be on alleviating older people's sense of social isolation, through for example, better contact with their families, and better leisure facilities for older people. More than a fifth (22%) specified the importance of policies to make older people feel less vulnerable, including better security and safer streets. About a fifth (21%) believed that an improvement in community care would be of greatest benefit to older people in cities. About one in eight (12%) mentioned a range of factors concerned with an enhancement of the position of older people within contemporary society, including greater respect for the elderly. It is notable that this ranking of preferences broadly reflected those survey respondents who were themselves elderly.

4. Disabled people

The overwhelming proportion of respondents (84%) to this question gave better physical access as their answer. Approaching one in five (18%) referred to issues concerned with equal rights for disabled people, and better societal awareness of their needs. More than one in eight (13%) thought that enhanced social and community provision for disabled people was what was most required.

e) Enhancing the role of the Church in the community life of the city

The questionnaire asked respondents how they thought their local Methodist Church could do more (if at all) to improve the quality of life for people in the local community. About a third of people who returned a questionnaire failed to answer this question, which might suggest that they thought their Church was already doing all it could, or alternatively that they could think of nothing else which it could realistically do.

Of those who did respond, over a third (35%) said that they thought their Church could be more welcoming, perhaps by staying open for longer hours during the week. A quarter (25%) thought that more could be done by their Church to develop better community links. One person, for example, commented:

> *"The Church should develop an awareness of what is happening within the community – where the real needs are! Perhaps we could do this via liaison with social services, neighbourhood schemes and voluntary organisations."*

Some people stressed the importance of better advertising of Church activities to the wider community. Two respondents said:

> *"The problem seems to be getting our activities known."*
> *"Perhaps we could start advertising locally – by contacting the local press or putting posters in GP surgeries etc."*

A fifth of people who answered this question referred to the need for their Church to engage in more active outreach work, including the provision of transport for elderly and disabled people who otherwise were unable to come to their local Church. A very similar proportion of responses (19%) called for their Church to do more to meet the needs of young people.

There were no significant variations in the ways in which men and women answered this question. However, there were some differences according to age. The 30–49 age group was particularly concerned that their Church should be more welcoming and should do more to develop better community links, compared with other respondents. The youngest respondents (those under 30) were more aware than other groups of the need for their Church to do more to appeal to young city dwellers.

f) How would you like to see life in the cities developing?

The final question asked people to look ahead and say how they would like to see city life developing. The highest proportion of answers to this question, more than half, (52%), referred to people's desire for an enhanced sense of community in the city. Under this heading people mentioned, for example, their hope for greater social equality; more mutual respect and acceptance between citizens, including those of diverse races and religious faiths; and more active participation by people in city life. Others (29%) specified their hope for a more vibrant and prosperous city life. One of these answers was:

"In this area there is a fear that the shops in the centre will not be commercially viable, with the proposed building of a large shopping centre on the outskirts. This will affect the whole region. Due to the change in retail provision, one suburb has already lost half of its shops which are empty and boarded up. I would like to see a reversal of this policy and a concerted effort to bring life back to the city centres."

About a quarter of respondents hoped for a better physical environment (26%) and for a safer and more secure city (26%).

Some people gave their own personal vision for the city, embracing several themes:

"I would like to see cities continue to grow along with the Church. People should not stop caring, but instead the community should pull together to wipe out crime and violence and make our streets safer for young and old alike."

"I would like to see development along the lines of the 'Sustainable Cities' BBC Reith lectures of 1995, by Sir Richard Rogers: more open spaces, less cars...cities built for people rather than vehicles. There should be a greater sense of co-operation rather than competition, and affirmation of cultural diversity rather than rivalry between different cultures."

The most significant difference in the answers given to this question by gender was that proportionately more women than men spotlighted the importance of the creation of a safer and more secure city. The most marked variation by age was that those aged under 30 were much more likely to have referred to their desire for a better physical environment in the city, than any other age group.

3. An overview of these survey findings

A number of themes which arise from the survey findings serve to reinforce some of the points which have already been made about city life. For example:

- The ordinariness of city life. Britain is now predominantly a nation whose population lives in urban areas, so city life is something many people take for granted as part of their everyday experience. Many people "just happen" to live in a city, for various reasons, and do not view this as something about which they have made an objective choice.

- The diversity of experiences of the city. People see the city in different ways and as a result of numerous factors, including the nature of the neighbourhood in which they live and the way in which they personally interact with their local area. As a result, some respondents cited 'friendliness' and 'the people' as features of city life which they liked, while others referred to "lack of community" as something they disliked.

- The different priorities of city dwellers according to age and gender. Having noted the diversity of attitudes to the city, it would also be fair to say that some distinct trends emerged from this survey by age and gender, in terms of perspectives on city life. For example, younger people were generally more conscious of the need for a sustainable city than older residents. Older city dwellers tended to place more emphasis on the importance of public provision such as libraries, health services and open spaces, rather than on the more individualistic pursuit of shopping. Similarly, women were generally more concerned about the need for safer cities than men.

The Working Party believes that just as the views of city dwellers should underpin the development of urban policy, so the views expressed in this survey set the agenda for this Report. The major themes which emerge from these findings provide the framework in which the realities of city life can be tackled, and the future for our cities explored. The Vision of the City which is suggested by this survey is one characterised by:

- An enhanced sense of community, in which there is more active participation by citizens and a sense of mutual respect between all city dwellers, irrespective of age, gender, race, disability or creed.

- Greater economic prosperity and vitality.

- A more equal, more socially just society.

- A greater sense of personal security.

- A cleaner, more sustainable city environment.

- The Church setting realistic goals for enhancing its role in the community life of the city, and taking practical measures in pursuit of these objectives.

It is notable that the overwhelming majority of people who responded to this questionnaire appeared to have no difficulty in conceiving of themselves as Christians on the one hand and city dwellers on the other. The fact that the most popular feature of city life for most respondents was shopping did not preclude many of them from expressing strong views about the need, for example, for their Church to do more to enrich the life of the local community. Therefore, while the apparent conflict between the spiritual and secular nature of the city is a major pre-occupation of academic theologians, it is an issue which most Methodists in cities today seem to have resolved for themselves in living their daily lives.

The remainder of this Report aims to investigate the extent to which the current policies and practices of Local and Central Government, Business, the Church and the Voluntary Sector are moving our cities towards a realisation of this Vision, and on what more needs to be done in order to attain it.

Part 3

FOCUS ON THREE OF THE MOST SERIOUS SETS OF PROBLEMS FACING CITIES TODAY

This Section is based largely on information gathered from the Consultation Meetings which the Working Group convened in Newcastle, Cardiff and Glasgow. These meetings were organised to gain some insight into the human reality behind abstract terms such as 'urban decay', and to understand more about how different cities are trying to address some of the most difficult problems facing them today.

The meetings each focused on different policy themes. The meeting in Newcastle concentrated on urban decay and its associated social problems, especially crime; the Cardiff meeting looked specifically at homelessness and housing need in the city; and the meeting in Glasgow examined transport and environment issues. The Working Group targeted these specific topics because they were three of the issues which emerged clearly from the Survey as of great concern to city dwellers. Although the discussion which took place at each meeting was geared to the situation in that particular city, many of the points which were made were relevant to cities everywhere in Britain.

While focusing on these three sets of issues the Working Group was also continually reminded that city life is the product of the interaction of all these factors and more, as has already been noted. The matching of themes with cities was entirely arbitrary, and should not be thought of as suggesting, for example, that homelessness is any worse, and the local response to it any less determined, in Cardiff than in any other British city.

1. Urban decay and its associated social problems

The Newcastle Consultation meeting was attended by representatives from local government (officers and members), the Church and the voluntary sector. The discussion which took place focused on life on some of Newcastle's very disadvantaged council estates, and on the efforts of individuals and institutions to generate positive change in these places.

Newcastle is a city of contrasts. Originally a Roman garrison town, it thrived first as a centre of the wool trade and later through coal mining and coal exporting, from the Middle Ages onwards. The 19th century added ship-building, steel production and engineering. The *Rocket* was built at George Stephenson's Newcastle works. Newcastle today is a city of about 192,000 inhabitants. The city centre retains many fine historical buildings, including the gently curving classical facades on Grey Street, which has recently been described as *"one of England's finest streets."*[67] Newcastle is a focus for the North East of England, and has a lively cultural life.

Like many other British cities whose prosperity was based on the trade of heavy industrial goods, Newcastle's local economy has suffered grievously from Britain's decline as an industrial and manufacturing nation. The attractive city centre contrasts starkly with the highly disadvantaged council estates which spread westwards out of the city. Meadow Well is the most famous of these localities, because it was the setting for major public disorder several years' ago. However, it is by no means the only deprived estate in the area. Newcastle is therefore a city in which the least prosperous neighbourhoods are not exclusively in the inner city, but include places further out towards the periphery of the city.

The Department of the Environment classifies disadvantaged city areas according to a standard list of criteria, and sorts them into four clusters of similar type. The majority of the most disadvantaged areas in Newcastle come under Cluster One.

Most of the localities in Cluster One are in the North of England and the Midlands and are places where:

> *"Population decline is high; benefit dependency and homelessness are relatively high; there is a low concentration of people from minority ethnic groups (though varying between individual areas); local authority housing is relatively high; crime rates and unemployment are both high and staying on rates at school are low; rates of new firm formation are particularly low; manufacturing employment remains well above average for inner city authorities as a whole."*[68]

The people who attended the Newcastle Consultation meeting explained what this meant in practical terms. While unemployment in Newcastle averaged 19% when the meeting took place (significantly above the national average), on the Meadow Well estate, for example, it was estimated to be at least 80%. Some families there are experiencing their third successive generation of male unemployment.

One person at the meeting said, *"When Vickers* (a firm which had previously employed many men locally in ship building) *went it left an urban wasteland. Where I live now is a 'municipal prairie' – a place that just warehouses people because there's no work for them to do."*

The meeting was told that young men had scarcely any hope of gaining a permanent full-time job in the area, they were effectively 'economically disenfranchised'. Good quality training placements and apprenticeships were almost non-existent. The ways in which men had previously earned a living were no longer available, and a generation of young men had been stranded by the decline in Newcastle's economic fortunes. They did not have the skills or the education to take advantage of the new job opportunities being created. There was a knock-on effect on their younger brothers and sisters still at school, many of whom had given up hope of ever getting a decent job and were disaffected from the education system.

The meeting heard that contrary to the media image of the area as an urban jungle, most of the population was law-abiding, but a small proportion of the local young men were engaged in major criminal activity, including drug dealing. Petty crime was common, and in the absence of a viable, legal local economy there was a sub-culture of 'graft'. Almost nine out of ten cases coming before the criminal courts in Newcastle involved young men. Some men who had never worked but had become heavily involved in crime had recently come out of prison, aged 25 to 30. These local 'lads' now organised much of the crime in the local area, sometimes recruiting younger boys to take a lesser role. Protection rackets often targeted building schemes on the estates. The impact on the local community was described by one person in the following terms:

"People's freedom of movement is constrained because they can't walk across the road safely to the chip shop for cars roaring up and down, or posses of young men who infuse a philosophy of intimidation across the neighbourhood they live in."

Fear was described as being widespread, of crime, the police and debt. It was suggested that even the trouble makers were sometimes frightened, but that they took refuge in a 'macho' image.

Many of the local people at the meeting were highly critical of the role played in local community life by the statutory services. These agencies were generally perceived to have withdrawn from the area. The police were described as being part of the same culture as the 'lads'. Their actions in the locality were said to be confined to chasing these young men in cars. There was too little effective, regular policing in the area, in the residents' views.

A local councillor attended the meeting. He lived in the area, and had stayed because although he could have moved away, he wanted to express his solidarity with the local community. He spoke of his frustration; like many of the residents he represented, he would have liked to have done much more for local people, but the council was constrained by lack of money.

The people who attended the meeting had very mixed feelings about government regeneration initiatives. Following the disorder on the estate, Meadow Well received a substantial amount of regeneration money. However, many were unhappy that in order to attract any major investment, the local authority and others seeking funding were compelled to 'hype up' the area's difficulties. As a result the people living there felt that they had became stigmatised.

Government schemes were often viewed locally as *"a political conjuring trick."* Some of the comments about City Challenge were:

> *"We've seen City Challenge set community against community....We've just been disappointed time and time again."*
>
> *"City Challenge was a con because it top-sliced budgets from different pots of money to make one pot. It turned community against community, fighting for funding."*
>
> *" They haven't thought about the long term. City Challenge goes in 1997 and what happens then? Who is going to pick up the tab?"*

Schemes like City Challenge were criticised for *"setting up communities to fail"* by raising hopes and then disappointing them, and for concentrating too much on capital as opposed to revenue spending. Some of the new buildings which had been constructed in the neighbourhood through government investment were under-used. The local authority was described as having to bull-doze structurally sound housing which could have been rehabilitated, because funding was only available for new building. This struck the local community as a serious waste of resources, when so much else needed to be done.

In the view of the people at the meeting the local community was continuing to be eroded. They spoke of how whole streets could degenerate with extraordinary speed, as if urban dereliction was a virus spreading across neighbourhoods. This urban decay afflicted owner-occupiers as well as tenants of the local authority or Housing Associations. Indeed, for home owners, the impact of community disintegration could be especially disastrous. In one road, for example, people who had bought their houses a few years ago for £24,000 found that the value of their most substantial asset had plummeted to only £1,000. Many people simply handed back the keys to the building societies and moved away. The houses were boarded up and often vandalised.

Once a neighbourhood acquired a reputation for dereliction, the urge to depart, if this was an option, could become irresistible. The 'penalties' for remaining included the fact that residents were sometimes deprived of services (including credit) because of their post code, not as a result of their personal circumstances. This was an example of the stigmatisation of particular neighbourhoods. People at the meeting believed that more needed to be done to help people to 'hang on', in such circumstances.

The Church had remained a living presence in the area, alongside the voluntary sector. Representatives from these bodies often worked together and in partnership with local people to try to improve the quality of life for the local community. Representatives from the Church spoke honestly of the difficulties of working with people who are often ostracised by others, and who respond to the harshness of the local environment by building a barrier of 'hardness' around them-selves. These people were also very clear that the appropriate role for the Church in the area was to work with and alongside the local community, not to view their activities as a 'quasi-mission' to a foreign land. If the Church was to be credible it had to belong in the community, and this might mean that some aspects of the usual Church hierarchies and structures would need to be adapted to fit local circumstances. Many of the people who worked so hard to try to improve their area were worn out with the effort; for them too, the temptation to give up and leave was sometimes hard to resist.

The consensus was that the key to regenerating Newcastle's most disadvantaged areas lay with huge improvements in education and training; and that much more needed to be done to support families and encourage children to stay at school and gain qualifications, so that the apparent inter-generational cycle of unemployment might be broken. The incidence of behavioural difficulties among children was said to be high, and health related problems were common across the community. The psychological effects of living in this environment took a heavy toll on people's well-being. One helpful response might be to organise an audit of the health needs of the community, carried out by local people but with the support of professionals and community workers.

It was also suggested that one of the major tasks for workers was to affirm the local people who could be linked in to community initiatives. A great deal of work was needed to help raise the self-confidence and self-esteem of local people so that they might be better able to take advantage of any regeneration programmes. The meeting heard that it was no good expecting immediate, measurable outcomes, as funders of regeneration schemes often seemed to do. The first requirement was for money to fund pre-vocational training: only later would many people feel able to engage in more formal employment training. It would take a long time to develop any meaningful partnerships between the local community and bodies such as the local authority. This would also require many more face to face workers in the community, and much greater consistency in funding and personnel.

This meeting left the Working Group in no doubt as to the size of the task facing the local authorities and other agencies and individuals seeking to regenerate the most disadvantaged districts in our cities. The Group was, however, immensely impressed by the commitment of the people and bodies in Newcastle who had stayed in the area, and who keep working to try to improve life for the local residents. One of the many important issues raised by the meeting was what more can be done to help support them in their efforts. This is a question to which the Report will return.

2. Homelessness and housing need

The Consultation Meeting which took place in Cardiff included representatives from the housing authority, housing assoc-iations, The University of Wales at Cardiff, the Church, residents associations, and the private and voluntary sectors. The subjects for discussion were homelessness and housing need.

Recent trends in housing provision in Cardiff are probably very similar to those in many other British cities. Most people, more than two in three of the citizens of Cardiff, now live in owner-occupied homes. The private rented sector has been in gradual decline over many years and now accounts for barely 8% of all homes in the city. The social housing sector provides about 24,000 homes and accommodates about a quarter (25%) of the 306,000 people who live in Cardiff. The local authority admin-isters 18,000 of these properties and Housing Associations, 6,000. The stock of council housing has diminished significantly in recent years as a result of the 'Right to Buy' and this trend continues. In the first nine months of the financial year 1994-5, a further 174 council homes were sold. In 1994, the only new homes being built in Cardiff were for owner occupation or for rental from Housing Associations.

Much of the remaining stock of council homes in the city is found on outlying estates which were hurriedly constructed in the decades after the Second World War, in response to the burgeoning demand for housing at affordable rents. As has already been pointed out[69], in many British cities these have left a continuing legacy of poor quality accommodation, isolated from the main sources of services and employment. This isol-ation appears to be characteristic of some estates in Cardiff. Two comments made at the meeting were:

"We're not just dealing in bricks and mortar. Beyond this, the quality of life is about facilities. Its about not designing the problems into communities, about what jobs are available, about the facilities for the community."

" One of the key questions is about all the things that go

along with housing. Do people always have to look beyond their area for their facilities? If so, people feel rootless."

Some of the people who lived and worked on estates in Cardiff felt that a further reason why these neighbourhoods did not always function very well as communities was that many council homes were massed together and segregated from districts in which there was a higher proportion of owner occupied homes. In housing jargon, there was 'insufficient tenure mix', making the communities on out-lying estates one-dimensional, and unable to sustain a range of facilities, such as banks. This too, appears to have been a consequence of poor planning, although the experience in Newcastle (see above) is that sustaining a mixture of housing tenures in an area can be extremely difficult, especially if house values tumble. People at the meeting were united in the view that in the future, housing should always be developed alongside the planning of jobs, services and other facilities.

Homelessness is a serious problem in Cardiff, as in most British cities. In the first quarter of 1995, the housing authority accepted applications under the homelessness legislation of 151 homeless households, but it had to turn away more than double the same number of people again. Most of the 151 households which were accepted were offered temporary accommodation. Until very recently, this was often accommodation in unsatisfactory 'bed and breakfast hotels', but in 1993/4 the housing authority in Cardiff was able to stop using this type of temporary housing solution, because it managed to lease sufficient self-contained flats for the purpose, (known as 'private sector leasing' in housing jargon). Whether it will be able to continue avoiding the use of bed and breakfast hotels once the new *Housing Act 1996* comes into force is highly questionable.[70]

Most homeless applicants whom the housing authority accepted were families with children. Cardiff also has a significant single homelessness problem. Unfortunately, single homeless people have very little chance of gaining access to the council housing stock under the current homelessness legislation.

The *Rough Sleepers Initiative* targets money (£73 million over the next three years) at cities across England to help voluntary sector organisations and local authorities meet the needs of roofless people, most of whom are single. However, neither Cardiff nor Swansea are part of this scheme. The explanation for this from the Welsh Office is that the scale and nature of rough sleeping in Wales is very different from that in London. However, other English towns and cities apart from London are set to benefit from this funding, so it seems anomalous that Cardiff is not able to do so too. It became quite clear at the meeting that there are homeless people on the streets of Cardiff, as there are in probably every city in Britain. One of the people at the meeting expressed his frustration in the following terms:

"Last night and tonight there will be young people sleeping on the streets of this city. There is an immediate need for beds tonight, not in five or ten years' time. There's nowhere for them to go, its an immediate problem."

A great deal of concern was voiced about the fact that as each year progresses with very few new homes for affordable rents being constructed, the gap between the demand and supply of social housing grows ever larger and becomes progressively harder to bridge. As one person at the meeting said:

"People are beginning to get used to the idea now that homelessness and housing need are insoluble problems, but they're not."

Lack of political will at central government level was blamed for the pursuit of this policy. On the whole, the people attending the meeting were supportive of the efforts of the local authority to improve housing conditions and alleviate homelessness in Cardiff, but with very restricted resources. The housing authority's capital budget, for example, has shrunk from £37 million in 1989 to £6 million in 1995, severely limiting the City Council's housing maintenance programme, and ruling out new building entirely. People at the meeting repeatedly called for Central Government to lift their current prohibition on the spending of capital receipts from the 'Right to Buy', by housing authorities.

From time to time, Cardiff City Council has gained some additional funding from central regeneration initiatives. For example, in 1992, money was made available from the Strategic Development Scheme (SDS) to fund a Renewal Liaison Officer post. The post holder supported a number of initiatives aimed at stimulating community involvement in planning. However, the Housing Authority's 1993-4 Annual Report states, *"1994/5 sees the end of the SDS funding for the Renewal Liaison Officer. Although seen as a valuable resource, the three year funding of SDS limits achievements to the short term, when longer term solutions are needed to bring about lasting community development,"* a criticism of many urban policy initiatives which has already been made in this Report.

The discussion about homelessness which took place at this meeting was realistic. People acknowledged that one of the reasons for the gap between the supply and demand for social housing was that there are more single person households now, partly because of a rise in the level of divorces, and also because more people are living longer, on their own in the community. However, they were also highly critical of the impact on ordinary people of the central government policies of encouraging young people to stay at home until they become economically independent; and of taking no concerted action to increase the supply of permanent homes at affordable rents. The meeting heard that families with adolescent children worried about whether their sons and daughters would be able to leave home, and if so where they would live. Representatives of an agency which worked with homeless young people spoke of their concern about the vulnerability of young homeless people who had left home prematurely, or who had been thrown out, or who had no home to leave, including many careleavers.

Some of the emotions which were expressed by community workers, Church representatives and others at the Cardiff meeting were similar to those in evidence in Newcastle. Many people in Cardiff are working hard to try to alleviate homelessness and address acute housing need, but they feel frustrated and hampered by what they perceive to be a lack of support from central government, and of resources which are in any way commensurate with the scale of the task facing them.

3. Transport and the related environment issues

The Consultation Meeting which took place in Glasgow focused on Transport and related Environment issues, and was attended predominantly by representatives of the voluntary sector and of community groups[71].

Perhaps to a greater extent than any other city in Great Britain, Glasgow currently demonstrates the paradoxes of contemporary city life. Once the second city of the British Empire, Glasgow has come through a long period of economic decline and has been renewing itself with considerable style and self-confidence for at least twenty years. Glasgow will be the UK City of Architecture and Design in 1999, and is gearing up for this event by restoring the Merchant City district at its centre. High quality, new architecture is juxtaposed with classical elegance. Fine Victorian streets filled with coherent terraces span out towards the city's West End. Glasgow is a relatively green city, with 8,000 acres of parks and open spaces, a country park and a well known Botanical Garden.

So far as its transport facilities are concerned, Glasgow appears, especially at first glance, to be rather well served. There are innumerable bus services. The underground system is limited in terms of where it reaches through the city, but is reliable and clean, especially in comparison with its counterpart in London. An overland railway system links Glasgow with much of the surrounding region. From the city it is possible to gain access to beautiful Highland countryside in less than two hours, via Scotrail's famous *West Highland line*. Hills fringe the outskirts and are visible from most points of the city. Glasgow's airport is only about twenty minutes' drive from the centre of the city, via the motorway, the M8, which goes through the heart of the city.

It became clear during the meeting in Glasgow, however, that by no means all Glasgow's citizens are currently able to enjoy the city and its environment in the ways described. In Glasgow, as elsewhere, the forces of social exclusion and spatially distributed poverty appear largely to be to blame. As in Newcastle, many of Glasgow's most disadvantaged areas are on the periphery, in what are known in Scotland as housing 'schemes' rather than estates. Glasgow suffered particularly badly from the surge of council house building following the Second World War. There was massive enthusiasm for demolishing former slums in the city centre, and for moving people out of the highly polluted inner city and towards the fresher air of green field sites, ringing the city. More recently, it has been recognised that many traditional tenement buildings are highly appropriate for today's pop-ulation, once renovated, and the focus has switched to rehab-ilitating, rather than demolishing them.

The usual problems of peripheral estates in terms of poor plan-ning of services and facilities, and isolation from sources of employment, already noted elsewhere, were compounded in Glasgow by an additional, pernicious factor. Many of the houses which were built in the post war period were unable to cope with the damp climate. The *1991 Housing Conditions Survey* showed that 104,000 homes in the city had signs of dampness and condensation, half of them in the public sector. Health problems are often the consequence, especially among children.[72]

Glasgow contains within its boundaries about two fifths of the areas of multiple deprivation in Scotland, mostly in these peripheral housing schemes.[73] The meeting heard that about two thirds of households in Glasgow do not have access to a car, and again these people live mainly in these same disadvantaged, outlying areas. Road traffic accidents are the third most com-mon cause of death in Glasgow, and the most common cause of death in people aged 1-34. About 120 people die each year from road traffic accidents, but these deaths are not equally dist-ributed across the city. The neighbourhoods in which car ownership is the lowest in Europe, are also the places where the number of road traffic accidents involving pedestrians are the highest in Europe, namely on the peripheral housing schemes. In the former Strathclyde region as a whole, children account for half of all pedestrians injured in road traffic accidents, rising to four fifths in the most disadvantaged areas. People attending the meeting pointed to the cruel paradox that more affluent Glasgow citizens seem to gain the benefits, and socially excluded people, the drawbacks, from cars.

Glasgow City Council's Transport Strategy currently states that its priorities are to:
- Give pedestrians a better deal
- Promote the use of public transport
- Encourage more people to use cycles
- Provide good access to the city centre for commercial, business and tourism activities
- Improve access for those with mobility difficulties
- Improve the appearance of the city's streets and open spaces, and create opportunities for more activity throughout the day and evening
- Reduce pollution caused by traffic.

However, some of the people attending the meeting were highly critical of the ways in which they perceived transport policy to be developing in practice, in the Glasgow area. At the time the meeting took place, some community groups represented there were campaigning against the proposed extension of the M74 motorway. They felt that this plan symbolised the way in which local decisions about transport policy continued to be dominated by the interests of car users, as opposed to those of pedestrians. Because car ownership is relatively low among residents of the peripheral housing schemes, people at the meeting felt that investing further resources in roads, as opposed to public transport, served to reinforce social exclusion, not alleviate it.

Those attending the meeting were also highly critical of the consultation process which the City Council had carried out concerning the M74 extension. One group, for example, reported that three quarters of the construction work for the new road had already been completed by the time one particular local community was consulted about the plans.

The general view of people at the meeting was well expressed by one person, who said,

> *"We need to redesign cities around people, not cars."*

Local authorities are faced with a number of dilemmas in this respect however, and Glasgow City Council is no exception. As one person at the meeting said,

> *"You can't say to people 'Get out of your cars' unless there is a viable alternative."*

Glasgow City Council's desire to create an integrated public transport network has been severely hampered by the deregulation of the city's bus services. There are currently 16 different bus operators, and the Council has little control over routes or prices, which vary from operator to operator. There are more than a hundred different services, although they appear to come and go with considerable frequency. On popular routes there is much duplication. There are so many different buses in the city centre that some streets have banks of bus stops, with would be passengers having to run from one to another. The system is extremely confusing and is especially difficult for many older and disabled people to use. People at the meeting said that the peripheral housing schemes are not sufficiently well served by public transport to compensate for the low level of car ownership there. There are particular difficulties for those seeking to travel by public transport from one outlying area to another. On the whole, most routes radiate out of the centre and it is often necessary to come into the city centre and go out again.

Glasgow is relatively unusual among British cities in having a major road network which runs right through the city centre. In most comparable cities it was too expensive to buy up city centre land for major road construction, so underground or overground railway systems were created to provide suburban areas with appropriate transport. In Glasgow, the demolition of inner city slums in the decades after the Second World War provided the opportunity to buy land cheaply for major road construction, Glasgow's transport infrastructure is therefore more heavily dependent on the car than many other comparable cities.

There are 'park and ride' schemes at some outlying railway and underground stations, but the incentive to bring a car into the centre of the city remains.

Vehicle exhaust fumes are a major contributor of atmospheric pollution. Many cities are now taking steps, often through partnerships with local environmental voluntary agencies, to measure their effects on the environment by setting up monitoring sites, based on an analysis of traffic flows. Glasgow has recently done so too. One of the aims of this initiative is to identify areas where nitrogen dioxide levels are particularly high because of vehicle emissions. This information can then be used to inform future transport planning decisions.

Glasgow City Council has a Parks and Open Spaces strategy, a City Wildlife policy, and a Landscape strategy. There is a multi-agency approach to urban renewal, and much of the city centre has been sensitively restored. The major environmental challenge for the city is to create a city which is *attractive throughout, and to remove the causes and effects of poor environment and unsightly urban fabric*", as its consultative City Vision document says.

Once again, as in most other British cities, the hardest tasks are to regenerate Glasgow in an inclusive way. Meanwhile, for all Glasgow's apparent success in terms of urban renewal, the population of the city continues to shrink; from 885,000 in 1975 to a projected 600,000 by the year 2,000. The challenge for the city authorities is therefore not only to maintain, but also to improve the city's infrastructure against the context of a declining population.

Part 4

SALFORD – A CASE STUDY OF REGENERATION IN ACTION

Earlier sections in this Report have set out the current urban policy framework in simplified form, and explored the nature of some of the most serious problems facing our cities today. How in practice do local authorities and the other key players go about trying to regenerate their city? The aim of this section is to provide some insight into this question, by focusing on the efforts in one particular city. Every city is different, but it is hoped that themes of wider relevance to other British cities will emerge from this brief analysis of urban renewal in Salford. Some of the material which informs this case study is drawn from a Consultation Meeting which the Working Group held in Salford. Other useful information came from meetings with officers and members of the City Council, and discussions with local people. The Working Group is very grateful for all their contributions.

Salford borders Manchester, on the west bank of the River Irwell. It currently has a population of about 229,300. The Greater Manchester Region as a whole has a total population of about 2.5 million. The origins of settlement in the Manchester area date back at least to Roman times. The region's industrial prosperity began in the 14th century, based on weaving, first of wool and linen, later of cotton, which was imported from the Levant by the 17th century. At the beginning of the 18th century Salford was a town with a population of about 7,000. However, within a hundred years Salford became a city of more than 220,000 inhabitants.[74] The major cause of this rapid urban growth was the rise of the Lancashire cotton industry, which was stimulated by a climate which has been described as 'moist'; by improvements in machinery and by a convenient local coal supply[75]. Salford was never solely a textile town however. Other major industries based there at this time included engineering, chemicals, leather and felt works. Brewing was also important to the local economy.

The transport of raw cotton, coal and finished goods was aided by a system of waterways which began with the Duke of Bridgewater's canal in the mid 18th century, and by the early 19th century, linked Manchester and Salford with Ashton and Oldham, Bolton, Bury and Rochdale. The Manchester Ship Canal which was opened in 1894, stretched to the Mersey estuary and made Salford a major inland port. The docks became a major source of employment in the city. Meanwhile, steam transport had been also been introduced to the Region, with the opening of George Stephenson's Liverpool and Manchester Railway, in 1830.

Such rapid industrialisation resulted, as in other cities in Britain, in areas of intense poverty and deprivation. Houses were built close to factories. Many people lived in cramped terraces, back to back and forty to the acre. In the middle of the 19th century Frederick Engels held interests in cotton mills in Salford, and described one local area in 1844 in the following terms: *"The...district between Oldfield Road and Cross Lane where a mass of courts and alleys are to be found in the worst possible state, vie with the dwellings of the Old Town in filth and overcrowding."* [76]

Salford prospered however, and more affluent suburbs were constructed. Conditions in the poorest districts undoubtedly improved, but by the early part of this century were still very disadvantaged and insecure. We know this partly because they have been painstakingly documented in a book called, *The Classic Slum: Salford life in the First Quarter of the Century* by Robert Roberts, based on his childhood memories of growing up in the area. The book makes clear that on the whole, *"life was far from being the jolly hive of communal activity that some romantics have claimed."* [77]

The decline of the textile industry in the decades after the Second World War left Salford with empty mills, mass unemployment, sub-standard housing and a polluted environment. In the 1960s, Salford still contained 20,000 houses classified as slums. In 1971, Robert Roberts described the area he had grown up in, as follows, *"That little world between the railway lines...had now been swept away. Except for a factory here and there, desolation remains."*[78] This was the legacy left to those seeking to create a viable and sustainable local economy in the city of Salford, in the post-industrial age.

Like Newcastle, Salford is classified within Cluster One of the Department of the Environment's criteria for grouping the designated Urban Programme authorities, (see above for the general characteristics of these areas). Salford has a potential labour force of over 100,000 people, of whom 77,400 are currently in employment. In the third quarter of 1994, un-employment in Salford was 11.1% overall, compared with 9.6% in Greater Manchester and 9.3%, nationally. However, as in other cities, unemployment in Salford was not evenly distributed but concentrated in particularly disadvantaged neighbour-hoods. Long term unemployment is a serious problem in Salford, with 41% of unemployed people in the city being unemployed for more than a year, compared with 36% in Greater Manchester and 33% in Britain as a whole.[79] In addition to relatively high numbers of unemployed people in Salford, there are similar numbers of residents who are 'economically inactive'. This group includes many people who have retired prematurely, often because they feel they have little realistic chance of obtaining work.

Within Salford's economy there has been a considerable increase in the proportion of the workforce employed in the banking and finance sector, and a slight rise in the numbers working in the distribution and catering industries, over the last twelve years. Employment in manufacturing has fallen. Since 1981 there has been a trend towards increased part-time working, with male part time employment increasing and female part time employment decreasing.[80]

Salford's urban regeneration strategies are multi-faceted and ambitious. They include some initiatives targeted at areas of most disadvantage, alongside others of application to the wider city population. Salford is pursuing some high prestige projects, but also laying much emphasis on 'capacity building' within deprived neighbourhoods; ie. helping to improve the skills and self-esteem of socially excluded communities. 'Partnership' is a theme which constantly recurs in descriptions of the large and small scale projects being undertaken: partnership for example, with local communities, with the private and voluntary sectors; and with the other two local authorities – Manchester and Trafford City Councils, and the two Urban Development Corporations, Central Manchester and Trafford Park, which have contributed with Salford to Manchester City Pride[81] .

Salford's economic future is inextricably linked to that of the wider economy in Greater Manchester, and the North West of England. Most of the trends in Salford's local economy mirror those in the wider Region, across which fewer than one in five employed people now work in manufacturing industry, an extraordinary shift, bearing in mind that Manchester was the world's greatest industrial city less than a century and a half ago.

Manufacturing will not return to Greater Manchester in the foreseeable future, at least not on anything like the scale of the Victorian era, because most British manufactured products are uncompetitive in the new global economy. The much lower wages paid in other parts of the world mean that British companies are finding it increasingly difficult to compete in terms of price. They may however, occasionally have a competitive edge over producers elsewhere in the production of 'high value added' goods, ie. products for which most of the profit derives from features concerned with the quality of their finishing, such as their design flair or their innovation. This kind of production generally employs relatively few people (usually with high skills). It is important that the Manchester Region fosters the development and growth of companies of this nature, but realistically, such firms are unlikely to make more than a limited contribution to the local economy, particularly in terms of employment.

Like most other British (and European) cities, Salford has concluded that the future lies not, on the whole, in manufacturing but in pursuing a range of 'consumption-oriented' city activities, based on the inherent advantages of the city compared with other places, which are as:

- a forum for meeting and for exchanging information
- a centre for tourism, leisure, creativity and culture
- a learning environment
- a varied and physically attractive place.[82]

Salford and the other constituent authorities of Greater Manchester are pursuing a number of schemes, often in partnership with each other and with other bodies such as the private sector and TECs, aimed at maximising these competitive advantages. The long-term strategic vision towards which the Region is working and which provides the framework for the area's regeneration is set out in the first part of Manchester City Pride mission statement:

"By 2005 Manchester and the neighbouring areas of Salford and Trafford will be unchallenged as:
- *a European Regional capital – a centre for investment and growth, not regional aid*
- *an International City of outstanding commercial, cultural and creative potential*
- *an area distinguished by the quality of life and sense of well-being enjoyed by its residents"*[83]

Greater Manchester has identified the fact that in the new global economy it will increasingly be competing not only with Liverpool or Leeds, for example, but also with other medium sized European cities, such as Barcelona and Stuttgart. In seeking to increase the Region's attractiveness to in-coming businesses and to tourists, both European and British, the various City authorities identified that the Greater city had several features of relatively unexploited potential, two of which happen to be situated in Salford: first, a large dock area, Salford Quays; and second, the largest collection in existence in Salford City Art Gallery, of the paintings of LS Lowry. Lowry was a local artist, most of whose pictures portray the early 20th century industrial landscape, and are of considerable popular appeal.

In other British cities, most notably Liverpool and London, dock areas which were until relatively recently desolate and decaying, have been brought back to life as attractive, affluent neighbour-hoods, and as a focus for culture and leisure activities. So too in Salford, where there is already substantial new owner occupied housing, and a large luxury hotel in Salford Quays. In February 1996, Salford was awarded a £64 million grant from the National Lottery to construct *The Lowry Centre*, a new, purpose built home for the City's collection of Lowry paintings, in Salford Quays. The Lowry Centre is the only joint project to date between the Millennium Commission, the Arts Council of England and the National Heritage Memorial Fund. Salford City Council is co-ordinating the project, donating land and providing financial and technical support. The project has been developed through a partnership approach, incorporating the private sector, among others. The scheme is a quite brilliant exploitation of the area's competitive advantages, and one which has managed to attract the necessary matching funding from, among other sources, the European Regional Development Fund.

The Lowry Centre will aim to integrate the visual and perfor-ming arts and is being planned to maximise its appeal to all sections of the population, beyond those who generally visit museums. Alongside a gallery to house the Lowry collection there will also be a Study Centre; two theatres, one with 1,650 seats, one with 400; and the first ever children's 'hand on' gallery, to encourage young people to experience the arts in an exciting way. There will also be a public plaza in which outdoor performances can take place (weather permitting), and the national *Centre for Virtual Reality* will be located on an adjacent site. The latter is to be a research facility as well as a tourist attraction, and will place Salford University at the cutting edge, so far as the development of this new technology is concerned.

Projections suggest that the Lowry Centre and associated developments will generate a further £100 million in private investment; create 6,500 jobs in the office, retail and leisure sectors; regenerate the remaining derelict land in Salford Quays; attract over 2.5 million visitors and bring in approximately £4 million a year to the local area.[84] The Lowry Centre is a high profile development which has raised the profile of Salford, regionally and nationally, and is also a key strategic project within the Manchester City Pride Initiative.

Good communications are increasingly important to the success of post-industrial, urban economies; in terms of roads, railway and air links, and also, increasingly, in terms of mechanisms for transferring information almost instantly and with great accuracy, through the interaction of telecommunications and computing. Technological advances in information technology are changing the world we live in many different ways. Employment is likely to depend increasingly on the manip-ulation of data derived via computerised communications. The development of such an 'information society' carries with it a serious danger of polarisation between those who are 'computer literate and adept' and the rest of the population. People who are unfamiliar with computer technology will be at increasing risk of unemployment and social exclusion. In an effort to minimise the chances of this happening in Greater Manchester, and to maximise the economic opportunities presented by computer technology, an initiative called *GEMESIS 2000* is under way. *GEMESIS* stands for *Government, Medical, Industrial and Social Information Superhighway*, and although it is currently being developed in Salford, it will be extended eventually throughout the Greater Manchester area.

Under the *GEMESIS 2000* project, a 'fibre-optic net' is being created to link together businesses, universities, schools and others in the Salford area. The only other such net currently in existence in Britain is located in Docklands. The *GEMESIS 2000* project is jointly funded with money from, for example, the SRB, the European Development Fund, and Salford University. The leading private sector organisation which is involved is NYNEX, which is a major telecommunications company. The *GEMESIS 2000* fibre optic net is being installed at the same time as

NYNEX lays cables for cable television throughout the district. The idea behind integrating schools into the system was to give children ready access to the latest communications technology and thereby encourage them to develop their skills in this area, perhaps leading some towards further education in this field. Some of the more tangible short term benefits include the fact that the system includes a video conferencing facility linking schools to native foreign language tutors in local universities.

The development of the Lowry Centre and Salford Quays, and the *GEMESIS 2000* project are examples of the types of high profile initiatives which are designed to make Salford (and Greater Manchester) an attractive and creative place. Marketing has a very important role to play in this new vision of urban economics. As the City Pride document states, *"To compete effectively with other major European cities, it is not enough merely to provide an appropriate infrastructure – equally important is the creation of a positive image for the City Pride area and the promotion of its benefits and attractions to diverse audiences."*[85] This helps to explain why Manchester has been so determined in its efforts to host the Olympics: simply pursuing this goal helps to reinforce the city's image as a successful, dynamic city on the international stage. In this sense, the 'hype' about a city can be a self-fulfilling prophecy. Although Manchester's efforts to gain the Olympics have so far been unsuccessful, the city will host the Commonwealth Games in 2002.

This is one of the aspects of city regeneration initiatives which can be particularly hard for local authorities and others to get right. The danger is that if the external Public Relations message conflicts with city dwellers' everyday experiences, the result is cynicism and disenchantment among the local population. This appears to have happened, to some extent, in Glasgow, where the message *'Glasgow's miles better'* alienated some people who felt left out of the city's new prosperity. The risk of public cynicism is something about which the bodies which have contributed to Manchester City Pride appear to be acutely aware.

The second part of the mission statement for the initiative says:

"...sustainable regeneration demands that the benefits of ... development... are experienced within the communities in which they take place and can be seen to have relevance to the lives of the people who live there."

Similarly, the City Pride document also states: *"Our marketing strategy has two themes – to promote the City on a regional, national and international basis to secure interest, investment and jobs, and to promote the City internally to residents and strengthen the sense of civic pride and ownership of the City."*

It would be easy for statements of this kind to be empty rhetoric, but in Salford, the City Council is trying hard to make them a reality and to bridge the gap between the city's population and the local authority, through the development and implementation of a Community Strategy. The Strategy's aim is to develop partnerships between the public, private and voluntary sectors, and local communities. It has three core values:

- Corporate working and partnerships, breaking down the barriers of who does what, developing partnerships at the local and city wide level, and ensuring the involvement of community representatives in addressing issues such as community safety
- Customer care and quality service – putting people first by ensuring service users are at the centre of actions
- Consultation and participation – planning and implementing decisions together.

Salford City Council has reorganised its service delivery in support of the Community Strategy. All council services are now managed and delivered on an area, rather than a departmental basis. Eleven service delivery areas were drawn up to cover the city. The idea of the new system is to encourage corporate working; enable local authority staff to develop a clear community focus to their actions; make the City Council more accountable and responsive; and facilitate the development of long term relationships between the local authority and the general public. One practical impact of the scheme is that if a person wants to contact the City Council about a local problem, they do not have to identify the right department to approach but can go straight to their local area office. A further element to the initiative is that Neighbourhood Co-ordinators are being appointed to en- courage a corporate approach in local areas, and to act as a single point of contact for the community.

Although the Community Strategy is relatively new in Salford, a number of community projects have already been developed as a by-product of the increased communication and co-operation which its implementation has fostered. These include: a *Disabled Access Guide* for people with disabilities using Salford shopping city; the development of a Resource Centre in a district of Salford called Ordsall, aimed at providing a base for local community groups, and business, training, and job search sup- port for local people; and *Salford Football Community Link*, a city wide project co-ordinated by the charity NACRO, which helps local communities set up and run junior football clubs.

The City Council is taking steps to try to ensure that people living in Salford's most disadvantaged neighbourhoods are also able to benefit from the new economic developments in the city. Salford has been successful in its bids for both rounds of the SRB. The successful round 2 bid is aimed at regenerating a district called Cheetham and Broughton, which straddles the Manchester-Salford city boundaries. The Cheetham-Broughton initiative is designed to create an unbroken ark of regeneration linking the Lowry Centre and Salford Quays in the west, to the International Sports Park, the central venue for the 2002 Commonwealth Games, in the east. Key partners include the City Councils of Manchester and Salford, the Housing Corporation, Greater Manchester Police, Manchester TEC, local community committees, and Man-chester Chamber of Commerce.

The Cheetham and Broughton area is a severely disadvantaged neighbourhood, with many of the characteristics already ident- ified in similar localities in other cities. There is high unem- ployment (20% compared to 14% in Salford and Manchester as a whole); particularly high unemployment among the ethnic minority population (36% compared with 20% among the general population); significant poverty (15 of the 69 Enumeration Districts in the area are in the most deprived 7% of such Districts in England); approaching 1 in 5 dwellings are unfit; the area contains 5% of all the derelict land in Salford and Manchester; there is high crime; low educational attainment and skill shortages (only 14% of pupils gained 5 or more GCSEs at Grades A-C compared to the average for England of 43%); and poor health (for men the chances of dying prematurely are twice those of the national average).

The SRB Cheetham and Broughton bid was for £25 million, this funding to be complemented by £62 million from private sector sources, and £48 million from other public sources. The programme is planned to last for seven years, and concentrates in the early years on providing a solid basis on which to develop the more physically based renewal in later years. Although this district has many problems, it also has considerable regeneration potential, because of its strategic location, diverse and rich multi-cultural community, strong investment base, and private sector investment opportunities. The SRB bid document makes clear that the intention is to build on the strong entrepreneurial tradition, which is closely linked to its role over the years as an arrival point in Manchester and Salford for immigrants from many different countries. All the key strategic SRB objectives (see above) are targeted in different ways.

However, some of the more basic 'capacity building', or community work elements of the scheme include measures to:

- develop existing networks and encourage broader community involvement in the future of the area;
- empower young people (through for example, developing services that address the needs of black young people, links with the economic programme elements for employment and training, and a self build housing project);
- support children and families (through programmes around parenting skills, family language and literacy development, assistance with children's behavioural difficulties, and reducing stress and anxiety among parents, especially socially isolated women);
- stimulate multi-agency approaches to tackling crime and fear of crime (including racial harassment and domestic violence).

The Economic programme component of the scheme focuses on measures to:

- develop enterprise in the community (in partnership with Manchester TEC and Business Link, to develop links between training providers and disadvantaged communities);

- support ethnic minority enterprises (by offering a range of business planning, start-up and on-going support services, delivered through bilingual consultants);

- identify and support small and medium sized businesses with significant growth and job creation potential (targeting the wholesale and distribution sectors centred in one part of the area);

- help companies address the linked problems of crime and insurance cost, through a business security package;

- improve the physical environment;

- develop business support and customised training in new information and communications technologies;

- enhance the local community's "access to employment", (through providing services including mentoring, vocational training and post training support to 14-19 year olds and the long term unemployed, a targeted approach to training local people in construction skills, and an outreach team and work in schools to encourage life long learning; job search support, especially for black people and those with language and literacy difficulties).

The projected outputs of the Cheetham and Broughton regeneration scheme include the creation of 1,100 new jobs; the delivery of 110,000 training weeks, leading to training and qualifications for 2,230 people; 260 business start-ups; 60 community safety initiatives; and the successful support of nearly 6,000 young people through personal and social development programmes.

One of the most impressive features of Salford City Council's approach to urban regeneration is the way that it appears to be managing to balance the pursuit of new economic opportunities, on the one hand, with a broadly based, inclusive approach to urban renewal, on the other. Both officers and members were honest enough to admit that they were learning all the time about what works, and that some of the apparently successful approaches of today were the result of having learned from the mistakes of yesterday. In the 1970s for example, the Salford district of Ordsall was the object of a major regeneration programme. In retrospect, the local authority believes that some of the approaches used at the time were over-professional and unintentionally excluded the local community. The result is that the scheme's outcomes have been less successful and long-lasting than they might otherwise have been. More broadly, officers suggested that until relatively recently, regeneration policy in Salford had failed to take into sufficient account the long-term effects on people of unemployment and social exclusion. If so, this is a criticism which could probably be levelled at the design of most initiatives, everywhere.

No doubt there are people living in Salford today who feel that the City Council's Community Strategy is a sham, and that all the power to take decisions about the future direction of policy lies where it always has done, with the local authority and other official bodies. One of the difficulties facing Salford and many other urban authorities is a long legacy of mistrust. People who have seen their local area degenerate, and whose hopes of improvement have been continually disappointed are unlikely to rush headlong into the formation of new partnerships. They will need time and information before they will be prepared to make the effort to become involved. Once having become involved however, many people will be highly committed. That is why the regeneration of the most disadvantaged neighbourhoods has to be a very long-term endeavour, which begins in a small way through the identification and support of active individuals and community groups.

From most people's point of view, the only thing that is worse than no consultation is tokenistic consultation. If local neighbourhood and community groups are invited to share in discussions, timescales will lengthen, and there must be sufficient flexibility to allow for this. If community groups take a role in decision making, the decisions which are eventually taken may not always be to the local authority's liking! Community groups need to be clear about the weight which is to be attached to their views when decisions are made. It is important that people's expectations are not raised, only to be dashed.

If a local authority instigates measures to encourage greater community involvement in regeneration plans, officers will need support as well as clear guidelines, especially since they are being asked to give up some of their power to the community. There can also appear to be an in-built tension between setting up new structures to help encourage community participation on the one hand, and the role of elected members on the other. What is the role of the councillor, if not to represent the views of their local constituents? These considerations suggest that officers at all levels, and members, need to be integrated into the task of planning community involvement, since their active support is vital to the success of these policies.

Notions of this kind seemed abstract and far away from the realities of daily life, as members of the Working Group walked around the Broughton area of Salford, which is scheduled for regeneration through the SRB. Some of the streets embodied what the Working Group had been told at the Newcastle Consultation Meeting: complete terraces of two up, two down brick houses were boarded up with wood or metal. The people who had once owned these houses had left, handing back the keys of their now virtually valueless properties to the building societies from which they had borrowed the money to buy them. Only a handful of people remained in a neighbourhood which once housed several hundred. The members of the Working Group were shown around the area by the Neighbourhood co-ordinator, and by a woman who lived nearby, who had been in the area for many years and was a linchpin of several local community initiatives.

The city of Salford clearly has a vision of where it is going, and people of intelligence and determination at all levels in the City

Council, and in many other organisations and groups, working to help take it there. After some earlier disappointments, Salford has recently succeeded in putting together project proposals which brilliantly exploit various government and European funding schemes, and which also manage to be attractive to other funders, including the private sector. Salford is striving to build a successful economic future for itself by being forward looking and progressive. Moreover, it is making a real effort to pursue these objectives in the context of a meaningful partnership with the local community.

In short, Salford appears to be doing everything right. Three uncomfortable questions, however, are raised. First, can Salford's efforts at regeneration, brilliant as they are, overcome the long term legacy that has been left it of urban dereliction, especially in the most disadvantaged neighbourhoods? Second, what is the economic future for cities which are less well led, and which lack the competitive advantages of a docklands area, and a major art collection of exceptional popular appeal within their boundaries? Third, how many equally needy and promising districts in other cities have to be neglected, in order that regeneration in Salford can take place? We will return to the issue of 'winners and losers' in the next section.

Part 5

TOWARDS A VISION FOR BRITAIN'S CITIES

Part Two explained that when the findings of the Working Group's survey of Methodists living in cities were analysed, a number of major themes emerged. These provide a framework for understanding how people would like to see our cities developing: collectively, they constitute a *Vision for the city*. Those themes are:

- An enhanced sense of community, in which there is more active participation by citizens and a sense of mutual respect between all city dwellers, irrespective of age, gender, race, disability or creed.
- Greater economic prosperity and vitality.
- A more equal, more socially just society.
- A greater sense of personal security.
- A cleaner, more sustainable city environment.
- The Church setting realistic, attainable goals for enhancing its role in the community life of the city, and taking practical measures in pursuit of these objectives.

The ideal city which these themes conjures up is one which is not so much a utopian, but a better balanced version of life in many of our cities today. There probably is not a single city in Europe which embodies all these attributes, although Amsterdam may come close. This list of objectives underlines people's desire for a new relationship between rights and responsibilities, the public and private, and the collective and the individual, in city life.

This Part of the *Report of the Working Group on the Cities* looks at how cities may be able to move closer to a realisation of the balanced, modern city, based on the evidence which the Working Group has gathered about the condition of our cities today, and an analysis of future trends.

To some extent, these features of the 'ideal city' constitute a 'virtuous circle', in which one positive element tends to reinforce another. For example, a city in which there is an enhanced feeling of community and a more equal society is also likely to be one in which there is a greater sense of personal security. Similarly, a city with a clean and attractive environment is more likely to attract and sustain new business activity. The challenge for policy makers is to devise strategies which can carry our cities towards a realisation of all these objectives, without pursuing one in a way that undermines another. Early Victorian cities, for example, were places of enormous economic vitality, but they were also badly polluted and socially unjust.

Any examination of the future of Britain's cities must begin with a review of their future economic prospects, based on inferences drawn from projections of current trends, because a degree of economic prosperity is a necessary, if not sufficient condition, for a successful city. Without prosperity, a city's attention becomes necessarily focused on survival, and other objectives which are crucial determinants of the quality of city life may have to be subordinated.

1. The pursuit of prosperity in Britain's cities

The impact of globalisation and technological change

Part 4, which examined current urban regeneration initia-tives in Salford, showed how technological advances are increasingly influencing commercial activities, so that infor-mation and communications technologies are becoming ever more central to the ways in which wealth is created. In Salford, the City Council and others are trying to harness these tech-nological developments to act as the engine of economic growth in the city, for the benefit of the whole community.

New technologies mean that work can increasingly be transported anywhere in the world. A particular component or sub-contracting operation can be sited wherever it can be most cheaply undertaken. For example, Neodata is a huge company which deals with magazine subscription orders. It is based in Boulder, Colorado, in the United States, but has back offices in County Limerick in Ireland for data entry, and the files produced there are sent to the headquarters in Colorado by satellite.[86] Technological change parallels and stimulates globalisation. It is the combination of these two trends which is already having an enormous impact on our cities, and one which is sure to increase as the pace of change accelerates still faster.

The notion of a 'world economy' is one which reflects a very old historical reality for most European countries, and especially for a trading nation like Britain. The current concept of 'the global economy' is qualitatively different. A global economy means an economy that works as a unit on real time, on a planetary scale. Capital flows, labour markets, commodity markets, information, raw materials, managements and organisation are all internationalised, and fully interdependent throughout the planet. The global economy covers the world, but not all regions and all people. Wealth, technology and power are concentrated in the North, while the South is increasingly differentiated. South East Asia is becoming integrated, under the leadership of Japan, while China is engaged in rapid economic growth. The countries of Latin America are described as inhabiting an 'in-between land', of semi-integration, alongside the daily reality of a marginal existence. Africa, however, is largely disconnected from this global system because most African countries currently lack the infrastructure which is the precondition for linkage to the global economic system.[87]

Globalisation sounds futuristic and abstract, but it is already having a significant impact on the commercial life of British cities. Europe's first response to globalisation has been 'economic convergence'; that is, companies across Europe are increasingly combining and merging in an effort to fight off competition from competitors in other parts of the world. This trend is largely the result of the decisions of individual firms, but is also stimulated by formal provisions in the European Union

Maastricht Treaty which encourage convergence between the national economies of the EU.

The practical impact of 'economic convergence' is that large companies are rationalising their activities across Europe. Instead of maintaining manufacturing plants and offices in most of the European Union countries, large multi-national companies are concentrating their resources in only one or two, and basing their decisions about where to locate on an analysis of the competitive advantages of different countries and regions within the EU. The consequences for individual cities can be devastating. A community which once had a secure place in a purely regional or national division of labour now needs to find a new role in a European wide labour market.[88] Some commentators have pointed out that Britain is relatively well placed when these decisions are being made, because generally, British labour costs in Britain are now lower than those in for example, Germany or France.

Globalisation and technological change explain why large scale manufacturing has left our cities, and why it will never return, except perhaps in a scaled down, high-tech form. At present there are 250 million workers in America and Europe earning an average of $85 a day. In South East Asia there are 90 million workers prepared to work for much less. In addition, over the next generation, 1.2 billion workers will enter the international labour market from South America, China and India. These people currently work for less than $3 a day. Manufacturing will therefore increasingly transfer to these parts of the world because labour costs are so much lower, especially probably to India, which has a competitive advantage because English is so widely spoken there – a somewhat ironic legacy of colonisation.

Opinion currently diverges between those who think that globalisation and technological change will seriously undermine the economic viability of our cities, and those who believe that these trends offer the hope of greater urban prosperity, provided that city administrations understand, and take steps to embrace, the new opportunities that they bring.

The pessimistic view of the economic future of our cities

Those who believe that the future of the British city is one of gradual economic decline point to several factors. First, they refer to the population losses which many British cities have experienced since at least the 1980s; the vacant office space in many cities, and the continuing drift of companies out of the city centre, to cheaper sites elsewhere. People who hold these views also point to projections of future economic trends within the European Union. Ominously for most of Britain, these suggest that the economic centre of gravity in Europe is slowly shifting south, towards the Mediterranean. Currently, the most economically vibrant parts of Europe describe a banana shape, from London and South East England, down through Paris to Milan, and through Switzerland to the cities of Germany. A new banana shaped area of prosperity may now be emerging, stretching along the coast from Florence and Valencia, and inland to Lyons and Madrid. If Eastern Europe becomes more prosperous, the focus for economic growth in Europe may also shift east, but this trend would be equally unlikely to benefit the majority of Britain's cities.

Secondly, the pessimists point out that the technological revolution is only in its very early days. Most commentators believe that new technology will fundamentally change the relationship between people and employment, with the result that far fewer people will need to travel into the city centre to work than today. Instead, their office may be at home, or entirely portable, moving wherever they happen to be. According to this theory, cities lose their rationale as places for exchanging information; much more happens via a computer screen. Here are several examples which have been given to support this view:

- A major merchant bank in the City of London is a subsidiary of another merchant bank in Frankfurt. To avoid the need for executives constantly to travel to and from Germany, the London bank is currently installing a 'video conferencing' suite on site, so that meetings can take place without everyone being physically present in the same place. This bank is also putting small cameras on top of the computers of certain key staff, who frequently need to talk to colleagues in Germany. It is only a small step from this to a totally portable video conferencing facility, which employees would be able to us anywhere.

- Mobile telephones mean that people need never be out of telephone contact, but they are quite expensive to run. A new system in one major firm of London accountants means that if there is an incoming call to the London office for a particular accountant, the switchboard automatically diverts the call to wherever that person is that day, say in a meeting in Leeds. With this kind of technology, again, the person's exact location is immaterial to the quality of the communication.

- Acknowledging the fact that people no longer need to be in the office on a regular basis in order to carry out most of their tasks, the same firm of accountants now has a "hot desking" arrangement, which means that executives no longer have their own office, or even their own desk. They only use a fixed space on the occasions on which they are on site, which are relatively infrequent. One consequence is that the company can operate with lower overheads, because it can manage its operations from a smaller building.

If fewer people have to travel in and out of our cities for work, this would certainly help to improve the city environment by alleviating traffic and the pollution this generates. However, this might also mean that city centres became less economically viable, since for example, the businesses which service these areas, for example cafes, dry cleaners etc. would lose much of their trade.

The optimistic approach

The optimists believe that these fears are exaggerated, and that a great deal of business will continue to be carried out on a face to face basis in cities, because the quality of the communication is so much higher than via computer or telephone. They point out that technological advances mean that it is no longer necessary for a bank to be within 500 yards of the Bank of England, as it was centuries ago, so that its officials could guarantee the safety of monetary transactions. The optimists also acknowledge that technology now allows the back up clerical workers to be physically located anywhere in the world, not merely elsewhere in the City of London. However, they point out that in practice, financial services are still dominated by big cities, especially New York, Tokyo and London. Half of the world's 100 largest banks by asset value, two thirds of those banks' net income and virtually all of the world's largest 25 largest securities firms are based in those three cities. Even where an element of the business has moved away it has tended to congregate elsewhere, as in Chicago so far as derivatives trading is concerned.[89]

The reason for this is that many of the skills which matter most in banking are personal. Face to face contact is essential, partly because this helps to promote the trust that is required to make an agreement but also because the informal exchange of ideas in banking and allied activities is unpredictable. The most valuable information may come from a casual conversation in a local winebar at lunchtime rather than through a formal meeting. What is true of banking is also applicable to all sort of other economic activities usually bracketed together as 'services', including the media, marketing and advertising.[90]

Furthermore, the optimists assert that big cities in particular have a competitive advantage in the new 'information based economy', on the grounds of their scale. In a big city, an employer ought to be able to find every possible combination of skill, age and background. When the European Bank for Reconstruction and Development set up in London in 1991 it needed people from 38 different countries speaking more than 50 languages, in addition to experts in banking, economics and administration. Three quarters of those who were eventually recruited were already living in London.[91]

It is also sometimes argued that as the knowledge based 'information economy' develops, improved telecommunications may serve to increase the attractiveness of a central city location rather than to diminish it. The growth of the electronic office is likely to reduce the cost of maintaining a relatively small elite head office, whilst admittedly leading to a continued reduction in unskilled and semi-skilled jobs. Moreover, technological advances tend to impact first on the cities, (it is in Docklands in

London, and Greater Manchester, that the first fibre optic nets are currently being developed in Britain) because this is where the market for such advances lies.[92]

Some commentators go much further, and suggest that the role of the cities, especially of the metropolises, is set to grow, as the nation state gradually declines. Some of these commentators are 'systems theorists' who believe that the global economy is increasingly becoming a linked system, in which the major cities will act as the critical nodes of communication. They point especially to trends towards greater economic and political convergence within the European Union, and suggest that these are likely eventually to result in the renewal of the role of regions and cities in Europe as locuses of autonomy and political decision making. Under this hypothesis, the more national states fade, the more cities will emerge as the driving force in the making of a new European society. [93]

Not all agree. Others believe that the nation state is set to remain the major force in politics and economics for the foreseeable future and in support of their argument, assert that there is no clear mandate for greater European economic political integration among the populations of the EU nations in general, and in Britain in particular.

The prospect of winners and losers among our cities

Whichever version of the future comes to pass, the optimistic or the pessimistic, or something in-between, the reality is that some British cities are clearly better placed to take advantage of current economic trends than others.

London is in a quite different position economically to all other British cities because it is the only British global city; in the first rank of European cities alongside Paris (with Berlin soon to join them); and also probably one of the three major world cities in economic terms, together with Tokyo and New York. London's economic advantages are in part historical (as has been described above) and stem from its former role as capital of a far-flung empire, its long standing function as the location for the headquarters of major companies, and its mix of governmental, cultural and business strength. Furthermore, London is particularly fortunate among British cities because it is a major hub in world airline networks, a feature which is increasingly important in the global economy.

It has already been suggested that Salford and Glasgow are successfully regenerating themselves, each by maximising their competitive advantages: Salford, by developing its dockside environment, based in part on its collection of Lowry paintings; and also by developing its telecommunications system, linked in with Greater Manchester's strong base in higher education and technological research; Glasgow by focusing more on the attractiveness of its contemporary and historic architecture, and its role as a centre for culture and tourism.

However, by no means all British cities are so fortunate in having this potential for growth, in terms of the current European prescription for economic prosperity. Not all, for example, have the necessary mix of universities and colleges to create a stimulating 'learning environment' of interest to new businesses, or a well-preserved, historic city centre, to attract tourists. If cities become increasingly competitive, there will be losers as well as winners. If Greater Manchester becomes the vibrant regional centre it hopes to be, what will be the future for Sheffield, or Liverpool? Equally balanced development across Britain's cities seems unlikely. This opens up the possibility of polarisation between not only regions of the country, but also individual cities. The question of the extent to which Central Government should intervene in this process to try to equalise some of the differences which may emerge, is likely to be of increasing importance in the years ahead.

The problem of unbalanced economic growth within Britain's cities

A further difficulty is the obvious lack of balance in terms of economic growth and prosperity within cities. If cities do succeed in attracting new investment and employment, a major task in itself, how can they ensure that all the people living there are able to benefit equally? As has been pointed out in the context of the Salford case study, this problem is made worse because the knowledge based 'information economy' tends to concentrate wealth and power within an educated elite, leading to increasing social and economic polarisation within cities.

Los Angeles is perhaps currently the best example of this phenomenon. Recent studies have shown that the economic expansion and restructuring of Los Angeles has significantly increased poverty levels and squeezed job growth upwards to a growing executive-professional-managerial technocracy; and downwards and in much larger numbers to the working poor who survive on public welfare, part-time employment and the informal economy. At the extremes of Los Angeles' income distribution, wealth is concentrated in protected communities with armed guards, while the urban poor are trapped in what have been called 'murderous landscapes of despair'[94]. Los Angeles may still seem to be a nightmare vision of the city of the future so far as Britain is concerned, but there is evidence of a similar trend towards polarisation here too, as became clear from our Consultation Meetings.

As has been observed[95], the process of city regeneration itself unfortunately tends to produce stark contrasts between adjacent districts. Although cities differ widely, there is a tendency in regenerating cities for the central business district to concentrate in 'directional activities' and to become empty of retail, commercial and residential land use. This is the centre of political power and economic growth. Nearby may be the homes of the 'new elite', the lawyers, brokers, managers and financiers, living in gentrified sub-areas which contain many bars, restaurants and other up market leisure facilities. Islington, just north of the City of London comes irresistibly to mind. (Some researchers have however, suggested, that the impact of gentrification on British cities has been exaggerated, and that its effects are largely confined to London[96].)

In some cities these areas are bordered by ghetto districts of acute deprivation. In these places however, and indeed scattered across the city, are pockets of economic vitality. These are often produced by immigrants from Asia and elsewhere, many of whom are engaged in small-scale entrepreneurial activities which demonstrate great resilience in the face of economic adversity. However, these small businesses are also often only viable because of the contributed labour of family members, which effectively subsidises their operation. Small businesses have an important role to play in enriching the commercial life of cities, and often provide a valuable service to local communities (for example, by staying open for long hours). They can constitute a first step on the ladder for talented entrepreneurs; all large businesses were small ones once. However, the contribution which small businesses can make to alleviating unemployment in our cities seems necessarily limited.

Out of town retail development and the decline of the traditional high street

Further away from the city centre, suburban sprawl is concentrating business services and other office and retail functions into 'Edge Cities', economic sub-centres which are often larger and busier than more central areas. These districts are often found near the interchanges of major roads and are generally accessible only by car. The trend towards the development of 'Edge Cities' came from the United States, where much laxer planning controls have stimulated their growth for many years. In Britain, once planning controls were relaxed and out of town shopping arrived, people appeared to like it just as much here too.

However, the problem of degenerating city centres and high streets, as economic vitality transfers to the outskirts of cities, is now beginning to attract public attention. To a great extent, our attitudes towards this phenomenon are hypocritical. Out of town shopping centres constructed of garish metal sheds, or even worse, mock Tudor beams, may not be aesthetically pleasing to look at from the outside, but they are thriving because most people find them convenient and reasonably pleasant places to shop in. We would like to maintain thriving high streets of small shops, but on the whole, we are not prepared to patronise these businesses, if offered the chance to shop in larger, out of town stores. Many people who work long hours and live in the suburbs like the fact that they can drive to a supermarket on an out of town site, park easily and often for free, and do all their shopping at once, without having to visit numerous small shops. Another feature which is popular with customers is the wide range of products offered in the largest stores, with which few small shops can compete.

Increasingly, out of town retail estates also contain leisure facilities such as multiplex cinemas. In some shopping malls the difference between shopping and leisure is becoming more and more blurred. The Metro Centre on Tyneside for example, now contain funfairs and other forms of entertainment, aimed particularly at children and families. It is entirely possible to spend a whole day in a mall of this kind, browsing, shopping, eating a cheap meal and perhaps watching a film, and many people chose to do so. However, no mall in Britain yet approaches the giant malls in the United States. In the Mall of America, for example, outside Minneapolis–St. Paul, you can purchase almost any product or service you can think of, including a wedding ceremony or a funeral.

One of the attractions of these shopping environments is that they are highly sanitised. Shopping malls are private property, with their own conditions of entry. 'Undesirables' will be kept out. Private security guards patrol them. They are places where people feel safe. Ironically, this may be deceptive. In one very large furniture superstore in North London, one of the major problems for the security guards is the fact that shoppers tend to drop their guard – they do not expect to have their pockets picked as they would on the street outside.

It may be that people are becoming more attracted to the pseudo-cities of out of town shopping malls, because they feel less at ease in the real city. While there may be an element of truth in this, out of town shopping is thriving principally because it is more practical for car owners, and cheaper than shopping in town. The economics of 'Edge Cities' work to reinforce their position and weaken that of the smaller shops in city centres. Economies of scale, plus the fact that land is cheaper on out of town sites, mean that prices in out of town stores invariably undercut those of smaller, city centre enterprises.

Although many think the trend is unfortunate, it would seem that out of town shopping is here to stay. Now that most people have become used to shopping in this way, it seems unlikely that they will willingly return to their previous consumption patterns. The challenge for small, city centre shops is the same as for other small city businesses: namely, to secure a 'niche market', in which they can offer a valuable service to local people. They can usually not compete in terms of price, but they may be able to do so in terms of quality of service, or of product. However, even if future planning mechanisms are less accommodating to out of town businesses than they have been recently, it is hard to see the average suburban high street surviving the onslaught of the larger, out of town developments which are already in place. New small businesses may, however develop out of the ashes of the old, to meet the emerging needs of local communities. Empty properties may be susceptible to conversion for other uses.

Meanwhile, under current arrangements, many people on low incomes are unable to take advantage of the lower prices in many out of town stores, because they do not have access to a car. This is an issue which is examined further, below.

Long-term labour market trends in Britain's cities

As manufacturing industry has declined in British and other European cities, the service sector has grown. In 1993, 7% of the European Union's Gross Domestic Product was generated by services, and this is projected to grow to over 10% by the year 2000[97]. These 'people centred activities' are expected to become ever more important constituents of city economies. Managerial and professional jobs are projected to increase by the greatest amount. There are also expected to be more jobs created in the catering, tourism and leisure industries, many of them part time and relatively poorly paid. Projections suggest that public sector employment (ie. jobs in local government and the civil service), still an important feature of most city labour markets, will continue to fall.[98]

The overall tendency in terms of skill levels is towards higher-level skill requirements, with increased demand for engineers and other professionals. There is also increasing demand for an up-grading of skills at intermediate and lower occupational levels; and more emphasis on flexibility and social skills, alongside formal qualifications. The demand for unskilled and semi-skilled employment is expected to go on falling. The proportion of women in the labour force is projected to carry on increasing, as is the prevalence of part-time working.[99]

The need for measures to help everyone, but especially people living in disadvantaged areas, to improve their educational achievements and qualifications, is obvious. The development of a flexible system of 'lifelong learning' is also likely to become more pressing, as people will increasingly need to requalify and up-grade their training, in line with technological advances and changes in labour market demand.

Conclusion

This brief survey of current thinking about economic trends in British cities suggests that the future is likely to be one of increasing uncertainty and change, as individual businesses continue to restructure in response to the impact of globalisation and technological innovation. We seem to be only at the beginning, rather than the end, of this process of adjustment.

No city can take its future economic prosperity for granted. The imperatives of encouraging inward investment, stimulating indigenous business growth and generating local jobs are shared by city administrations of all political complexions. Few can be in any doubt that they are engaged in the toughest of competitions with other British and European cities, for business and prosperity. It is beyond the power of local governments to protect city populations from the full force of future economic uncertainty, but they can do a great deal to help by creating an environment which encourages wealth creation, and by equipping people with the skills to enable them to take advantage of the opportunities ahead. Salford City Council seems to be a very good example of a local authority which is putting into practice, the current European prescription for city success.

The current competitive system for allocating urban regeneration moneys may be an efficient, meritocratic way of distributing scarce resources, but it also ensures that there will be losers as well as winners (as well as creating other problems, discussed above). Some of the places which are proving to be unsuccessful in this competition are areas of great unmet need. One of the responsibilities for central Government is to ensure that these cities and neighbourhoods are not left to manage on their own. The quality of life for populations in these places must not be allowed to deteriorate to an intolerable degree. This may mean that new funding regimes, in which the key criterion is the depth of social and economic need, have to be introduced to complement those currently in operation.

Projections make clear that some people are much better placed to benefit from current labour market trends, than others. Over the next two decades, employers will place a higher premium on flexibility, solid educational attainment, computer literacy and good communication and social skills, even than they do today, and this can only enhance the competitiveness of already advantaged groups in the labour market. People who are less well endowed with these attributes are likely to lose ground, rather than gain it, and they are especially likely to be concentrated in the most disadvantaged areas of our cities. Unless measures are taken to reverse these trends, there is every reason to fear that there will be increased polarisation within city populations, and between city districts.

If the economic trends identified here take effect, it seems that all the efforts of local authorities and other local groups and individuals may be unable to create the more socially just city societies which most people want. Much more fundamental change will be required to reverse these trends, and it would appear that central government will have to take the lead. This crucial issue is explored in detail in the next section.

2. Creating a more socially just society in our cities

Since most of Britain's cities became recognisably modern, through the processes of industrialisation, there has been enormous social progress. As a historian of urban planning has pointed out, society has changed shape over this period. It is no longer a pyramid, with few at the top and many at the bottom, but rather an old fashioned spinning-top, with a big bulge in the middle. The problem is no longer the one the first Fabians posed in 1884, *Why are the Many Poor?* However, it is beyond dispute, and has been demonstrated again in this Report, that a substantial proportion of people in British cities still live in poverty, often clustered together in especially disadvantaged inner city or peripheral urban areas, and excluded from many of the benefits of city life. For example, official statistics show that a quarter of the population currently live on less than half of average income, after housing costs are taken into account. This is often regarded as a surrogate measure of poverty[100].

The continuing existence of social disadvantage in our cities has led some to argue along Malthusian lines, that 'the poor are always with us', or that this problem is explained by the existence of an urban 'underclass'.

The notion of 'the underclass' has become a topic of popular debate, first in the United States and now in Britain. In the 1980s, Charles Murray propounded the theory that a dependent 'underclass' had developed in America, created by an over-generous welfare system. He asserted that this group, made up of predominantly black, feckless single parents, criminals and drug abusers, had become structurally detached from mainstream society, with their own deviant value system, which is passed down from one generation to the next.[102] Murray also claims that a similar group, albeit with slightly different characteristics, has come into existence in Britain[103]. Murray's theory has however, been much criticised, and recent research in Britain refutes the idea of a distinctive dependency culture, independent of mainstream society. It also tends to show that socio-economic disadvantage attaches to areas, rather than to individuals. If people are able to move, they are much more likely to secure employment and improve their situation.[104] If the underclass theory was valid, one would expect these residents to transfer their disadvantage with them, when they moved.

As a recent, Government published analysis points out, with particular relevance to what the Working Group heard during the Consultation Meeting in Newcastle, *"This is not to deny the cultural differences, in part spatial, within urban areas. They develop partly in response to economic and social disadvantage and are, in part, a coping mechanism. They serve to reinforce the polarisation and distance between sections of the inner city population and 'mainstream' society. But they are largely a product of, and maintained by, structures of disadvantage."* [105]

'Structural disadvantage' is what the first urban policy practitioners, the CDP teams sent into the inner cities, identified as the root cause of urban poverty and decay in 1969. If this is still the problem more than twenty five years later, why has it proved to be so enduring?

The factors which reinforce social exclusion in our cities

Research shows that social exclusion in disadvantaged areas has, in the main, been produced and reinforced by the combined effects of four forces: housing allocation processes, the labour market, poverty and low incomes, and racism. The aim of the following paragraphs is to 'disentangle' the effects of these elements, to explain why it has been so hard to regenerate the worst hit neighbourhoods in the inner city and on the peripherary.

I) The housing market

Living and housing conditions in disadvantaged city areas differ from those in other neighbourhoods in several important respects. Although the tenure mix within these areas varies across the country, they generally have lower rates of owner occupation, a larger proportion of total dwellings in municipal ownership, and significantly more homelessness enquiries than other localities.

They also tend to have a higher proportion of their properties in disrepair. Traditionally, the private rented sector has offered the poorest housing conditions, but in recent years there has been a marked trend towards more owner occupied homes being in serious disrepair. One of the reasons is that the increase in the elderly population has led to an increase in outright owners, the poorest of whom lack the money adequately to maintain their homes. Many of these older people live in inner city areas. It has been suggested that another factor contributing to the increase in poorly maintained, owner occupied housing is the recent expansion of home ownership into sections of the population who cannot really afford this form of tenure[106].

Housing authorities in disadvantaged city areas often face major problems in maintaining the quality of their housing stock. This problem is compounded by the fact that most of the more attractive council homes have been sold to their tenants under the Right to Buy scheme. Some of the system-built housing developments from the 1960s and 1970s have structural problems, and much of the council housing which remains from the major construction programmes of the inter-war years now needs rehabilitation. As became clear during the Cardiff Consultation meeting, housing authorities often lack the resources to invest adequately in cyclical maintenance and repair.

Many forces have operated together to concentrate socially excluded people into relatively poor quality, council owned homes, in the most disadvantaged neighbourhoods in our cities. In order to understand how this has happened, it is important to examine trends across the housing market as a whole, including the private and owner occupied sectors. This is because the composition of the population living in council owned homes today is the result of the different housing choices made by other people, coupled with their own lack of ability to choose to live elsewhere.

Throughout the post war period, until about fifteen years ago, Britain has had relatively large public rented housing and owner occupied sectors, and a very small private rented sector, in comparison to other European countries.[107] More recently, the public rented sector has diminished in size and the owner occupied sector has increased, so that two thirds of UK dwellings are now in owner occupation[108]. In general terms, more affluent people who previously lived in public rented housing have moved away, or bought their council homes under the Right to Buy. One of the reasons why this had led to concentrations of socially excluded people in disadvantaged areas is because on the whole, most of the council homes which have been purchased have been in districts away from the two areas of maximum disadvantage – the peripheral estates, and the inner cities.

The movement of more affluent people out of public sector renting and into home ownership has been an important, but by no means the only factor, concentrating social exclusion in disadvantaged city areas, and especially within the diminishing public sector housing stock. An additional factor has been increasing demand for this accommodation from poor house-holds. The largest proportion of new public sector lettings are to homeless applicants, most of whom are dependent on welfare benefits. As has already been explained, economic restructuring within cities has left some disadvantaged neighbourhoods with few employment opportunities, and deepened social exclusion in the area. This is particularly pronounced in public sector housing estates which were highly dependent on a single employer, such as the Hartcliffe and Withywood estates in South Bristol, which once employed several thousand people but which is now closed. A similar phenomenon was described in Newcastle at the Consultation Meeting which the Working Group held.

A further crucial factor has been changes in housing subsidies. Over recent years, the system for subsidising public sector tenancies has gradually become one in which rents have been allowed to rise to market levels, with means tested housing benefit becoming the mechanism to help those unable to afford these rents. This has made public sector tenancies relatively less attractive to people on middle incomes who are not eligible for housing benefit, and reinforced the link between low income and council home rental.

The changes which have occurred in the public rented sector since 1980, as a result of these forces, have been described in the following terms:[109]

- Fewer economically active residents
- Fewer multiple earners
- Fewer higher income households
- Declining level of car ownership
- More households with no earners
- Declining role as family housing
- Increase in female headed households
- Increase in unskilled manual workers
- More elderly people
- Ageing dwelling stock
- Declining proportion of 3/4 bed houses
- Increasing proportion of flats
- Increasing proportion of lettings to homeless people
- Increasing proportion of tenants on state benefits.

The primary factor which has deepened the element of social exclusion for most public sector tenants in disadvantaged city districts, is their inability to move away to areas where job prospects may be better and the quality of life, higher. Most of these people are unable to buy a home of their own because they cannot afford a mortgage. Nor are they generally able to improve their housing situation by transferring to a more favourable public sector tenancy elsewhere, because of the pressure on the stock, its overall low quality, and the fact that it is generally now found in disadvantaged city areas.

Research suggests that the recent trend towards the growing

concentration of socially excluded people in the public sector housing stock, has been much more pronounced in Britain than in most other European countries, and that one of the main reasons for this is the small size of the private rented sector here[110]. In most European cities, the social role of the private rented sector has had a positive impact on residential structure. Partly because of rent control and regulation, this sector has often housed a mix of households, including the very poorest. This has relieved the pressure on the public rented sector and prevented it from becoming a resolutely residual form of housing provision, as it is increasingly in Britain. It has also made it easier for public sector tenants to move away from declining city areas. Recently published Government statistics support the notion that private sector tenants are much more mobile than local authority tenants[111].

Many owner occupiers in disadvantaged city neighbourhoods also find it difficult to move away. The decline in the housing market hit house values hard, especially homes which had recently been bought under the Right to Buy. In particularly badly affected city districts, house prices can plummet, with homes becoming virtually worthless. Many of these purchasers have been pushed into negative equity, and 25,000 homes were re-possessed by mortgage companies in 1994[112].

These considerations suggest that future housing policies should concentrate on increasing the mobility of people living in disadvantaged areas, and improving the state of repair of property in these neighbourhoods, both rented and privately owned. In other European countries, the private rented sector plays a valuable role in offering greater housing choice to people on low and middle incomes, and has prevented council housing from becoming an entirely residual form of housing tenure. Over the last few years there have been repeated attempts to revive the private sector in Britain, but without any great success. The public housing sector has benefited from the contribution made by Housing Associations, but this has been too small to counterbalance the overall decline in the quality and quantity of the sector as a whole.

Much more needs to be done to help restructure the housing market so that it better meets the needs of people living in the most disadvantaged areas of our cities. This is partly a matter of ensuring that there is a sufficient quantity of better quality, affordable housing near sources of jobs and services. It is also important that this housing reflects the changing composition of households in Britain. There is a strong trend towards the formation of more single-person households, and away from the traditional nuclear family. Housing must adapt accordingly, through the creation of more one and two-bedroomed homes.

2) The labour market
Although the ways in which housing allocations processes work can have an independent effect on disadvantaged city districts, it is the compounding effects of poor housing in poor environ-ments, coupled with geographical and structural barriers to employment, which reinforce social exclusion in these places.

The difficulties faced by people living in disadvantaged city areas, in obtaining and maintaining employment, differ accor-ding to the city and the district in which they live. In many ways, people living on peripheral estates are worse off than those in the inner city, in this respect. The peripheral estates are often physically cut off from the main sources of jobs. Job search may be hampered by low car ownership and poor public transport links. As has been noted, estates which were built to meet the needs of a single employer, who has now departed, are probably the most disadvantaged of all.

Levels of unemployment in disadvantaged city neighbourhoods will depend, to some extent, on the demand for labour across the economy as a whole. However, recent research suggests that unemployment in cities is becoming increasingly concentrated in the least favoured districts on peripheral estates and in certain inner city neighbourhoods. In Coventry for example, the worst five wards in terms of percentage unemployment rates increased their share of the whole area's unemployment from 31% in 1986 to almost 34% in 1991[113]. It appears that these areas not only suffer from particularly high levels of unemployment, but also from a poor quality of employment. Research shows that most inner city residents are likely to be restricted to low paid, insecure employment, possibly part-time, and with poor promotion prospects. They are also much more likely to experience periods of unemployment than other city dwellers[114]. It has been argued that our economy depends on an infrastructure of low wage, non professional jobs – secretaries, cleaners and maintenance workers, for example – and it seems that it is people living in disadvantaged city neighbourhoods who are often employed in these activities[115].

The populations of working age in these areas are disadvantaged in labour market terms, partly on account of their relative lack of formal qualifications. Yet on the whole, the majority of jobs which are available to inner city residents are semi-skilled or unskilled, and require little formal training. It has been suggested that an even more important factor is the significance attached by employers to recent, and relevant work experience[116]. In this sense, the experience of periodic unemployment is self-reinforcing: a patchy employment record is often viewed as suggesting unreliability by city employers.

A further factor which works against inner city residents searching for work is the subtle discrimination of informal recruitment channels[117]. Especially when unemployment is high, employers often do not bother to advertise vacancies for relatively low grade jobs. Instead, they rely on word of mouth, internal adverts and other informal networks to recruit new staff. People who have been out of work lose touch with these lines of communication, and so never hear about vacancies.

Certain characteristics of inner city labour markets contribute to higher levels of unemployment in disadvantaged neighbourhoods. The labour markets in which inner city residents are competing tend to be large, and because they are located in the city centre, the whole city population often has access to them. Moreover, inner city residents are more likely to be employed in temporary or unstable service sector employment, so they are also more vulnerable to redundancy and unemployment.

Although disadvantaged inner city populations have often suffered from unemployment caused by manufacturing decline and other forms of economic restructuring, it has been suggested that the main problem in these areas is not a shortage of appropriate employment, but rather the barriers to employment encountered by these people[118]. This is shown by the fact that local measures designed to increase employment in disadvantaged city areas have not usually been very successful, despite the best efforts of those running the schemes[119]. For the reasons already described, inner city employers tend to recruit on a city wide basis, with only limited benefits to inner city populations[120]. Most job vacancies also arise from job turnover rather than job creation.

These facts suggest that the emphasis in schemes aimed at tackling unemployment in disadvantaged city neighbourhoods should be on job preservation, and on removing the barriers to unemployment (such as poor self-esteem, lack of recent or relevant experience, and reconnecting people with recruitment channels), rather than solely on job creation. Measures should be especially targeted at helping unemployed young people, and the long term unemployed.

3) Poverty and low incomes

Poverty interacts with other factors to prevent some citizens from taking a full part in city life. The measurement and mapping of poverty in our cities is a complex task, made much more difficult by the fact that there is no official definition of poverty in Britain. Various surrogate measures are generally used instead, such as the proportion of the population receiving certain means tested benefits. The measure of poverty used by the European Union is 'below half average income'[121]. Surveys, including those commissioned by the *Breadline Britain* television series, have adopted as a poverty measure, lists of necessary goods and services, based on the views of ordinary people. If a household is unable to afford to purchase a significant number of these essential items, they are deemed to be living in poverty. *Breadline Britain* surveys found, for example, that 32% of the population of Manchester and 40% of the population of Liverpool were living in poverty in 1987 and 1989, respectively. Poverty was not evenly distributed across these cities but clustered in the inner city, and especially in Liverpool, on the edge of the city[122].

A 1991 survey in London ranked wards according to the percentage of households suffering overcrowding, in households with no car, the percentage of the economically active population unemployed, and living in rented housing. This found a marked concentration of disadvantage in inner east London, either side of the River Thames, and a smaller cluster in the inner north west part of the city.[123]

The *Family Expenditure Survey* and the *General Household Survey*, provide some broader insights into the distribution of poverty across Great Britain. Analysis of these figures shows that the poorest households in Greater London and other cities, are both absolutely and relatively poorer than the poorest households in other areas of the country[124]. Similarly, a comparison of the proportion of households receiving Housing Benefit across England reveals that 49% of all households receiving Housing Benefit are in inner city areas, although these districts only house 31% of all English households[125].

Official statistics show that people within the population who have the lowest disposable incomes tend to share certain characteristics. The five largest groups (largest first) are pensioners, the unemployed, those employed but on low incomes, single parent families, and sick and disabled people[126]. These groups are strongly associated with disadvantaged city neighbourhoods. Inner urban areas have a slightly lower concentration of older people than the country as a whole, but they tend to be poorer than older people in general.

In recent years a number of demographic and economic forces have operated to deepen poverty and disadvantage, in city districts as elsewhere, and most of these trends are projected to continue. They include high unemployment, concentrated in households and areas. Although nationally, unemployment in the UK has fallen slowly from a peak of 10.9% (3 million) in 1993 and this trend is expected to continue, long term trends suggests that the 'residual level of unemployment' to which unemployment drops at the peak of the business cycle, has been increasing over the years[127]. Moreover, official unemployment statistics omit certain groups, such as young people aged 16 to 18. Male unemployment fell by 2 million between 1977 and 1991, but only half of this change was reflected in the unemployment figures. About 1.8 million men disappeared from the statistics because they were economically inactive, and many of them retired early[128]. The operation of the 'benefits trap' has led to a situation of unemployment being increasingly concentrated within households; in 1992, nearly 60% of married women whose husbands were working were themselves employed, compared to only 24% whose husbands were unemployed[129].

It is sometimes suggested that official statistics on the level of unemployment, paint an unnecessarily gloomy picture of the economic vitality of individuals and disadvantaged areas, by failing to take into account the 'informal economy'. The argument is that many people of working age who are officially out of work and dependent on means-tested benefits, are working, mostly on a part-time, casual basis. Studies have suggested however, that the informal economy may be smaller than often supposed[130]; that it does not play a particularly important role in inner city areas[131]; and that the high unemployment and low incomes usually found in disadvantaged city neighbourhoods, reduce the demand for local goods and services, and discourage illegal, economic activity[132].

Yet another trend is the rise in lone parenthood. The proportion of lone parent families in Britain increased from 8% in 1971 to 21% in 1992[133]. Lone parenthood is strongly associated with poverty, mainly because of lone parents' dependence on benefits: the lack of affordable child care provision makes it very hard for many lone parents to work[134].

A third trend is that towards increasing inequality. A number of studies show that inequality in terms of both income and wealth has risen substantially in Britain in recent years. For example, the *Joseph Rowntree Inquiry into Income and Wealth* found that although the real incomes of the population as a whole rose significantly between 1979 and 1992, the poorest 20% failed to benefit at all, leading to a growing gap between those on the lowest incomes and the rest of the population[135].

More people have become dependent on means-tested benefits as a result of both higher unemployment and demographic changes, and the income gap has widened between these people, and those with earnings[136]. Health inequalities strongly mirror those of wealth and income; for example, life expectancy at birth is about 7 years higher for people in Social Class 1, compared with those in Social Class V[137]. A number of factors are believed to be responsible for this, including nutrition[138].

The role of labour market disadvantage in reinforcing the exclusion of people on low incomes living in the most disadvantaged areas, has already been discussed. Clearly, this is especially relevant to the situation of economically active people of working age. However, for other groups such as the elderly population, those who are sick or disabled, and lone parents, the level of welfare benefit entitlements and their eligibility criteria are key determinants of quality of life. Numerous studies published in the last few years have demonstrated the difficulties of living on means-tested benefits.

Recent research carried out by NCH Action For Children alone, has focused on the inadequacy of benefits for young people living independently, for pregnant mothers, and for children with disabilities and their families[139]. These difficulties often lead to debt. Only 3% of households with income above £400 per week have debt repayment problems, compared to 28% of those with incomes below £100 per week[140]. The extent of debt problems in the most disadvantaged city districts is also demonstrated by the reappearance of pawn brokers – a commercial activity which had all but disappeared for many years.

Low income statistics show a strong correlation between poverty and living in rented accommodation, the form of tenure which is over-represented in disadvantaged city districts. Poverty and housing market mechanisms work together to deepen social exclusion in disadvantaged city neighbourhoods.

4) Racism

Britain's black population lives predominantly in the cities. In part, this reflects settlement patterns which were determined by the immigrant population's role as a replacement labour force in the 1950s and 1960s[141]. Black people are over-represented in the South East, especially in terms of a concentration of Afro-Caribbeans, Bangladeshis and East African Asians; and in the West Midlands, where there are particularly high proportions of people of Indian and Pakistani origin. There are also significant populations of mainly Pakistanis in the North West and York-shire and Humberside, and of Indians and East African Asians in the East Midlands.

Within these regions, black people are often concentrated in the most disadvantaged city neighbourhoods. It seems that this persistent inequality results mainly from the interaction of two factors, namely, processes of discrimination in the housing and labour markets. These forces greatly magnify for many black city dwellers, the difficulties which all residents of disadvantaged city neighbourhoods tend to face.

It has been suggested that this disadvantage has been deepened by a racially based dual rental market in the private rental sector, and the discriminatory practices of estate agents[142]. Research has shown that allocation policies for council housing are often discriminatory. It has been demonstrated, for example, that the points systems for council house allocation have indirectly discriminated against ethnic minority families, which may score less well in categories such as length of time on the list, and long association with an area. Larger council homes are usually in short supply, and this may discriminate against some ethnic minority families[143]. A significant proportion of the black population arrived in Britain only relatively recently, and was housed through the operation of the homelessness legislation. This has meant that these people have tended to be accommodated in the poorest quality housing, and in over-crowded conditions. In 1988, only 1% of England's white population was living at densities of more than one person per room, compared with 9% of the non-white population as a whole, and 30% of those of Pakistani or Bangladeshi origin[144]. The scope for these people to be subsequently re-housed has often been limited.

The Cash Incentive Scheme has offered a feasible route out of social rented housing for some black tenants, although most of these schemes are in the South of England. Housing Associations in general and Black Housing Associations in particular, have also played a valuable role in recent years in housing black people in better quality accommodation. However, it was recently announced that the Housing Corporation's special funding initiative for Black Housing Associations is to end.

Disproportionately high numbers of Asian households are owner occupiers. It has been suggested that this is partly a result of discrimination in other sectors of the housing market, which leaves Asian people with no realistic housing alternative[145]. These owner occupiers are often on a low income, however, and their property is quite often in poor condition and in severely disadvantaged city districts[146].

An examination of the position of black workers in the labour market shows that here too, discrimination has often operated to place them at a severe disadvantage. Unemployment rates among the black and other ethnic minority populations are significantly higher than among the white population.

There are significant differences between the unemployment rates of different black and ethnic minority groups. Unemployment is especially high in the Pakistani and Bangladeshi populations, more than three times the white unemployment rate[147]. Youth unemployment is very high among young Afro-Caribbeans, more than double that of the same age white population. Analysis of official statistics shows that these differences are not due simply to differences in qualifications, or the age profiles of different population groups. Research suggests that indirect and direct racism are important determinants of these trends, and that black workers often suffer as a result of employers' recruitment practices and concepts of suitability, and their use of informal information networks and recruitment channels[148].

One of the factors which contributes to the vulnerability of many black workers living in disadvantaged areas in our cities is their concentration in sectors and occupations which are more vulnerable to job loss. Analysis of longer term trends in unemployment among the black population suggests that there is a disproportionate tendency for black workers to be squeezed out of work during a recession. This may partly be because when unemployment is high, employers have a greater choice of potential workers and are more likely to rely on informal recruitment methods[149].

The adverse position of many members of the black and ethnic minority populations in the labour and housing markets, living in disadvantaged city districts, is also reflected by their incomes and wealth, relative to the rest of the population. More than a third of black Britons are in the poorest fifth of the population, compared with 18% of white people[150].

The most disadvantaged city districts: is decline irreversible?

This analysis of how structural disadvantage has been reinforced in the most disadvantaged areas of our cities, explains why government funded regeneration initiatives have largely failed to 'solve' the problems in these places. On the whole, urban regeneration schemes have not managed to compensate for the other detrimental forces impacting on the people living there.

Some of these adverse forces are the direct result of other government policies. This is most obviously true of recent government housing policies, which have led to the public housing sector becoming an increasingly residual form of housing tenure, so deepening the disadvantage attached to particular neighbourhoods. Similar criticisms could be made of the current benefits system, which has tended to produce 'benefit traps'. These have hindered people from re-entering the labour market, and provided those who are economically inactive with a standard of living which is impoverishing. In the past especially, urban policy often appears to have focused on the wrong objectives, and has failed to tackle the structural barriers to employment faced by many residents of the most disadvantaged city areas. It is encouraging that current initiatives appear to be much better targeted at the problems facing these districts. However, the concerns about the in-adequacy of available funding compared to the scale of the task, and about other features of funding regimes, have already been explained.

Looking to the future, it is hard to disagree with the conclusions of the study which the Department of the Environment itself commissioned, which says: *"There is very limited evidence to suggest that inner city problems overall are diminishing. On the contrary, it seems most likely that existing resource allocation mechanisms, both market and bureaucratic, will continue to reproduce spatially concentrated disadvantage. The likely future, based on current trends is, if anything, one of increasingly marked inner city problems, increasing spatial concentration of disadvantage in inner city areas and outer estates and increasing polarisation and lack of social and economic cohesion between inner cities and other areas."*[151]

Although some disadvantaged areas may be buoyed up by the economic performance of the wider region of which they are a part, even this cannot be taken for granted. For all these city neighbourhoods, measures are required to reconnect them with broader economic and labour market processes, measures which address the adverse factors set out here. Some suggestions for the direction of future policy are given in the Recommendations section at the end of this Report.

Hope for the future: community-based approaches to regeneration

There is a danger that the content of this Report to this point, gives the impression that the most disadvantaged districts in our cities are sterile places, devoid of activity, where the local residents are passive victims of forces beyond their control. This is far from the intention of the Working Group. Although it is important to acknowledge the nature and scale of the problems facing these areas, it is also crucial to recognise that a great deal is currently being achieved by people in every city in Britain in turning around their own neighbourhoods.

If the most disadvantaged parts of our cities are to regenerate it is probable that they will have to do so largely as a result of their own efforts, albeit with substantial help from local government, local businesses and from voluntary sector organisations. This may not be quite as fanciful as it first appears. The Working Group has become aware of numerous examples of grass-roots activity of this kind during the process of preparing this Report, many of them led by the voluntary sector.

There is a great range of different types of community-based initiatives, but a common characteristic is that they are largely run by groups of local people, who have identified and res-ponded to local needs. The range of organisations that have become involved in community regeneration is wide, but include: community development trusts, housing associations, faith communities (such as the St.Paul's Church Centre in Marylebone, London), voluntary organisations and settlements (for example, the Manchester Settlement). Their work prog-rammes include: childcare and youth work, family centres, adult and out of school education, provision and management of workspaces, crime prevention, health projects, environmental improvements, carnivals and arts initiatives.

Some black and ethnic minority groups have come together to meet the needs of groups within their own communities, needs which they have identified are otherwise not being addressed. In

Birmingham for example, a black group is running a range of education support services for black children and young people, including Saturday schools and mentoring schemes.

Many schemes focus on providing training opportunities for local people. The fact that they often operate in the neighbourhood, in a community centre or Church hall perhaps, makes them much more accessible to the local population than larger scale initiatives run by TECs or Further Education Colleges. Local training schemes are not only more accessible in geographical terms: people who have, for example, been out of the education system for many years or who had a bad experience of education in school, or who have been unemployed for a long period and lack self-confidence, often find it much less intimidating to begin training through this less formal route. Once they have gained more confidence, they may then wish to pursue formal qualifications through a College course. This is an example of how community-based schemes often manage to reach local populations with which more bureaucratic initiatives fail to engage. Training schemes of this nature seem to be exactly what is required to reconnect people living in disadvantaged communities, with formal training and employment networks.

One of the most important effects of these community regeneration schemes is that they 'build capacity' in disadvantaged areas; that is, they increase people's self-confidence so that they, and the neighbourhoods they live in, are more likely to be able to benefit from more formal regeneration initiatives. However, they can also have a direct and immediate effect on the economic well-being of a disadvantaged area. This is especially true of those projects which are developing and implementing local economic strategies. Some local schemes have promoted 'micro businesses' (businesses employing three people or fewer), established broader based, commercially viable companies, or attracted companies on the move. In some cases these enterprises have been shown to have created sustainable employment in hard pressed areas, and to have helped to remove the stigma associated with them, which is often a barrier to successful regeneration[152].

Some of the most exciting community-based regeneration schemes currently in operation are enterprises which have resurrected notions of 19th century, self-help capitalism. One example of this type of activity is the Credit Union. In some of the most disadvantaged city neighbourhoods, commercial banks and building societies have departed because the area is too disadvantaged to sustain them. People receiving Income Support may be entitled to a loan from the Social Fund, but only if there is sufficient money in the local Benefit Agency's fund and only if the person concerned is considered likely to be able to repay the debt. For some residents, loan sharks are the only realistic source of a loan, but they usually charge prohibitively high rates of interest.

Credit Unions are a much more economic (and safer) option for people on low incomes. Each week a member pays in a small amount. If members keep up regular payments they become eligible for a low interest loan. Every year, a dividend is paid out to members (typically 8% in 1995). There are now 600 Credit Unions across the country, with assets of £65 million. Fifty new Unions came into being during 1995. However, there is clearly enormous potential for many more to be established. Ireland, for example, has a strong tradition of Credit Union activity, and it is relatively unusual for an Irish village not to have its own Union. Unions do not have to be based on a geographical area, they can also be established at a workplace or around any other shared affinity (eg. a Church). The staff at one of Britain's major commercial banks are reported to have formed their own Credit Union, a clear example of the financial advantages of these schemes[153]. Once people join a Credit Union they are often surprised how much more attractive their terms are, compared with those of building societies and banks. This is because all the benefit is shared by the members. Today's Credit Unions therefore behave like building societies did in the 19th century.

One drawback of traditional Credit Unions for people on the lowest incomes is the need to be able to make regular savings. Some Unions have tried to address this difficulty by creating a new type of scheme, called a Debt Repayment Scheme. Members who are in financial difficulty have their debts 'bought out' by the Union. This is not a gift and has to repaid at an interest rate of 1% per month. As the money is repaid, other debts are bought out. A scheme of this kind operates on the Ely Estate in Cardiff. South Glamorgan County Council invested £3000 to start up the initiative, and did so for sound financial reasons: people who are hard pressed are likely to become dependent on the local authority's services in the future, unless they receive help of this kind.

A second form of community economic activity is the LETs scheme. An estimated 40,000 people in Britain now belong to these. LETs stands for 'local exchange trading schemes' and are effectively, a bartering system, which enables people to exchange goods and services without money changing hands. To repay a 'debt' incurred through having obtained a service, a member offers her or his own chosen services to other members. Services have a LETs price and are netted off centrally, so the scheme works like an alternative currency. Like the Credit Union, the LETs idea has something to offer everyone, but it is particularly useful in very disadvantaged areas because it may allow people who are on very low incomes to obtain goods and services which would otherwise be entirely beyond their means. There are LETs schemes running in disadvantaged parts of Manchester, Bristol and Newcastle. The London Borough of Hounslow was the first local authority in Britain to sponsor a LETs scheme, as part of its anti-poverty strategy. Many others are reported to be considering following Hounslow's example[154]. One distinctive form of LETs scheme which has been developed in Minneapolis in the United States, has huge potential here. Newly retired people help care for very elderly, infirm people and help them to stay in their own homes. In so doing, they build up 'hours' of care which they can then trade in for support in the years ahead.

The community networks which these local projects often create have a potentially important role to play in linking the people in a local area, with the organisation of more formal urban regeneration schemes, such as SRB bids. However, it is time and energy consuming for, typically under resourced, local groups to engage in the process of working up these bids, and then helping to implement them if they are successful. This is one reason why the voluntary sector is often marginalised in these schemes. The recognition that engaging in formal regeneration schemes carries a considerable cost so far as community groups are concerned, has led to the suggestion that special funding should be available to local groups to facilitate and sustain their involvement in local networks. A structured grant system could, in particular, aid the participation of groups which are often invisible and unrecognised by policy makers, such as networks of women's and black groups[155].

Networks of this kind can also provide immense support to the dynamic pioneers engaged in community regeneration. Research has demonstrated that these individual 'social entrepreneurs' are often the driving force behind successful community regeneration schemes[156]. These are the people who have the ability to assemble skills, form alliances and raise funding to deliver specific projects or initiatives. They use these skills to transform under used and neglected assets; help other local people to develop their own interests; and attract more cautious developers to invest. In Salford, the local authority has made a considerable effort to implement their regeneration strategy around these activists.

However, the Working Group heard at the Newcastle Consultation Meeting how easily these pioneers can become isolated and exhausted. People working in disadvantaged areas are also often exposed to personal risks. They may, for example, challenge the viability of local criminal activities, including those of drug dealers. The murder of a vicar in the Anfield area of Liverpool during the Summer of 1996, demonstrated the vulnerability of those who seek to offer an accessible, personal service in communities which lack sufficient, statutory support services.

These considerations show that it is vital that community regeneration organisations should support and appropriately supervise the activities of the people who work for them, whether in an employed or voluntary capacity. This is also an issue for larger organisations which employ staff to work in very disadvantaged city neighbourhoods, especially if they are often working on their own. This is as relevant to the Churches, as it is to Housing Associations and charities like NCH Action For Children. These agencies must recognise the special stresses experienced by staff working in very disadvantaged areas. The questions which need to be addressed in each case probably include the following. What support structures and systems of accountability are in place? What are the risks to personal safety which are likely to be encountered, and how can they be lessened? How can the service which is being offered be made most effective, without the person delivering it being over-whelmed? What opportunities are there for the person to have time away periodically?

Conclusion

Previous paragraphs have demonstrated the depth of structural disadvantage in the worst hit neighbourhoods in Britain's cities, caused by a pernicious mix of housing market mechanisms, labour market processes, poverty and racism. On the whole, regeneration schemes have failed entirely to address these problems. More recently, there is evidence of a more focused approach towards trying to reconnect people living in dis-advantaged areas with city labour markets, but regeneration programmes leave the problems of the housing market, poverty and racism, virtually untouched. Government policy could fairly be accused of having actually worsened the first two, and of having had no positive impact on the third.

If a more socially just society is to be created in our cities, these policies will have to change. It is a waste of resources to invest regeneration moneys in disadvantaged city districts, unless other government programmes are also developed at the same time, to restructure the housing market, alleviate poverty, and tackle institutionalised racism.

While regeneration schemes have failed to address the structural disadvantage in the worst hit neighbourhoods, the people living there have quite often got on with the task of regeneration themselves, by setting up community based projects of various kinds, often run in partnership with local authorities and voluntary organisations. Many of the most exciting of these are based on traditional notions of self-help capitalism. Government regeneration schemes seem now to be taking much greater account of the need for 'capacity building' schemes of this kind, but it has taken a very long time for this lesson to be learned. The efforts of these social entrepreneurs – often the true heroes of local regeneration – could yield even greater results, if they were provided with more government support. Community based initiatives, appropriately linked to wider regional, national and international regeneration schemes, are the best chance which the most disadvantaged city districts have.

3. Creating a greater sense of personal security in our cities

Crime and fear of crime in our cities: the scale and nature of the problem

Crime was the negative feature of city life which was chosen by more respondents to the Working Group's survey of city dwellers, than any other. Some of the individual comments which were made referred to people's fear of crime preventing them from engaging in community activities, particularly on dark evenings, in areas which effectively shut down once the shops have closed.

These findings are reinforced by those from the Government's *British Crime Survey*[157], which is regarded as the best source of national information about crime rates and trends, and is based on interviews with about 15,000 households across the country. The most recent Survey, carried out in 1994, shows that most people are more worried about becoming a victim of crime than about anything else in their lives (including suffering a serious illness or accident).

Overall, people's first concern is that their home will be burgled. Women are especially worried about being the victim of rape or burglary; men's main anxiety concerns the risk to their cars. Fear of street robbery means that about 2% of the population never go out after dark. Older women are most likely to avoid going out at night, as many as 11% of those living in inner city areas, according to the Survey. This reinforces the Working Group's finding that many more city dwellers avoid going out after dark, for fear of attack.

There is a widespread perception that cities are much less safe places than they were some years ago. To some extent, this view is reinforced by statistical evidence, although it is notoriously difficult to gauge the true level of crime, because many offences are never reported to the police. Over the past 25 years, recorded crime figures have risen, on average, by about 5% per year. In

1994, there were 5.3 million recorded offences in England and Wales, about 95% of which were non-violent property crimes. The actual number of offences is likely to have been much higher[158]. The 1994 *British Crime Survey*, for example, estimated that there were 18 million crimes committed in 1993. Between 1979 and 1994, *British Crime Survey* findings suggest that the risk of becoming a victim of burglary or violence trebled, while the chance of becoming a victim of car crime, doubled.

Crime does not, however, have an equal impact across the country; people are much more likely to become victims of crime in some areas, compared with others. The *British Crime Survey* found that people living in the most disadvantaged city districts—in the inner city and on peripheral estates—were the most likely of all to be victims of violence and of car crime. This was also the population group which was the second most likely to suffer a home burglary. Residents of gentrified city districts, which are often adjacent to disadvantaged neighbourhoods, were actually the most frequent victims of burglary[159].

Once a household has suffered one burglary, the *British Crime Survey* suggests that their chances of being victimised again are much increased. Burglars may wait a few months to allow time for the replacement of stolen items, and then break in and repeat their previous thefts. It is therefore very important for burglary victims to improve their security arrangements, in order to prevent this 'repeat victimisation' from occurring. However, people on low incomes are much less likely to be able to do this than more affluent households.

Certain groups within the population are more often victimised than others. People of ethnic minority origin in our cities are much more likely to be the victims of crime, especially violent crime, than other city dwellers. Asian people are at disproportionately high risk of vandalism and victimisation by groups of strangers[160]. Differentiating a racially motivated attack from other assaults is difficult, but even official statistics demonstrate a rise in the incidence of these crimes – from 4,383 offences in 1988, to 7,780 in 1991, for example[161]. As Britain's ethnic minority population is concentrated in cities, it is fair to infer that the great majority of these assaults must have occurred in urban areas. It is, however, also beyond doubt that official statistics seriously underestimate the incidence of racial attacks, as the efforts of various voluntary monitoring groups in city districts, have demonstrated[162]. Although the Asian community appears to have borne the brunt of most racially motivated crime, it is also important to recognise that other groups have suffered too, including, for example, Afro-Caribbeans and Irish people[163].

Women are at high risk of becoming victims of domestic violence. Nearly 1 in 30 women across Britain reported to the *British Crime Survey* that they were concerned about being attacked by a member of their own family. Among women under 30, the figure rose to 1 in 10, and in disadvantaged city districts, to 1 in 5. More than a quarter of all women respondents to the Survey aged under 30 had received abusive comments in the street, and 1 in 5 had been followed. The Survey concluded that the domestic violence, harassment and sexual insults that women have experienced fairly routinely from men, have contributed to their fear of crime to a far greater extent than the chance of life threatening attack.

Parental fear of crime, especially Stranger Danger, (and of traffic, for more information about which see below) has led many families to withdraw their children from the streets. A recent Mori poll[164] found that 85% of adults think it is less safe for children to play outside than it used to be. More than two in five of those interviewed, said that their children never or hardly ever played outside, without adult supervision. In fact, the chances of children being abducted or molested by a stranger, are minute.

Young people do appear, however, to be at significant risk of becoming victims of other forms of crime. A recent study[165] of the experiences of 11 to 15 year olds in Glasgow and Edinburgh found that only 10% had never been the victim of crime. Of the sample 82% said that they had been victimised during the current year. More young men had been victimised than young women. Theft and assault were the offences most often suffered by young men; harassment and sexual offences, by young women. The *British Crime Survey* confirms the fact that young men are the most frequent victims of violent crime.

Older people's fear of violence is understandable, given their vulnerability and the horrendous nature of some of the attacks on them which have occurred, but in fact, their statistical chances of becoming victims of violent crime are very slight.

The impact of crime and the fear of crime on city life

As any city dweller will tell you, crime is a serious problem in our cities. Crime is spatially distributed alongside social exclusion: people living in the most disadvantaged parts of our cities are most likely to be the victims of crime, and are usually least well equipped, on account of their low incomes, to prevent it. There is no doubt that in some of these neighbourhoods, crime has a disastrous impact on residents' quality of life. This would seem to be the case, for example, in some particularly disadvantaged areas of Newcastle, as the Working Group heard during the Consultation Meeting it held in the city (see above), but Newcastle is not unique in this respect.

The misuse of drugs is perceived to have increased in recent years, especially among children and young people. It is very difficult to obtain an accurate picture of trends in drug abuse, but on the whole, research tends to support the view that young people are being initiated into drug abuse at a progressively younger age, and that drug abuse is particularly prevalent in disadvantaged city districts[166]. A drug abusing, criminal, sub culture appears to embrace some residents in these neighbour-hoods. Drug abuse is often associated with other forms of criminal behaviour, on the basis that drug addicts need to commit offences to fund their habit. Recent research suggests that while this may sometimes be the case, the links between drug abuse and wider offending behaviour are not all one way: young people who offend may also be attracted to drugs[167].

In many city districts, and for many city residents, the risk of becoming a victim of crime is something to guard against, but not a routine experience. This does not prevent almost all city residents from worrying about crime. In some ways, the fear of crime has an equally serious effect on the quality of city life as crime itself, because it can have just as profound an impact on individual behaviour. The fear of crime is largely responsible for many people deciding that they and their children, are safer indoors than outside. It has been argued that fear of crime can be a self-fulfilling prophecy. As people generally, and children in particular, withdraw from the streets, this makes them less safe socially, because if children are absent there is an increasing breakdown in local links and in the sense of belonging[168].

This process is highly conducive to urban crime[169]. Conversely, if a city's streets are busy with different kinds of people enjoying themselves, in the evening as well as during the day, a sense of public confidence and well-being is generated and criminally motivated people find it much harder to act, unobserved and unchallenged. A local authority which manages to generate more 'street life', through encouraging pavement cafes and outdoor arts events, is likely to find that crime falls, at the same time as the sense of well-being increases.

So far, this section has concentrated on the impact of crime on individuals in cities, but it is important to recognise that crime also has a huge, adverse effect on city businesses. It is estimated that during 1993, retail businesses nationwide were the target of almost 180,000 burglaries, at a total cost of over £1 billion. Research suggests that some shops are much more likely to be burgled than others; the risks are highest in groceries, electrical shops, gas showrooms and music shops[170]. These figures apply to Britain overall, but given Britain's population distribution, it is probable that most of these offences will have been committed in cities. People who run small city shops on their own are particularly vulnerable to robbery. This is an especially frightening experience. Many owners of small shops in British cities are Asian, so it is possible that some robberies may be partly motivated by racism.

Crime can make the difference for hard-pressed city businesses, between viability and bankruptcy. A serious burglary or robbery may persuade a company which is barely surviving, to shut down altogether. In particularly disadvantaged neighbourhoods, high levels of crime are a very serious disincentive to businesses which might be considering moving in and setting up there.

Who commits crime?

The task of developing measures to make our cities safer must begin from an understanding of who commits crime, and from an awareness of the factors which tend to encourage offending. On the whole, although the statistics in this area are quite hard to interpret, the popular stereotype of most crimes being committed by young men, is largely correct. This is not new. A Home Office analysis of the criminal records of a random sample of people born in 1953 showed that one in three men had been convicted of an offence by the age of 35. Most young men's offending was short-lived however; the consensus of view has been that young men tend to grow out of crime, once they settle down with a job and a family[171].

According to Home Office statistics, more than four fifths of all convicted offenders are men, and more than two fifths are aged under 21[172]. The peak ages of offending in 1994 were 18 for men and 15 for women; and the commonest offences committed by young offenders were theft and handling stolen goods[173]. Over recent years, the peak age of offending for men has risen gradually, having been 15 for a long period. This may reflect the increased use of informal cautioning by police forces, rather than changes in the offending behaviour of young men. The rate of known offending among the population aged 10 to 17, fell by 17% between 1981 and 1991, but again, it is believed that much of this decline may be due to demographic changes, increases in informal cautioning and declining police detection rates, rather than to an absolute fall in offences committed[174].

Research suggests that young offenders tend to share common features of background and experience. Some of the key correlates are: family poverty and social exclusion; poor parental supervision; inconsistent parental discipline; family conflict; low educational achievement, truancy and school exclusion; strong peer group pressure; and the involvement of parents, siblings or other relatives in criminal behaviour.

Although it is popularly believed that children from single parent families are more likely to commit offences than those from nuclear families, the research is equivocal about this. American research, for example, has shown that homes that are intact, but unhappy and neglectful, are more likely to produce delinquents than those which are 'broken' but where the children are consistently nurtured and loved. The direct influence on children's behaviour appears to be the quality of the relationship with and between their parents[175].

There is no evidence to suggest that young black men are particularly inclined to commit crime, in comparison with other groups within the population. Being young, unemployed, disadvantaged and from an ethnic minority is associated with a high probability of being subject to search and arrest by the police, and black youth perceives itself as being harassed by 'over policing'[176]. It has been suggested that these differential arrest rates may be partly due to racism within police forces, but they are also partly explained by differential rates of offending attributable to age and deprivation factors[177]. The final result of institutionalised racism in the criminal justice system and of these other factors, is that young black people comprise 15% of the population of young offenders in prison, while forming only 7% of the population of British youth, overall[178].

It is important to recognise that the factors listed above are only indicative. Criminologists are still unable to predict which, of two young men with similar backgrounds and personal experience, will commit offences, and which will not. Similarly, while there is a strong correlation between living in a disadvantaged city district and involvement in crime, many criminals come from other places, and most people who live in deprived neighbourhoods are not engaged in crime.

Trends in crime and in unemployment

The 'causes of crime' have often been the subject of heated political debate. In particular, controversy surrounds the question of whether poverty 'causes' crime. The previous paragraphs show that it is more meaningful to refer to 'correlations' than to 'causes', when looking for a relationship between crime and other factors.

Research has shown that there is a strong correlation, or association, between trends in crime and trends in unemployment in Britain. When unemployment is high, levels of property crime are also high.[179] Disproportionately high numbers of young offenders in prison have been found to be unemployed[180]. Some commentators have suggested that one of the most important reasons for this association between unemployment and crime, is the fact that we live in a manifestly consumer society in which 'luxuries' are widely seen to be necessities. Young people in particular, may be inclined to view the possession of the 'right' pair of trainers, for example, as essential to their status and self-respect. Yet, unemployment and lack of income debar some people from obtaining these things through legal means. These considerations lead to the conclusion that, *"when poverty and associated disadvantage are linked with monetary success as a dominant cultural goal, high rates of criminal behaviour are the normal outcome"*[181].

Similar thinking lies behind theories which link together levels of inequality, crime rates, and society's sense of well-being. In very unequal societies, people on the lowest incomes become miserable because they feel socially excluded on account of their economic exclusion, and those on higher incomes worry about losing what they have, through unemployment or illness, or theft. This misery and anxiety then translates into higher crime rates, and mental and physical ill-health[182].

Research findings that suggest that various social and family factors are often correlated with the commission of offences, have led some people to develop broader theories, based on notions of 'the underclass'[183] or more recently, of the 'demoralisation of society'[184]. The Working Group repeats what was said earlier in this Report, namely that it found no evidence of the development of deviant value systems in disadvantaged city neighbourhoods, to support these theories.

Strategies for preventing and alleviating crime in cities

If cities are to become safer places the implementation of a range of responses will be required. However, prominent among these must be strategies to prevent young men from becoming involved in offending; and to help prevent crime in the most disadvantaged parts of our cities.

1. The need to alleviate youth unemployment in disadvantaged city neighbourhoods

During the Newcastle Consultation Meeting in particular, the Working Group heard a great deal of testimony about how young men had become economically and socially disenfranchised in city districts where there was very high unemployment, and how some (but by no means all) had become involved in crime.

Recent research carried out on peripheral estates on Wearside has looked at the way in which some young people drift into crime, in more detail[185]. It shows how some young people, especially young men, can become very disillusioned with school during their early teens, because they see no prospect except unemployment ahead of them, and then drift into an anti-school, anti-work culture. Some of the young people in this study lost contact with the school system when they left school at 12 or 13, and found neither regular employment nor a YTS place. Many of them viewed YTS as 'slave labour' or 'pretend jobs'. They form part of the estimated group of 50,000 16 and 17 year olds in Britain who are neither employed, in education or on YTS, and who therefore have no visible means of support[186]. As has been suggested, these youngsters are very vulnerable to drifting into crime, to secure an income; and into illegal drug taking, to compensate for the lack of meaningful activity in their lives. These are significant risks for all young people who are idle, bored and poor[187].

Although the conventional view of criminologists has been that young men tend to grow out of crime, Home Office research[188] now suggests that the delayed entry of young men into the labour force, caused by high unemployment, is leading to a situation in which many young offenders are continuing to offend for longer than they used to, into their twenties. The Home Office surveyed one thousand 14 to 25 year olds in this study. More than a quarter of men aged 22 and older admitted committing property crime, compared with only 3% of women. Young women aged 14 to 17 were almost as likely to commit offences, but they grew out of their offending behaviour much more quickly.

This study found that many of these young men in their early twenties remained dependent, socially and economically, and lagged behind the young women who took part in the research, in terms of maturity. The inability of many of the young men in the study to find work, traditionally one of the main ways of providing a sense of direction, was identified as a key factor in the development of offending behaviour.

Other commentators too, have described the increasing infant-ilisation of young men, for whom the traditional routes to adult-hood are being denied, and have pointed out that if they are unable to make an economic contribution, young women will in-creasingly decide that they are better off without them[189].

Projections suggest that we are moving towards a world in which paid work will be concentrated in the years 25 to 55[190]. Most of the jobs that are being created are part-time and low-paid, traditionally 'women's work'. Overall, women's participation in the labour force is growing, and men's decreasing. Unless young men with few skills begin to compete for those jobs or obtain better qualifications, male youth unemployment seems set to rise above its current level of 1 in 5 16-19 year olds[191].

Seen from this perspective, solving the problem of youth unemployment is likely to be the most effective means of preventing youth crime, and this is the conclusion reached by the authors of the Home Office study. Some local authorities, TECs and voluntary sector projects have developed imaginative schemes to help unemployed young people living in disadvantaged city neighbourhoods into meaningful training and work, (see above) but there are huge difficulties in doing this in the hardest hit districts, and much more needs to be done to overcome these.

2. Longer term crime prevention: better community support for children, young people and families

The study discussed above, concerning the lifestyles of alienated young people on Wearside, shows that any effective strategy to prevent youth crime must include measures aimed at supporting adolescents, children and their families, and at preventing young people from drifting into crime. The following paragraphs set out some ideas about how this can be done, based on initiatives which are already running with some success in British cities. The benefits of these schemes are long term, but they offer the possibility of very good value for money.

Education has a vital role to play in the long term battle against social exclusion in disadvantaged city areas, and in reducing crime. Extra tuition for children who are failing at school can help raise their level of achievement, and also enhances self-confidence. Mentoring schemes, Saturday Schools and the *Children's University Project*, which runs through the summer holidays in Birmingham, are all good ways of doing this. Schools have a broader role to play supporting local communities and acting, for example, as the focus for crime prevention strategies. Imaginative solutions are needed to the problem of providing a high quality education to children who persistently truant, or have been excluded from school: at present, these youngsters are among the most at risk of becoming young offenders[192].

The problem of providing meaningful and affordable leisure facilities for young people, was one which was raised by some respondents to the Working Group's survey of city dwellers. In certain other European countries such as Denmark, the Youth Service is truly national and provides a wide range of activities for children and young people.

In Britain, the Youth Service has been in steady decline for many years, as a result of successive budget cuts[193]. Some local authorities have hardly any youth service provision at all, even in the most disadvantaged city neighbourhoods. This long-term decline needs to be reversed, and steps taken to ensure that the resources invested in youth provision are well spent. There is no point, for example, running a service between 9am to 5pm during weekdays, if the main demand is in the evenings and at weekends. Highly skilled, detached youth workers (who engage young people on the street, rather than operating out of a project base, waiting for young people to come to them) are more likely to reach groups of alienated young people in disadvantaged districts, than any other group or body.

A restoration of the Youth Service might help to fill the current gap for support services for parents of adolescents who are at serious risk of offending, but who have not yet attracted the attention of the police or the courts. More specialised support services are needed in the case of families in crisis, to help them 'hold on' to very difficult or damaged young people, and to provide support for young people living on their own in the community, where family life has broken down and the young person has left, or been thrown out. Special drug education initiatives, aimed particularly at vulnerable young people in disadvantaged city neighbourhoods, should also be further developed. In all these cases, it is vital that young people are actively involved in the development and running of services.

Pre-school programmes for families and children, such as the Headstart programme which operates in the United States, can have long term benefits and should be expanded[194]. There should also be more community based family centres in hard-pressed city areas; these provide valuable support to parents in difficulty and help keep families together.

3. Other community crime prevention strategies

A wide range of community crime prevention strategies can make a real impact on crime rates and the fear of crime, at local level. On the whole, it is now accepted that these projects are most likely to succeed when developed and run in multi-agency partnerships, involving key players such as the police, local authorities, the probation service, business and the voluntary sector[195]. A cornerstone of these projects should be the active participation of local people, since they are in the best position to assess what the main problems are, and how they can best be addressed. Community based crime prevention projects can help restore the self-confidence of local communities, something which may have been lost through the isolating and alienating effects of high crime, and the fear of crime.

The importance of crime prevention to successful community regeneration is recognised in the SRB bidding guidance, within which it is an identified strategic objective. The local partnerships which come together through the SRB process, and which were also encouraged by the *Safer Cities* initiative (part of the *Action For Cities* programme, launched in 1988), are as relevant in the context of crime prevention, as they are to economic objectives. Many local authorities have developed Community Safety policies; incorporated crime prevention into their strategic objectives or 'vision statements' (as in Manchester City Pride's); and set up crime prevention projects (such as those described in Salford), funded in a variety of ways.

Typical crime prevention schemes in disadvantaged city neighbourhoods include projects to 'design out' crime on council estates and in shopping centres, by installing better lighting and closed circuit television systems, to improve people's self confidence and to deter crime. Some local authorities and police forces have given security advice to tenants and then organised schemes to provide security devices at affordable prices, such as improved door and window locks. A demonstration project on the Kirkholt Estate in Rochdale in the late 1980s shows what can be achieved. Analysis of burglaries on the estate showed that those who had already been burgled were four times more likely to be victimised again, than those who had not. A package of measures was developed to protect these households. These included an upgrading of home security, property postcoding, removal of prepayment meters, and 'cocooning' (ie. getting neighbours and others to keep a special eye on particular homes). A major improvements programme on the estate was also undertaken. The effects were dramatic; burglaries on the estate fell by 75%.[196]

Various schemes have been developed aimed at discouraging domestic violence. These include public education programmes such as the 'Zero Tolerance campaign', run recently in Scotland and in Islington, and provision of advice and support for victims, a feature of several community safety programmes in London boroughs, including Hackney, Islington and Hammersmith.

One of the factors which has sometimes increased crime and conflict on council estates, has been the concentration there of families generally perceived as disruptive by other residents. The fact that public sector housing has increasingly been allowed to become a residual form of tenure, is largely responsible for this trend. The issue of 'problem families on estates' has recently generated media and political interest, and resulted in new powers being given to housing authorities, to move these households out if they are causing a significant nuisance to others.

The Working Group is in no doubt that the quality of life on some estates is badly damaged for the majority, through the criminal behaviour of a small number of anti-social, sometimes dangerous, residents. This is a serious problem and demands a determined response, but housing authorities and the police must act fairly, and make sure that vulnerable households are not unfairly scapegoated. The Working Group is also concerned that the 'solution' to this problem of transferring these families elsewhere is really no solution at all, since this succeeds only in moving the problem elsewhere. In some cases, 'neighbourhood mediation schemes', such as those running in Glasgow, may be enough to resolve the problem[197]. In other, more serious cases, schemes like the project which NCH Action For Children has recently established in Dundee, in partnership with the local authority, may prove to be valuable. This initiative moves 'problem families' out of their existing neighbourhood, but then works with them to try to resolve the difficulties which lead to the development of their anti-social behaviour, in the first place. The Dundee Project is in its early stages, but will be worthy of careful evaluation to see if it is a model which could be usefully replicated in other cities.

4. Policing Britain's cities

Effective law enforcement is obviously a crucial factor in increasing community safety in Britain's cities. So too is an effective criminal justice system, in a wider sense; and support for the victims of crime.

The Working Group agrees with the suggestion[198] that policing needs to be preventative and local, carried out by officers working in the communities from which they are recruited, and in which they live. These goals may be hard to attain (for example, because of the career structure in the police forces operating in larger cities, which mean that officers may move between districts every few years, due to promotion); but they should be actively pursued. One of the advantages of 'local policing by local police', is that it helps to increase the accountability of police forces to the people whom they serve. Other steps should also be taken to further police accountability, by for example, further reforms to the system of Police Authorities.

Police officers in our cities are called upon to perform an ever wider range of roles. As other statutory services have been cut, the police have often been left to carry out a variety of welfare roles. It is often they who have to deal with seriously mentally ill or intoxicated people who are a risk to themselves or others, on city streets. At the same time, the police are being called upon to develop the expertise to respond to 'high tech' crimes, such as child pornography on the Internet, and to sophisticated frauds. These competing priorities pull the police service in different directions, and mean that difficult decisions have to be made, since resources are inadequate to do everything.

Research suggests that the public would like to see additional investment in foot patrols, while police officers themselves believe that 'high tech' responses, such as the installation of closed circuit television, are better value for money[199]. The same study showed that both police and public agreed that burglaries, street robberies and large scale drug dealing should be high policing priorities, but the public placed greater importance on domestic violence, vandalism and vehicle crime, than did the police. Statistics are sometimes produced to show that the 'Bobby on the Beat' only very occasionally comes upon an offence being committed, but her or his physical presence may deter crime, and certainly raises community confidence and diminishes the fear of crime, something which can in itself reduce crime in a neighbourhood, if people are thereby encouraged to 'reclaim the streets'.

Several policing ideas from American cities have recently attracted interest among British journalists and politicians, as possibly worthy of imitation here. One is that the police should prioritise the prosecution of petty offenders, such as vandals who commit minor acts of criminal damage, and 'aggressive beggars'. The theory is that if people commit minor offences and go unpunished, they subsequently graduate to more serious crimes. This scheme was tried out in New York at the instigation of the Republican Mayor, Rudolph Guliani, and has been trumpeted as a great success, since crime levels have reportedly fallen in the city. However, critics suggest that this may be due more to economic and demographic factors, than to this particular initiative. A second suggestion is the introduction of curfews for young people, as a way of seeking to diminish the scope for their involvement in disorder, and crime. Again, many have expressed scepticism about the feasibility of this. Whether or not schemes such as these are eventually piloted successfully in British cities, it is difficult to envisage them making more than a marginal difference to the level and nature of crime. They are certainly no substitute for the wider reaching approaches already discussed.

While many policing issues are contentious, few would disagree with the importance of measures being taken to help the police to raise their 'clear-up rates'. At the moment, Home Office figures show that only about one in four notifiable offences are 'cleared up', although the proportion is much higher for violent offences (3 in 4) than for burglary, or car crime (1 in 5)[200]. It is certain that racial attacks very often go unreported to the police, yet they can have a devastating attack on the sense of well-being in a neighbourhood, as well as on individual victims. New laws on racial violence, and the development of a new strategy for preventing and deterring racial violence, are urgently required.

Conclusion

Crime and the fear of crime seriously erode the quality of life in our cities, especially for vulnerable households living in disadvantaged districts; for people of ethnic minority origin, and for women, fearful of domestic violence. Previous paragraphs have shown the enhanced role which a range of crime prevention interventions could play in combating these problems. But ultimately, the research suggests that measures targeted at vulnerable young people, especially socially excluded young men, would do more to help solve the problem, than anything else. New ways have to be found to provide them with high quality training placements and work, and a system of structured incentives to move them from the first to the second.

4. Towards a cleaner, more sustainable city environment

There is an almost universal desire, demonstrated for example, in the survey which the Working Group carried out for this Report, for our cities to be cleaner, more pleasant places. The term 'sustainable development' is often used to describe the transformation that is required to achieve this. Sustainable development is sometimes viewed as antithetical to economic growth, but this is a misunderstanding: rather, sustainability demands that city initiatives which meet the needs of today must not jeopardise the next generation's capacity for meeting theirs. Pursuing policies which stimulate economic growth but damage the environment, generates a cost which will have to be met either now, or later, by our own population and sometimes also by others. Sustainability therefore demands that the ecological costs and benefits are computed as well as economic ones, and that decisions about development refer to both. It also requires a world view, rather than a purely domestic one, on the basis that the world's environment is an interrelated system.

Almost everyone agrees that sustainability is crucial to the future viability of city life, but are we all as individual citizens prepared to make the significant lifestyle changes which this inevitably requires? In 1991, the Club of Rome made the following judgement, *"The transition to a sustainable society is technically and economically possible, maybe even easy, but it is psychologically and politically daunting."*[201]

The most important and challenging issues for British cities are the nature of the changes which have to be made to city life, and the strategies which need to be employed to engage the whole population in this process. But before addressing these questions, it is necessary to analyse briefly the environmental problems which presently affect British cities, in global and more local terms; and to look at what is already being done to try to solve them. Many city responses are being made within the context of 'Local Agenda 21'; this is examined in the section which then follows.

Global threats to sustainability

Four main threats to sustainability world-wide, have been identified[202]. These are:

1. **Global warming**, caused largely by the burning of fossil fuels, leading to a build up of carbon dioxide in the atmosphere – 'the greenhouse effect'. Global warming is believed to be resulting in significant changes to the climate and weather patterns.

2. **Ozone depletion**, resulting from the release of chlorofluoro carbons (CFCs). These break down ozone in the upper atmosphere and allow more ultra-violet light through. This slows plant growth and causes various cancers, including skin cancer.

3. **Deforestation**. Tropical rainforests mop up carbon dioxide, and therefore mitigate the effects of global warming. They also provide habitats for many plants and animals, some of which may prove to be sources of medicines. Human activity, particularly logging, has severely depleted the world's rainforests.

4. **Soil erosion**, leading to desertification, after which the land becomes incapable of food production. The usual cause is overly intensive methods of agriculture, boosted by artificial irrigation, which exhaust the soil and groundwater reserves.

Environmental issues facing our cities and current policy responses

1. Atmospheric pollution

Contrary to popular belief, air quality has actually significantly improved in Britain over recent years. The main reasons for this have been the switch of British power stations away from coal and towards gas, a much cleaner fuel; and the introduction of progressively tougher EU standards for vehicle exhausts, linked to increased use of catalytic converters. In the past, the main constituents of atmospheric pollution in our cities were noxious discharges from factories and domestic chimneys. Today, these are a much smaller, and still declining part of the problem. Pollution from vehicles now causes more than half of all air pollution in cities, and for some types of pollutant, such as carbon monoxide, this is by far the greater contributor.

Atmospheric pollution damages the people, wildlife, plant life and buildings in our cities. There has been a significant increase in the incidence of asthma in British cities. Although atmospheric pollution is not proven, scientifically, to cause asthma, it is known that it can trigger an attack in people who already have the disease, and it increases susceptibility to lung infection and damages bronchial cells. Atmospheric pollution has been estimated to lead to 20,000 hospital admissions each year[203].

Air blows about over the whole continent, and pollution blows with it. This is why the only response to atmospheric pollution which is likely to be successful in any single European county, is a European wide policy. There have been major achievements in reducing the levels of some pollutants as a result of concerted EU action; for example, carbon monoxide levels have fallen by 17% and sulphur dioxide levels by 27% across the continent, over the last five years[204]. The European Commission has recently published proposals to improve fuel standards and tighten up vehicle emission standards still further.

Projections of road traffic emissions suggest that levels will fall until around 2010 as a result of the impact of higher emission standards, but will then rise again because this effect will be more than counter-balanced by the projected increase in traffic[205]. It seems that the only way of avoiding this longer term increase in atmospheric pollution is to change patterns of movement; still tighter emission standards are unlikely to be enough.

The British Government is contributing to European wide initiatives aimed at combating atmospheric pollution. It has recently published a consultative document setting out a national Air Quality Strategy, which goes beyond the 1990 Environmental Protection Act and proposes that local authorities should have powers to control atmospheric pollution in response to local needs. Critics have suggested that the motivation behind this is to hand the most difficult problems over to local government is to solve, without giving them the resources to accomplish this; while others feel that this task can only be carried out at a local level, by local authorities[206]. Many local authorities in cities are now monitoring air pollution, especially in places where air quality is believed to be particularly poor, on account of heavy traffic. These exercises are often carried out in partnership with local environmental groups.

2. Traffic

The problems of atmospheric pollution and traffic are inextricably linked, as the previous paragraphs have shown. It has been suggested that, *"At the heart of urban planning lies the relationship between where people live, where people work, and how they travel between them. Transport is the most difficult policy area within the wider sustainability argument. The critical issue is the balance between private and public transport."*[207]

Our over-reliance on the car has been identified as lying at the root of many current city problems. The 'car economy' is a major cause of noise pollution and of traffic accidents, as was discussed during the Working Group's Consultation Meeting in Glasgow. It is also largely responsible for the development of 'edge cities' of retail development, and the decline of the traditional high street. Traffic congestion in our cities adds an external cost to business and impedes economic activity.

Parental concern about traffic is the major reason, together with fear of 'Stranger Danger', for children being withdrawn from the streets. Research in 1971 found that 80% of seven and eight year olds in England travelled unaccompanied to school. A similar survey in 1990 found that fewer than 10% did so[208]. Fear of traffic has led to a situation in which cycling by children has become a recreational activity, rather than a mode of transport, to a greater extent than is the case in many other European countries, and in contrast to the position in Britain in previous years[209]. It has been suggested that the decline in children's independent mobility and outdoor play, has adversely affected their physical fitness[210] and psychological well-being[211].

The Government's consultative Air Quality Strategy document has been produced by the Department of the Environment, but it has been pointed out that the extent to which it manages to bring on board the Ministry of Transport and the Treasury, will be crucial to its success[212]. Public policy towards the control of the car remains equivocal, reflecting widespread ambivalence about the issue. In most cities, initiatives have recently concentrated on 'traffic calming measures', such as the construction of 'sleeping policemen'. Road pricing and tolls have been discussed but not implemented. Many city public transport services are perceived to be declining rather than improving, so many people feel that there is no viable transport alternative to the car.

3. Waste

The ways in which we currently produce and consume goods generate enormous amounts of waste, which then has to be disposed of. In Britain, about 90% of all waste is disposed of by landfill[213]. This process leads to further environmental problems however; for example, the production of methane gas, which contributes to global warming; and the contamination of underground water supplies. More recycling facilities, the reduction of superfluous packaging, and the development of alternative means of disposing of waste materials, are initiatives which are being explored to try to deal with this problem. The Government's 1990 *White Paper on the Environment* set a target of recycling half of all recyclable household waste by the year 2000. Although statistics suggest that the proportion of households items such as glass and aluminium cans which are recycled is growing, this target looks fairly ambitious, on current trends.[214]

4. Energy

Energy is often generated and used in our cities in expensive and wasteful ways. Lack of effective insulation, and of energy conservation measures, contributes substantially to this problem. At the same time, people living in disadvantaged city districts often find that they cannot afford to run the heating systems installed in their homes. Fuel poverty is a serious risk to health, especially for the more vulnerable sections of the community, including the elderly, disabled and long-term sick people, and children. Some local authorities, among them Glasgow City Council, have initiated programmes to upgrade energy conservation and home insulation, but their efforts are often hampered by inadequate resources.

5. Urban layout, the built environment, and public spaces

The design and appearance of cities can make an important contribution to sustainability. Earlier sections have shown that the layout of many of our cities today is partly the consequence of the development of the car; suburbanisation was only possible because the car, and to a lesser extent the train, make commuting viable. Almost all cities in developed countries have separated out the principal city functions of commercial activity, administration, shopping and housing, into discrete areas. Typically, the business and administrative functions are in the city centre, and housing further out. Shopping facilities are now often found both in the centre, and on the peripherary.

This form of urban layout both encourages and predicates a great deal of movement from one part of the city to another, leading to traffic congestion and pollution. It has been suggested that a much more sustainable form of city layout would be one in which there is a much greater mix of different activities within a single area. Sir Richard Rogers, for example, envisages an ideal city of the future in which *"living, work, shopping, learning and leisure will overlap and be housed in continuous, varied and changing structures."*[215]

The difficulty for planners today, is developing strategies for moving towards this vision, on the basis of current city patterns. Opportunities to do this however, sometimes arise in unexpected ways: for example, in Manchester, the recent, partial destruction of the 1960s Arndale Shopping Centre and nearby bus garage and office blocks by a terrorist bomb, has given Manchester City Council and its partners, an unusual chance to create a new, mixed development. An architectural competition has been held and the shortlist of five share the common characteristics of encouraging more pedestrianisation, opening new green spaces and extending the shopping area[216].

Today, there is enormous enthusiasm for the idea of creating new urban neighbourhoods, and of sustaining old ones. This is not a new idea. One of it earliest proponents was Jane Jacobs, in the United States[217]. In the 1960s, based particularly on her experience of Manhattan, she advocated the establishment and maintenance of city neighbourhoods of mixed functions and therefore land uses, to ensure that people were there for different purposes, on different time schedules, but using many facilities in common. She believed that the city should have conventional streets on short blocks, and a mixture of homes of different age and condition. The main problem with this prescription however, is that it tends to encourage gentrification, and can intensify the social exclusion of people on low incomes, unless very firm measures are taken to prevent this from happening[218].

The quality of a city's Built Environment contributes significantly to the quality of life of its residents and workers, and can also, as has been shown in Glasgow, stimulate tourism and economic activity. Almost all Britain's cities contain wonderfully attractive buildings, but they also invariably have districts of run-down housing and dilapidated estates. Great improvements have been made to these areas in many British cities, but much more still needs to be done.

The proposed construction of any new public buildings in our cities, including the development of housing, should be viewed as an opportunity to improve the aesthetic quality of the environment, as well as meeting more obvious functions. Boring, off the shelf 'design and build' Housing Association schemes, squeezed onto city sites with no room for 'greening', do little to improve the quality of life for the wider community, regardless of the attractiveness of their interiors. It is entirely possible to construct innovative, delightful and cost effective public buildings, which can be a source of pleasure to local people. Architects should be encouraged to create stimulating buildings of this kind. An obvious example is the Lambeth Community Care Centre, in south London. Run by the West

Lambeth Health Authority, the Centre offers a new-style version of the 'cottage hospital' service to local people in the inner city. This concept of a community based health resource was praised in the *Tomlinson Report* in 1992. The architecture is also imaginative and sustainable, and the building is set in a lovely garden, which is tended by local people. The Centre and its garden provides a valuable health service to patients, and much needed visual relief to the residents of the local tower blocks and dense terraces.[219]

Public spaces are important in cities, because they are the places where people can meet and be together with others. Modern urban life is incomplete without them; they are one of the things that creates 'buzz' and makes cities fun. On the whole, the British climate means that public interiors are even more important than exteriors in this respect, although parks and squares can also fulfil the function of public space. In medieval times, churches were important public interiors, as were taverns, and later, coffee houses and pubs. In the Victorian era, railway stations became significant as public interiors and as symbols of civic pride and identity; magnificent Victorian examples include St.Pancras in London, and Central Station in Glasgow. The new Eurostar Terminal at Waterloo, designed by Nicholas Grimshaw, continues this tradition into the current age.

The most important meeting places in British cities are now, invariably but not always, privately owned public interiors, particularly bars, cafes and restaurants. Over the last 30 years, Britain's dining habits have changed enormously, and eating out is now a major pastime. A recent survey of a thousand households in Bristol, Preston and London found that 94% had dined out in the past twelve months, on average once every 3 weeks[220]. Eating out choices in cities have expanded to cover most tastes and incomes, ranging from the ubiquitous American hamburger bar to highly sophisticated restaurants. Immigrants to British cities from abroad, especially from Hong Kong and Bangladesh, have hugely enriched British domestic and restaurant cuisine.

Shopping malls and entertainment complexes, such as the new

Trocadero virtual reality centre in London, are also important city spaces. Deyan Sudjic has described the Trocadero as, *"what passes for the public space at the heart of London in the nineties. It is the virtual incarnation of the public realm. The piazza has been supplanted by a giant mall where, for the price of admission...an escalator shoots you through a barrage of sound and light.."*.[221]

The new 'cafe/themed leisure/shopping culture' that has developed in many of our cities, above all in London, is much enjoyed by many city dwellers. However, based as it is on a range of consumption activities, most of which require a relatively high level of disposable income, it is effectively out of the reach of people on the lowest incomes.

6. Green space and wildlife

Throughout the twentieth century, plants and trees have been valued as 'green lungs' for cities, and as enhancements to the city landscape. Currently, there is growing awareness of their importance to the sustainable city as, for example; filters for dirt, dust and atmospheric pollutants; and as means of controlling and purifying water. For people living in densely built up areas, the accessibility of nature and green areas is of great importance for recreation and leisure. Plants and trees make a city a better place to live in, are of significant cultural and historical value, and contribute to city identity and character. They have also been shown to have measurable effects on mental health and to speed recovery from illness[222]. These are crucial components of a healthy urban society, as well as potential contributors to a city's economic success by attracting inward investment.

On the whole, urban fringe horticulture and fruit growing has largely vanished from Britain. In contrast, in many of the world's major cities, a very substantial proportion of food is grown locally. One example is the United States, where the 1990 census found that urban metropolitan areas produced 40% of the dollar value of US agricultural products, up from 30% in 1980. A second is Berlin in Germany, where there are 80,000 community gardeners on municipal land, with a waiting list of 16,000. In the

UK, the National Food Alliance's project Growing Food in Cities, highlights the potential for regenerating the city environment, improving public health and contributing to community development through food growing in cities, or on the urban fringe[223]. The inspiration of small groups of city dwellers is usually the decisive starting point, but the readiness of local authorities to lend support is crucial in fostering the potential of these local initiatives.

Green cities also help to sustain wildlife. Urban habitats provide homes for different kinds of animals and insects, and for native flowers, especially in undisturbed areas such as railway lines and sidings, derelict sites and even large gardens. 'Green corridors' can link the city with the surrounding countryside, and allow endangered species to spread and to strengthen their numbers through colonisation and migration.

The local authorities in many of our cities have active Environmental and Wildlife policies. However, there is widespread concern that the trees and parks dating generally from the Victorian age, are disappearing with no clear strategy for their replacement. Many public parks are decaying because local authorities lack the resources to maintain them, and it has been estimated that in some urban areas, 50% of street trees are dying because of the activities of cable laying gangs[224].

UK wide, local authority led responses: Local Agenda 21

Local Agenda 21 is the policy umbrella which brings together most of the sustainability initiatives being carried out at a local level. It starts from the premise that our current levels of production and consumption are unsustainable and encourages global thinking, coupled with local action. Local Agenda 21's message is that everything is connected, that ecology and the economy are interwoven locally, regionally, nationally and globally, in a seamless web of cause and effect.

Chapter 28 of Agenda 21 (the action plan for the 21st century, agreed at the United Nations Conference in Rio on Environment and Development in 1992 – the *Earth Summit*) encourages local authorities to adopt a Local Agenda 21 for their community, by 1996. The UK local authority associations are working together to meet the 1996 target. Local authorities are working together with business, voluntary and community sectors to identify what sustainable development means, at local level. Many city authorities have appointed Local Agenda 21 co-ordinators, to facilitate this process. The Department of the Environment is helping to fund a programme of regional seminars to bring together these groups. The national Local Agenda 21 steering group has also sent out briefing packs to help local authorities in their task. Many sustainability initiatives were already under way in cities before 1992, but Local Agenda 21 provides the framework for following these up. Activities being carried out at local level tend to fall into the following categories:

- energy efficiency measures, for example in local authority buildings, street lighting, transport fleets and public sector housing;
- work to minimise the use of resources and maximise the use of the least environmentally damaging products in purchasing and specifying contracts;
- traffic calming, bus lanes and other bus priority schemes, pedestrian- isation, cycle lanes and other urban traffic management schemes;
- waste minimisation and recycling schemes;
- initiatives involving the local community, or raising community consciousness about environmental issues.

Each local authority has been asked to report back on the development and implementation of its Local Agenda 21 action plan to the national Steering Committee, by the end of 1996. In 1997, the UN Commission on Sustainable Development will examine the impact of Local Agenda 21, world-wide.

Local Agenda 21 has undoubtedly stimulated the development of some very useful local sustainability strategies in British cities, and given added momentum to others which were already under way. Three of the most imaginative and exciting are in Edinburgh, Leicester and Knowsley. Edingburgh has an Urban Forestry strategy, based on a detailed analysis of all the trees and open spaces in the city. The aim is to develop urban forests as nodes in a wider 'Forest Habitat Network', linking woodland ecosystems across Scotland[225].

Leicester[226] was designated Britain's first Environment City in 1990 by the Royal Society for Nature Conservation and the Civic Trust. Under the leadership of Leicester City Environment Trust, eight specialist working groups have been developing and implementing a city-wide sustainability strategy. Specific initiatives include the creation and maintenance of the Riverside Park, a linear site of 1,000 hectares which runs through the city centre and contains a variety of prime habitats; and the adoption of a package of measures to encourage cycling and to enable streets to be safe for children's play.

In Knowsley[227], on Merseyside, the Knowsley Wildflower Project is a joint initiative between a voluntary organisation called *Landlife*, and Knowsley Borough Council. It is working to improve the local environment by converting wasteland into large scale flower meadows. The local community is involved through a schools programme. The project is becoming self-supporting through income gained from the sale of wildflower seeds and topsoil. The project is helping to create an attractive environment, in which the people living in this disadvantaged area can take great pride.

A notable national initiative which has been fostered by Local Agenda 21 is the Groundwork Foundation, which seeks to encourage sustainable enterprise across Britain. There are 33 Groundwork Trusts, each backed by a local authority, working with 6,000 small and medium sized companies at local level. Fifteen themes of work are supported by major firms, including for example, Shell UK. A wide range of activities have been stimulated by Groundwork Trusts, all concerning environ-mental, economic regeneration. They include 'Brightsite schemes' to green factory and commercial environments, and the carrying out of 'Environmental Reviews', which enable small and medium sized enterprises to appraise their environmental policies and management systems.

The relative progress of cities in Britain

The previous paragraphs show that many British cities are taking positive measures in pursuit of sustainability, encouraged by Local Agenda 21. However, the transformation which is required to make our cities truly sustainable is on a much bigger scale than most British cities and their populations are currently envisaging. Throughout the developed world, nations, regions and cities are working towards sustainability, and some are further ahead than others. The sustainability programmes currently being developed by most Swedish cities for example, are far in advance of those in Britain[228].

One reason for this is that in Sweden, there appears to be more national leadership behind the changes required to achieve sustainability. *The National Vision – Sweden 2009*, and *The Vision of the Ecocycle Society*, are mission statements towards which Swedish cities are working. These are quite ambitious documents and set out requirements, for example, for all city planning to integrate measures to encourage biodiversity and to facilitate recycling. There is a national system for monitoring atmospheric pollution in Swedish cities, and economic incentives apply not only to unleaded petrol as in Britain, but also to heating fuels. Sweden has carried out an environmental audit and computed its 'environmental debt', the result of the pollution of the past. This process makes visible the costs of inaction, and reinforces the fact that the question is, not if people will have to pay when the environment is damaged, but when, how and who will be forced to do so.

In Sweden, as in Britain, local authorities are the bodies with lead responsibility for developing and implementing environmental policy, and about three quarters of them are doing so by reference to their own sustainability vision statements, developed within the Local Agenda 21 framework.

Practical measures are being taken in two Swedish cities, Stockholm and Gothenburg, in pursuit of sustainability. In Stockholm, the two major political parties signed the *Dennis Agreement* in 1992, named after the Governor of the Swedish

Bank, who chaired the negotiations. This pledges the active support of local government administrations in the city until 2006, for a range of measures designed to enhance the environment, improve accessibility and encourage economic growth. Public transport will be improved, peripheral relief routes will be expanded and vehicle tolls will be introduced (probably in 1997). Throughout this period, all road building will be financed by tolls on vehicular traffic. This multi-party agreement ensures continuity for these projects, regardless of any changes in local government.

Gothenburg has been actively pursuing greater sustainability since at least the early 1980s. One of the schemes that has been developed connects two thirds of all households in the city, to a district heating system. This system uses regained waste heat from sewage water to supplement the natural gas which is otherwise used, and accounts for two thirds of all heat production in the city. As a result, Gothenburg has some of the lowest carbon dioxide emissions in Europe. Gothenburg is also developing an advanced Waste Plan, with local composting sites for organic material, and source separation of non-organic waste into five fractions: glass, paper, metal, plastics and textiles. This makes recycling much easier.

It is much easier for central and local government to pursue sustainability in Sweden than it is in Britain. Sweden is an affluent country, has small cities with low population density, and does not have to contend with such massive problems associated with a post-industrial heritage, as those that face many British cities. In seeking to balance the priorities of economic growth and sustainability, the Swedes therefore have a significant advantage over the British, and one that it magnified by the fact that Sweden regards itself as a 'Welfare Society'. In the past, the pursuit of economic growth in Sweden has often been tempered by social justice concerns, so programmes which trade off economic growth for sustainability do not seem so radical there as they might in Britain. Moreover, environmental degradation is viewed as a long term threat to welfare, so reinforcing the importance in Sweden of adopting measures to combat it[229].

The more determined political support for sustainability in Sweden, at national and often, local level, are also important factors. But associated with this, and probably most important of all, is the greater public awareness of environmental concerns in Sweden, compared with Britain, and therefore of support for sustainability programmes.

Encouraging lifestyle change in British cities

Many of the recent improvements to city environments in Britain have been accomplished through enhanced technology; for example, the better control achieved over vehicle emissions through the development of cleaner fuels and catalytic converters. However, it appears that cities throughout the developed world are rapidly approaching a situation in which these technological advances will not be enough to compensate for other adverse forces, so that more fundamental changes will be required to city lifestyles and patterns of consumption. These will not come about unless and until individual city dwellers are prepared to take more individual responsibility for the environment by, for example, sorting their waste, or by travelling by public transport rather than by car.

Even in Sweden there are significant barriers to achieving these changes. A public attitudes survey in the city of Gothenburg recently found that while most people wanted strong measures against environmental degradation and were prepared to pay higher taxes to this end, they were not very supportive of policies restricting car use in the city, such as the introduction of tolls. Another recent survey in Gothenburg analysed the relationship between public behaviour and attitudes. It found that although there was widespread public support for the idea of an environmentally friendly lifestyle, people were vague about what this meant in practice. For the most part, this was certainly not established in their everyday life. A further finding was that the people who were least responsive to the idea of an environmentally friendly lifestyle, were households on the lowest incomes. People feeling that they do not have a great stake in society were least likely to be prepared to change lifestyles, for the common good[230].

There is no reason to suppose that the findings from a similar survey carried out in a British city would be very different. Here too, most people's understanding of 'green issues' is probably fairly hazy, although there is widespread support for the general idea of protecting and improving the environment, especially among younger people, as shown by the Working Group's survey and by other research. A survey carried out by the Department of the Environment in 1993 found that 85% of adults in England and Wales were 'quite concerned' or 'very concerned' about the environment, but only 10% for example, said that they had used public transport on a regular basis instead of their cars, for environmental reasons.[231] Education, for children in school and for the whole population through public campaigns, has a crucial role to play in furthering popular understanding of what sustainability means, and why it is so important.

A useful starting point for Government in encouraging lifestyle change, is the development and publicising of new ways of measuring sustainability. For example, in the city of Freiburg in Germany, the consumption of drinking water per citizen per year, is used as a sustainability indicator. It shows whether the city's water resources are used efficiently, which is important because extraction of ground water for drinking water has lowered the water table, and is damaging the forests near the city. It is very easy for citizens to behave in ways which are less damaging to the environment; for instance, by using a new type of tap or shower that limits the water flow, or by using rainwater collected in a butt to water the garden or wash the car. This is something that citizens can change themselves, without the help of government – but it helps enormously that this behaviour is officially monitored and publicised[232].

The concept of 'sustainable citizenship'

This heightened public awareness is a necessary precondition for attitudinal change, but it will not in itself, alter individual behaviour. For this to happen, a partnership is required, between the citizen, the holders of power in local government, business, industry and central Government. This has led environmental campaigners such as the Scottish Environmental Forum, to develop the idea of 'Sustainable Citizenship'. This has been defined as, *"a way of living in family and community which enhances the quality of life, is sensitive to present and future needs, and empowers the citizen to influence and participate in the economic, political and social changes necessary for sustainable development."*[233] The hope is that as people become more actively involved in local decision making, they acquire a greater stake in their area and become more prepared to make fundamental changes in their lifestyles.

If this process is to generate broader change across districts and cities, local authorities need to respond positively, and by fostering genuine partnerships between themselves and local communities. This means that they have to be prepared to devolve decision making to the lowest possible level, and take steps to involve individual citizens in the process of formulating and implementing local policies. Central government also has a role to play, by providing leadership at national level through regulation, and supporting local efforts through funding.

'Sustainable citizenship' sounds rather abstract and grandiose, but it is really about very practical things. It is strikingly similar to the idea behind the Community Strategy which Salford City Council has developed to involve the population in the regeneration of their city (see above for further information).

An example of sustainable citizenship in action, is the East Hall energy conservation project in Glasgow[234]. The project arose out of a struggle against damp housing, which was affecting the health of residents in East Hall. East Hall is part of Easterhouse, one of Glasgow's most disadvantaged peripheral housing schemes. People were accused of causing the dampness themselves, through cooking and heating in ways which led to a build up of condensation. They decided to take matters into their own hands and to prove that the real reason for the dampness was the poor design of their homes. The East Hall Residents' Association gathered information to show that it would be better and cheaper to improve people's living conditions in East Hall, through energy conservation. The City Council was initially unresponsive, but eventually developed a partnership with the local Residents' Association, and a company which specialises in energy conservation, called *Heatwise*.

A scheme was successfully carried out to improve insulation and energy conservation in East Hall. The project uses solar energy, and homes are now so well insulated that heating becomes a secondary factor. Fuel bills have fallen from a household average of £25 per week before the project began, to only £7, after its completion. The people who successfully campaigned in East Hall started with their own problems, but then made the connection to wider global environmental concerns such as global warming, and the need for international solutions. The Residents' Association became much more confident and active through this campaign, and have since formed links with a community development project in Nicaragua.

A key factor in the success of this initiative was the willingness of Glasgow City Council, albeit after initial reluctance, to respond positively to the Residents' Association. If a local authority is not willing or able to engage with local people in this way, it is very difficult to sustain a campaign and a valuable opportunity for fostering community support may be lost. This is reported to have happened in Liverpool, where local groups have been campaigning for the introduction of measures aimed at curbing high levels of atmospheric pollution, caused largely by traffic fumes. There has been no action in response to the concerns they have voiced, and the result is that *'People were very enthusiastic at first, but its like anything. They fall away after a while.'*[235]

Conclusion: the need for more leadership and support from central government

Raising public awareness of 'green issues' and creating a climate of opinion in which people are more prepared to countenance major changes to their lifestyles is a long term task, but one which should be being strongly encouraged now. Although it would not be helpful, let alone politically possible, for central government to initiate an environmental programme in our cities which was way ahead of public opinion on this issue, there are more modest steps which could be taken immediately. This is particularly true of a range of measures targeted at discouraging car use, and improving air quality in our cities[236].

Additional revenue could be raised to pay for these measures, in the following ways:

1 A tax could be introduced for non-residential car parking spaces, in places like city centre office blocks. The money raised would be substantial (at least £1 billion per year);

2 Fuel duties are rising annually by 5% above inflation rates – a deliberate measure to discourage car use which is already in operation, but at the moment the taxation generated in this way is not spent specifically on environmental improvements;

3 Higher vehicle excise duty rates could be set for bigger cars, that produce more pollution;

4 New taxes could be introduced to make it less attractive for firms and employees to run company cars;

The combined extra revenue could be spent on:

1 Significantly improving public transport services, including extra support for new, "green" public transport systems such as trams (already in operation in Manchester, and in development in Birmingham, Glasgow and Croydon) and guided busways (in development in Edinburgh);

2 Encouraging telecommuting and car-sharing;

3 Cleaning up bus exhausts, some of the heaviest pollutants of city air;

4 Persuading people to scrap "old bangers", in favour of newer cars fitted with catalytic converters;

5 Establishing and resourcing a system of frequent roadside checks, to identify and enforce the cleaning up of the minority of heavily polluting vehicles;

6 Encouraging the development of "green cars", including electric vehicles, by setting a zero vehicle excise rate for these vehicles.

A programme of this kind would help move public opinion in the right direction without requiring substantial additional public spending, and contains an appropriate mixture of 'sticks and carrots'.

5. Encouraging a greater sense of community in our cities

More than half of all the city dwellers who completed the Working Group's questionnaire, spoke of their desire for a greater sense of community in our cities. It is not surprising that this should have been such a heartfelt view, since many forces seem to be working together to fragment British society, and to push us further apart. Growing inequality, globalisation and technological innovation increase the sense of personal insecurity. As people and places struggle to adapt to these enormous changes, is 'a sense of community' in our cities, one of the casualties? Have we lost something precious, and if so, how can we get it back? Or is there a need to create new structures and patterns of organisation in our cities, ones which are better suited to the way in which city life seems to be developing? These are the important questions which this section aims to address.

What do we mean by 'a greater sense of community'?

'Community' is a word which is used much more often than it is defined. This may be because it is quite an elusive concept, but also one which has warm and comfortable associations. It has been suggested that, *"everyone, it seems (or nearly everyone) is in favour of community. This has become the intellectually respectable form of nostalgia, but also the propaganda of optimists, everywhere"*[237]. The concept of community has also sometimes been the subject of heated political debate, perhaps because people's attitudes to it often reflect their most deeply held beliefs about the characteristics of 'the good society'.

A community can be based on the shared experience of places, attitudes or loyalties, or on common interests. We can simultaneously belong to a number of communities, in all these different senses; for example, to 'the ethnic minority community', 'the gay community', or the 'Internet community'.

'Community' should be differentiated from 'identity'. The two terms are not synonymous, although a feeling of local identity may help to create a sense of community in a district or city. As vastly improved communications and the impact of mass consumerism threaten to weaken local distinctiveness, it is important that cities and their neighbourhoods retain distinctive features of local culture. In some cities and neighbourhoods, football rivalry provides a focus for local identity. In London, the traditional banter between people living North and South of the River Thames fulfils a similar function. A sense of belonging which is based on excessively strong notions of 'territory' (such as those which lead to 'gang rivalry' among groups of young people); or of religious exclusivity (such as the traditional Catholic – Protestant divide in Glasgow, now much less pronounced than it once was), is clearly unhelpful, however. These sorts of communities are defined as much by those who are kept out, as by those who are allowed in.

In the context of this Report , 'a greater sense of community' is connected to the way in which we relate to other people in our neighbourhood, or our city; and the desire for it indicates a dissatisfaction with how this relationship currently works. It may also suggest the need for a new balance between the public and the private, and the collective and individual, aspects of our lives. Everyone may have their own interpretation of what 'a greater sense of community' means, but in the context of the city, most people would probably agree that this relates to the creation of a greater sense of belonging, or of shared identity, by all city dwellers. It is an inclusive, not an exclusive concept.

The desire for a 'greater sense of community' may partly arise from a feeling that there is not enough to bind us together as city dwellers. Other, negative connotations of this condition are the sense of personal insecurity which many people feel, because of the fear of crime; of personal isolation and loneliness, because we do not know our neighbours, and our family and friends may live in another part of the city, or further away still; or of personal discomfort or even guilt, when we pass a homeless person begging on the street, if we are fortunate enough ourselves to have a home.

The undermining of 'community' in our cities

It is not difficult to identify a number of different trends, which together, may have undermined the feeling of community in our cities, by enabling people to lead increasingly individualistic lives, separate from those of others.

The first trend is the growing importance of home and home based leisure. Homes are warmer (mostly, because of the invention of central heating), more comfortable (due to generally rising living standards), and often endowed with multiple sources of entertainment, such as terrestrial, satellite or cable television, videos, stereos and computers. All these are in addition to more traditional, home based pastimes, such as reading, cooking, listening to the radio, gardening and caring for pets. Many city dwellers therefore have very good reasons for enjoying life at home and not engaging much with other local people, to a significant extent. If predictions about the growth in home shopping and 'telecommuting' via computer come to pass, home may play an even more important part in our lives in the future, than it does now.

In the earlier years of the 20th century, more people probably did participate in communal leisure activities in British cities than they do today, but this may have been in no small part because of the lack of alternatives. The hugely expanded home leisure choices we now enjoy, compared with those offered to our grandparents, are a marvellous thing, but they also mean that there are fewer common experiences which we all share. Although television viewing has declined slightly in recent years, it is still the dominant leisure pastime, occupying just under an average of 26 hours a week[238]. Watching particular soap operas on terrestrial television appears to be an important feature of adolescent culture, but otherwise, the range of choice on television militates against the sharing of even a common televisual experience (except on rare occasions, such as England versus Germany football matches).

The advent of television has been identified by the sociologist

Robert Putnam, as the major cause of the decline in what he calls 'civic society' in America[239]. Putnam argues that television viewing is 'privatising existence' in America, and has caused people, especially women, to withdraw from engagement in community activities. Referring to what he calls 'an impressive body of literature', he goes further, and suggests that heavy television viewers are unusually sceptical about the benevolence of others, and overestimate crime rates, for example. Television encourages passivity, he believes, and may also increase pessimism about human nature.

Theories which demonise the role of television, perhaps need to be counterbalanced by some reflection on the great pleasure which many people derive from television viewing, particularly city dwellers who might be excluded by low income or by mobility problems from participating in other leisure activities. Any nostalgia for the days of the past should also be tempered by the recognition that community life in our cities may not always have been quite so vibrant as we are sometimes tempted to think: in *The Classic Slum*, the author remarks that his abiding childhood memory, is of seeing working men leaning against their open front doors in the evenings, staring vacantly out into the street, for lack of anything else to do[240].

The second trend which has undermined 'community' in our cities, is increased personal mobility and transience. When we venture out of our comfortable homes and into the world, we often do so in our cars. Increased access to personal transport allows us to travel longer distances between home, work and play, and diminishes our dependence on local facilities and resources. The fact that many people move home more often than they used to, also serves to undermine community links. Ironically, this Report has also shown that one of the major problems for people living in the most disadvantaged districts of our cities, is their lack of mobility.

A third factor which may be undermining community life in our cities is long working hours – for working people. The pressures of globalisation and technological change have forced many companies to restructure, and to pursue productivity gains remorselessly. This has often resulted in longer working hours for individual workers. As growing numbers of women enter the labour force, this is increasingly true of women as of men. In families in which two partners work, this leaves very little time for leisure, and fatigue enhances the relative attractiveness of home based pastimes. People may simply have less time than they used to, for involvement in community life. This is not a consideration for people who are retired, economically inactive, or unemployed. Many people in the latter two groups probably feel that they have too much leisure time, rather than too little.

Home based leisure may be more and more attractive, but it seems that participation in various leisure pursuits outside the home, is also increasing. The growing popularity of eating out has been referred to in a previous section, and attendances at city cinemas, theatres and concerts are also rising[241]. This tends to undermine the notion that people are too busy to take part in local community life.

All these trends have interacted, to weaken the bonds between individual city dwellers and households in local areas. Other links may now play a more significant role in many people's lives, for example, working relationships. In the new information society which is developing, the Internet is likely to allow many city dwellers to develop 'virtual' relationships with people all over the world. But it would be unfortunate if these exciting new opportunities were enjoyed at the expense of a sense of community in local city areas.

The fourth factor which compounds the effects of all the others, to undermine a sense of community in our cities in a particularly insidious way, is the growth of inequality and social exclusion. As the gap grows between the lifestyles of those on the lowest incomes and the rest, it becomes harder to sustain mutual understanding, tolerance and respect. As this Report has shown, these divisions are frequently ones of race, as well as income. The gap separating people on the lowest incomes from others is now such, that the lifestyles of affluent people living in British cities more closely resemble those of similarly advantaged city dwellers in other developed nations, than they do those of the poorer residents of their own city. For example, while more affluent city dwellers can sometimes feel overwhelmed by choice – over which of the many thousands of product lines to purchase in a supermarket, or where to go for a weekend break; people living on the lowest incomes have very few choices at all – not even over their diet, or hobbies[242].

There are relatively few opportunities for people of all incomes in the city to meet and mix together. These are fertile conditions for the development and reinforcement of stereotypes, for example of 'scroungers', because there is a diminishing sense of common humanity to undermine them. If inequality continues to grow, it has been suggested that, *"our city of the future will seem full of lights and shadows. Information workers may grow wealthy but the other ranks will be poor indeed. Video cameras may reassure but at the expense of building walls between different sectors of society."*[243]

Community, citizenship and social exclusion

Eating out or going to the cinema may help bring our city streets to life and discourage crime, but this form of consumption-based leisure is individualised, and relatively exclusive: people on the lowest incomes are unlikely to be able to take part. The same could be said of shopping as leisure. This has led to the criticism that, *"What is lost, in this vision of the city as a shopping centre is the sense of a people joined together in a perception of common ends; who found their common life on procedures they regard, by and large, as just....What is lost, in a word, is the sense of the city as polity."*[244]

This view links 'community' with the concept of social justice, and implies people working together for common ends, under-pinned by shared values. Those who see community as connected to ideas of common purpose, also often refer to the importance of 'citizenship'. They do so particularly, when speaking of community in the sense of it as a shared experience of a place – the 'local community'. It is in the local community that most people have the greatest opportunity to exercise their 'citizenship'. David Marquand has written, for example, *"Citizenship is nothing if it is not public. The notion of the citizen implies a notion of the city – of the polis, of the public realm, of public purposes, publicly debated and determined."*[245]

Citizenship is the role which individuals play in a democratic society as political and social beings; it reconciles individualism and social justice; and it is crucially concerned with power and its distribution, the framework of public and collective decisions, and accountability for those decisions. Citizenship is also about the exercise of responsibilities, particularly the responsibility to pay taxes and to obey society's laws.[246]

Social exclusion undermines the exercise of citizenship, just as it undermines a sense of community. Voices of people who are on very low incomes, and who live in disadvantaged city districts are often not heard when decisions are taken which affect their lives. For example, if a major bank decides to shut down a branch in a disadvantaged area, there has traditionally been little that the local population have been able to do about it. As has been suggested, *"If we listened to the poorest, not only those living on minimum income but those who never take part in anything, those who feel inadequate and excluded from mainstream society, they would reveal everything in our society that crushes or tramples people down....Their experience could teach us the demands of a true democracy, where all citizens have rights, where all citizens are heard, because they are human beings."*[247]

This view of community, seems to come close to what the city dwellers who completed the Working Group's questionnaire generally wished to see develop in their city, associated as it is with notions of mutual trust, common purpose and citizenship[248]. This type of community is characterised by tolerance, acceptance and respect between people of all faiths, cultures and creeds. These values are hard to retain in a society of growing inequality and fragmentation.

Restoring 'community' in our cities

Tackling inequality

A critical factor in rebuilding community in our cities has to be measures to reduce inequality and combat social exclusion, especially of people living in the most disadvantaged districts in the inner city and on the periphery. As this Report has shown, this is a huge but not impossible challenge, given the political will and resources commensurate with the task of overcoming the structural barriers to integration which have, in many cases, developed over many years.

In these disadvantaged city neighbourhoods, the Working Group has seen how local people are working in voluntary associations of various kinds, to improve life in their area. They are often reviving 19th century notions of self-help capitalism in the process. The formation of little local networks and partnerships may be almost invisible at national level, but locally, this Report and others have demonstrated how effective these initiatives can be in stimulating economic and social regeneration, and in reaching parts of cities and city populations that more formal regeneration programmes often miss.

Grass-roots community campaigning

Bringing people together at local level to spur social and economic regeneration can also sometimes have a further consequence: it can help people exercise the rights of citizenship in their area, by providing the conditions in which local people begin to engage in community-based campaigning. Some groups operate specifically with this as their aim. The Citizen Organising Foundation is one of them, and has about 60,000 members, nationwide. Most come from disadvantaged city districts, including those in Liverpool, Bristol, Sheffield and London. These groups have very little interest or past involvement in party politics and are composed of faith communities, community groups and tenant associations, amongst others. They hold meetings and train local leaders. Their achievements are local: they have, for example, succeeded in changing the policies of supermarkets and building societies (persuading some to return to disadvantaged areas they had left); forced local authorities to clear illegal tipping sites; campaigned on homelessness and repossession; and helped to alter policing tactics. They have done this by being legal troublemakers, and by haranguing local politicians and company directors whenever the opportunity arises.[249]

This is one of the aspects of grass-roots community activism which is beginning to attract the interest of journalists, academics and politicians. Andrew Marr suggests that this is because, *"as globalisation intensifies, almost every serious political thinker appears to be investigating the web of social relationships below the level of the state - religious groups, clubs, societies, campaigns - and concluding that this social capital is important both to economic success and to sustaining decent, low-crime communities."*[250] Marr argues that this community activism is mainly a product of profound disillusion with conventional politics and a reaction against the long term effects on disadvantaged city neighbourhoods, of both market individualism and municipal socialism. This certainly echoes much of what the Working Group has heard around the country, during the process of preparing this Report.

People-based solutions to city problems

At first glance, this form of grass-roots, community campaigning might appear antithetical to the mechanisms of local government, but as the Working Ground found in Salford, the more far-sighted local authorities are trying to harness the creativity of these groups, and build their regeneration strategies around them.

It has been persuasively argued by Landry and Bianchini, that this is not an 'optional extra' for local authorities, but set to become their central activity in the years ahead. They suggest that, *"In the period after the Industrial Revolution the priority was to respond to immediate problems by creating physical infrastructures... what was needed then was the particular creativity of engineers, planners and scientists... But today, the focus on the physical has gone as far as it can... We know that crime will be solved less by physical control and more by establishing a sense of place and mutual responsibilities, in communities and neighbourhoods."*[251]

Implications for local authorities

As previous sections in this Report have shown, it is clear that more sustainable city environments will not be created only by looking at specifically environmental dimensions; it will also be necessary to encourage people to take more personal responsibility and change their lifestyles.

In the new, knowledge based global economy which is developing, cities are competing with each other as centres of innovation and creativity, and the sense of well-being or 'liveability', is an important ingredient in their success. This depends on objective factors like housing and transport, but also on more subjective features such as what the city feels like, for the people who live or work there. Creating what Landry and Bianchini call these 'soft infrastructures', is something which local authorities can only do in partnership with local people, and is a task which requires very different skills from those of traditional city planners, who have been trained to find physical solutions to city problems. Local authorities do not necessarily have a monopoly of local expertise about this, and may be highly dependent on the actions of 'social entrepreneurs', as has been discussed in an earlier section.

This requires a fundamental change of approach from local authorities, from the one which they have traditionally employed. The emphasis has to be on a local authority working in partnership with local people, to encourage their participation in regenerating their districts; on the 'enabling authority' working to 'empower' local people, as the jargon would express it. Ironically, these phrases themselves tend to exclude ordinary people, when the intention must be that they should describe a new, inclusive approach to local government. Local authorities will have to find more accessible ways of talking about what they are trying to do, if they are to engage local people, effectively. This is just one of the challenges which they face, in moving towards a radically different way of working. (Others are discussed in earlier sections which focus on regeneration in Salford).

Making good the democratic deficit in city government

The partnership approach to local government which is increasingly required in our cities, should not be viewed as entailing a reduction in its power and influence. The reverse is true: a system of local government in which people take a more active part would strengthen local democracy in our cities. This might constitute one step towards making good what might be described as the 'democratic deficit' in British local government.

In the words of two Government reports: local government exists *"in order to give outward form to the inward unity of a living community"*; *"local government is government by communities, rather than of communities and is the means by which local communities may take decisions affecting the delivery of public services in their area."* [252] However, local government is widely perceived to be moribund in Britain, as reflected for example, by the typical 30-40% turnouts at local elections, which are lower than anywhere else in Europe.

Low election turnouts are, in no small measure, the public's response to the fact that local government has been gradually denuded of its influence over local affairs. In recent years, the creation and development of unelected bodies, and privatisation, have shifted power away from local authorities, in the fields of, for example, training (the establishment of TECs), and water supply and drainage (the creation of water authorities, and their subsequent privatisation). Local government expenditure has been increasingly centralised: more than 85% of it is now controlled by central government [253]. These factors have severely limited the scope for local initiative, and have therefore discouraged the participation of politically committed people in local politics, as well as dampening wider interest among ordinary people in local government. This is concerning, because as the economic libertarian, Frederick von Hayek has written, "Nowhere has democracy worked well without a great measure of local self-government, providing a school of political training for the people at large as much as for their future leaders."[254]

There is a pressing need in Britain, for local democracy to be reinvigorated. Great steps could be taken in this direction by restoring to local authorities, many of the powers which have taken away from them. The principle of subsidiarity (the notion that decisions should be devolved to the lowest possible level), should be acted on. 'Subsidiarity' is a term which is usually associated with the policies of the European Union, but in fact, the idea behind it belongs to a much older political tradition.

The 19th century, political philosopher, Alexis de Tocqueville, wrote, "It is difficult to draw a man out of his own circle to interest him in the destiny of the state, because he does not understand what influence the destiny of the state can have upon his own lot. But if it be proposed to make a road cross the end of his estate, he will see at a glance that there is a connection between this small public affair and his greatest private affairs; and he will discover, without it being shown to him, the close tie which unites private to general interest. Thus, far more may be done by entrusting to the citizens the administration of minor affairs than by surrendering to them the control of important ones, towards interesting them in the public welfare, and convincing them that they constantly need one another in order to provide it."[245] This remains broadly true today. Citizenship is a habit which can be lost, especially in today's complex cities, in which our mutual interdependence is generally much less transparent than it was in earlier times.

The decline of local government in Britain is in marked contrast to current trends throughout most of Europe. Every other state of the European Union has all or most of the following: local discretionary taxes, freedom to buy and sell property without government permission, freedom to raise commercial loans, discretion to fix pay and conditions for their staff, the administration of public health. German Lander can veto national legislation; Italian regions can levy income and transport taxes.[256]

The belief that local democracy must be strengthened may be perceived as left-wing, but in fact, people from very different political perspectives have agreed about the importance of this principle, albeit sometimes for different reasons. Britain's cities will need strong local governments, moving towards a coherent vision of the future, if they are to survive in the new global economy. Sir Chris Patten has therefore written, from his vantage point as Governor of Hong Kong that, *"I am convinced that an important factor in ensuring the competitiveness of the developed countries of Europe and North America in the next generation will be to reduce the proportion of their national incomes consumed by the state. Doing this, while enhancing the authority of governments and preserving the fabric of our communities, will be an immense political challenge, which will be a little easier if we manage to secure a closer constitutional relationship between decision-making, money-spending and revenue-raising."*[257]

Some people have suggested that a step in the right direction would be the development of a system of mayors in Britain, similar to those in, for example, the United States and France. The argument for mayors is that they provide cities with an obvious centre of leadership, elected on the basis of a clear policy platform. One of the potential drawbacks is that mayors in both these countries have sometimes proved to be corrupt, but this criticism could be made of any local government system.

If the system of city government throughout Britain is to be reinforced, London, Britain's dominant city, surely needs a city-wide government of its own. This would make it much easier to take strategic, democratically accountable decisions in the capital. At the moment, London's borough councils negotiate over issues of common concern. In some ways, this process works surprisingly well, but it is susceptible to inertia, especially in the case of policy proposals which would benefit the city as a whole, but are not in the best interests of one or more, individual London boroughs, which are then able to block progress.

Many might think that the establishment of a strategic authority and the election of a mayor for London, would be a considerable advance on the current position in the city. However, some people have argued that these ideas are now old-fashioned and far too passive a version of local democracy. They want more radical steps to be taken[258], such as the greater use of local referenda, or of 'citizens' juries' – small groups of citizens, selected to represent the general public rather than any one interest or sector, who meet to discuss a policy question. They are informed about the issue, take evidence and cross examine witnesses, discuss what they have heard, and then reach a decision. The idea is that citizens' juries help to develop the habit of active citizenship and bring into the local decision making process, understanding and practical experience which is often otherwise lacking.[259] Citizens' juries are therefore, an attempt to reach over many centuries of human history, back to the original notion of Greek, participative democracy.

Citizens, consumers and communities in the city

At the same time as power has gradually shifted away from local authorities, and towards central government, there has been increasing emphasis on the role of the individual city dweller as a consumer of goods and services. Individual choice and consumer accountability have been promoted by greater rights to information and to complaints procedures, and by the publication of tables of national performance indicators.

The Citizen's Charter was developed as a means of ensuring that public services were of high quality and more responsive to consumer demand. The rationale was to *"raise quality, increase choice, secure better value, and extend accountability."*[260] A new standard for the delivery of quality was published, the *Charter Standard*, and those public services which met the standard have been awarded the Chartermark. Individual Charters have been produced for individual public services. *The Citizen's Charter* has however, been criticised because it is based on a notion of passive consumerism, rather than of active citizenship. When a consumerist perspective is applied to local government, some have objected that it has served to depoliticise the role of local authorities, one of the most important tasks of which is to promote collective well-being, by balancing competing local interests. [261]

Many people have welcomed the moves to increase the accountability of public services to individual consumers, pursued in the ways described here. There may indeed be scope for further measures of this kind. Some local authorities have, for example, sought consumer feedback about proposed policies and service delivery, through local surveys. However, these schemes cannot be a substitute for the strengthening of local democracy, because they are about something entirely different. Services need to be accountable to individuals and communities, directly and politically. At best, consumerist schemes such as the Citizen's Charter, give the individual consumer power and choice, but only as much power as her or his income permits, and only as much choice as is left by the tendency to monopoly. The promotion of consumer choice may be a necessary, but it is certainly not a sufficient condition of democratic freedom, as Simon Jenkins has pointed out, paraphrasing de Tocqueville.[262]

Safeguarding democracy while rebuilding a sense of community

Amidst all the talk about 'active citizenship', it is easy to get carried away. The reality is probably that even if all the steps canvassed in previous paragraphs were implemented in our cities, only a minority of city dwellers would really wish to become actively involved. It is important to remember that there is a democratic right not to be an active citizen, in the sense, for example, of participating in a local self help group. Many people are quite happy going about their individual lives and should be allowed to continue to do so, provided that their actions are not harmful to the wider community.

The task of encouraging greater involvement and more personal responsibility must involve the use of both carrots and sticks, as has been suggested in the context of sustainability. Education also has an enormous role to play in this; if people are informed about public policy issues, they are much more likely to take an accompanying opportunity to take part in a consultation exercise, or to consider adapting their lifestyles to encourage sustainability. Measures to reinvigorate local government, through application of the principle of subsidiarity for example, would help to remind city dwellers of their mutual inter-dependence.

Some of the current debate about the need to restore a sense of community to our cities verges uncomfortably close to authoritarianism. This criticism has been levelled at some versions of 'communitarianism', an idea developed by the American academic, Amitai Etzioni. Etzioni's own rationale for communitarianism is that *"free individuals require a community, which backs them up against the encroachment of the state and sustains morality by drawing on the gentle prodding of kin, friends, neighbours and other community members, rather than building on government controls or fear of authorities."*[263] Communitarianism rejects individualism and stresses the importance of individual responsibility and civic duty, and in this the Working Group believes it is much to be welcomed.

However, some versions of communitarianism have been criticised for being fundamentally intolerant of difference. At its most extreme, communitarianism could mean that a self-selected community shames miscreants into conformity by the force of majority opinion, backed up by the option to eject, as the last resort. As Anna Coote has asked, *"Where does communitarianism leave the dissenters and non-conformists, the artists and innovators, the misfits and migrants...?"*[264] Communitarianism sometimes seems to be more concerned with setting and maintaining boundaries, than with civil rights. For Coote, it also fails to take into sufficient account the way in which power is unevenly distributed within society, in terms of race, gender and class, for example.

The reality is however, that at present, almost any grouping together of people – whether from self-interest or through wider concerns – is to be welcomed as a small contribution to overcoming the community-less ethos of some city districts. Most successful community endeavours are small scale and area specific, and are at least partly inspired by self interest and community regard.

One of the sentiments that lies behind the populisation of the communitarian ideal, is clearly an understandable desire to regain old certainties, at a time when everything seems to be changing so fast. Yet, as Coote points out, the 'communities' which some older people today think of when they remember the city life of their childhoods, were produced by very different conditions to those which apply today. These communities were the product of an industrial economy; they were geographically fixed and based on families in which men were bread winners and women generally stayed at home, sustaining the infrastructure on which production depended. This had a great impact on people's personal relationships and attitudes towards others. Economic necessity reinforced this way of life. To reconstruct this model now, without the incentives which produced it, would be virtually impossible. The challenge for cities and people today, is to build a new, more inclusive sense of community which fits with the more dynamic, economic and social conditions which now prevail.

Communities therefore cannot be forced into being, but they can be stimulated by the right policy mix. Similarly, in a democratic society, the Working Group is clear that individuals cannot be compelled to be active, model citizens, but we believe they can be encouraged to take more personal and collective responsibility, by some of the measures suggested here.

6. Enhancing the Church's role in community life

One of the questions in the Working Group's survey of city dwellers, asked how people thought their Church could play a more active role in the community life of their city. Many respondents seemed stumped for an answer. Statistics suggest that the membership of the Methodist Church is falling in the cities, as indeed across the country. This is part of a wider trend within Britain's mainline Churches, membership of which have fallen by a quarter since 1970[265]. This may have fuelled the perception that the Church will do well to hang on to its current position in terms of community participation in our cities, let alone expand it. The high proportion of non-responses to the question about the Church in the Working Group's question-naire, may therefore reflect a broader pessimism about a de-clining Church. Many congregations in city Churches are very small and comprised of older city dwellers. How can it be possible for the Church to enhance its role in the community life of our cities, from this shrinking and ageing, membership base?

Answers to this problem seem to be emerging from the churches themselves. No longer able to imitate the larger congregations with their minister-preacher, choir, organ and multiple activities, some urban churches have begun to see in their very smallness, some strategic advantages. Their congregations have learned to function in an alternative way, as churches of the street, more like the base ecclesial communities of Latin America than the more typical 'building based' congregations in Britain. New patterns of ministry, mission, worship and grass-roots political activity have evolved. The Methodist *Mission Along-side the Poor* has assisted many such alternative projects[266]. It has also been suggested, based on an analysis of East London, that the development of multi-faith communities in our cities sometimes encourages the indigenous white population to practice their religion, thereby stimulating the growth of Christian congregations[267].

The Working Group believes that there are practical measures which the Church can take to expand its role in city life, and indeed, that it is vital for both the Church and our cities that it should do so. The Church can learn many useful lessons from highly successful Church initiatives which are already under way; from secular institutions in our cities; and from its own history and traditions. In seeking to move forward towards a vision of greater community involvement, it could strengthen its resolve by reflecting that the Church remains by far the best supported voluntary association of individual city dwellers in the country, and that its contribution to community life in our cities, is probably much more significant than is generally appreciated, perhaps by itself, let alone by others.

Before moving on to consider some of the practical steps which the Church might take in the cities, it is important to acknowledge that all the Church's work needs to be underpinned by a clear theological understanding of what it is doing and why. This may be particularly pertinent for city Churches which are heavily involved in community development. As has been asked, *"How do the bread and wine shared on a Sunday relate to the children's play in the nursery, the toy library and the creches, and the human drama which unfolds just a stone's throw away from the table on which they are offered?"*[268] Part Six addresses this question, by discussing a range of theological perspectives on the city.

The Church's role in building bridges across and within communities

The Church is well placed, perhaps now uniquely placed, to enable city dwellers who are otherwise divided, to meet and mix together, on neutral ground. By doing this, the Church can help discourage the increasing fragmentation within our cities, which is undermining a sense of community. It has been suggested for example, that, *"one aspect of the polarisation which bedevils so many aspects of London life and politics is that some ministers and politicians... speak and act without much personal experience of the inner city. Without the imaginative understanding of what life is like for lone parents on crime-ridden housing estates, it is easy to believe that they could improve their lot 'if they were really trying'. Churches can offer the possibility of gaining this indispensable personal experience."* [269]

The Church can also perform a similar function, in wider contexts. First, the Church is a truly national (and of course, international) force, with Churches in different parts of our cities and beyond, throughout the country. It is important that the understanding of city life which City Churches develop is taken wider, throughout the Church. In this way, people living in the suburbs, provincial towns and rural areas are likely to become much better informed about the realities of life in disadvantaged city districts – the challenges and achievements – than they will be if their exclusive source of information is the mass media.

Secondly, the Church has a responsibility to share its insights about city life, with the wider, national public. It is well placed to gather information about city trends and problems, perhaps in partnership with others. Its long tradition of doing this probably began with the publication of the Rev. Andrew Mearns' penny pamphlet, *The Bitter Cry of Outcast London* in 1883. The Working Group hopes that this Report will be seen as continuing the tradition to the present day, following in the steps of *Faith in the City* and the *Petition of Distress from the Cities* [270].

In disadvantaged city districts, characterised by significant racial tension, the Church has a particular responsibility to encourage the forces of mutual toleration and respect, in partnership with other faith communities. A recent report from David Haslam of Christians for Racial Justice sets out very clear and relevant policies about how this may be done [271]. What this means in practice is likely to differ between cities and neighbourhoods: in Glasgow for example, it suggests particularly, the need for a closer relationship between the Church of Scotland, the Catholic Church and other Christian denominations, while not forgetting of course, the contribution of non-Christian faith communities [272].

There is a danger that these words sound hollow, especially given the fact that the bulk of Christians of Afro-Caribbean origin in our cities are now outside the 'mainstream' Churches, in contrast to the situation in the Caribbean before immigration. The growth of the black led, mainly Pentecostal Churches is a response to the negative experience of black Christians in the 'mainstream' Churches.

It has been suggested that there has been growing consciousness and action in relation to racism by Christian groups in our cities, but that racism goes deep within the Christian community itself. *"Churches are far better at attacking sleazy and sordid groups of back-street thugs uttering racist slogans than at combating the reputable racism of those who smile, speak well and are charming, and are most likely Church members."* Similarly, Church initiatives to address race issues have been criticised as tokenistic 'add ons', which do nothing to influence the marginalisation of race within the power structures of the 'mainstream' Churches. The appointment of 'chaplains to black people' (like chaplains to industry, universities and hospitals) has been cited as evidence of this[273]. A truly multi-ethnic Christianity would rather be appointing black chaplains to white people – as indeed, is done by present mainline denominational practice in appointing black clergy from Britain and overseas, to churches of mainly or solely white membership.

The future lies with mutuality, not chaplaincy, and the struggle against racism must be seen as deriving from the heart of the Gospel, and must be at the heart of the structures and total life of the Church, not on the margins[274]. *"Racism threatens Christian faith at its very foundations: it threatens the renunciation and the covenant made at baptism, just as it threatens the equality and sharing of life in the Eucharist... for the Church to engage with racism seriously is to open a Pandora's box of unfinished theological and spiritual business,"* it has been claimed[275]. Nonetheless, the Working Group believes this must be done.

Giving a voice to people
who are socially excluded

This Report has referred repeatedly to the many ways in which people living in the most disadvantaged neighbourhoods of our cities, are socially excluded. One aspect of this is the fact that their voices are often not heard in discussions about, for example, the causes of poverty, or even about what it is like to live in poverty. This is rather amazing, given that they are clearly in a position to know more about this subject, than anyone else. Ironically, those who seek to advocate on behalf of the poor sometimes inadvertently do them damage by reinforcing stereotypes, or by overplaying the extent to which socially excluded people are helpless victims[276]. The danger of this happening is much lessened, if socially excluded people themselves are given the opportunity to advocate for themselves.

The charity ADT Fourth World has probably done more than any other organisation in Britain to encourage this process, and locally and nationally, the Churches have taken some important steps in the same direction. The *Bradford Urban Hearings*, organised by the *Bradford Metropolitan Faith in the City Forum*, are an impressive example of what can be achieved. The Forum is composed of representatives from seven Christian denominations. In 1993, they decided to carry out a piece of research about city life in Bradford, in the spirit of the original *Faith in the City* document. As well as referring to statistics, the Forum wanted to draw on the experiences of the people living in the inner city and outer estates of the city. They took the model of 'Hearings' from an experiment in the Diocese of Liverpool, and set up four of them, in contrasting districts of Bradford. One essential ingredient of the 'Hearings' model, was that it provided an opportunity for local people to speak about their lives, directly to the people who were the major decision makers in their local area. The findings from the Hearings were written up, and form the major part of the Forum's report, *Powerful Whispers* which is about city life in Bradford, but care has been taken to broaden its relevance to Churches, and communities in other British cities.[277]

The ecumenical organisation, *Church Action on Poverty*, has recently completed a three year initiative – *Local People National Voice* – which has given people in poverty an opportunity to speak out at Poverty Hearings held across the country. These culminated in a National Poverty Hearing at Church House, Westminster, in 1996, attended by national politicians and by Church leaders. The event was addressed by people living in poverty, from cities throughout the UK.

These initiatives have begun to change the climate of opinion among campaigning groups in Britain, about what might be an appropriate style of advocating on poverty issues. Their success has emphasised the importance of working in ways that provide people living in poverty, with the opportunity to express their own views and feelings about their lives, rather than putting words into their mouths. Those who spoke at these events seem generally to have found it a rewarding and empowering experience, and the National Hearing certainly made for powerful listening, as members of the Working Group can attest. What the longer term impact will have been on the national politicians who attended, is perhaps more doubtful; however, the challenge for Church Action on Poverty and other campaigning agencies is clearly to follow up these events in a sustained way. At least when one of these MPs next takes part in a debate about poverty, she or he may recall an image of one of the people who spoke at the National Poverty Hearing, rather than a stereotype devoid of humanity, drawn from the popular press.

Giving a voice to the voiceless is being increasingly seen as a vital part of the Church's task, in terms of its mission and theology. In this way, Christian theology ceases to be an interpretation of realities from outside, and becomes a testimony based on the discipleship of those on the inside. Recently, the Urban Theology Unit has published a book called *Faith from the City*, in which the experiences and testimonies of people in often stressful urban situations are claimed as contemporary manifestations of the way in which biblical people see the action of God, in events in their own contexts[278].

Participation in public life and individual Christian responsibility

Creating a better balanced, more inclusive and more socially just society in our cities requires political as well as personal action, a social as well as an individual response. These are tasks both for the Church and for individual Christians. So far as the former is concerned, *Faith in the City* remarked that, *"while many members of the Church of England have generally found it more congenial to express their discipleship by helping individual victims of misfortune or oppression, fewer are willing to rectify injustices in the structures of society."* [279]

It has been suggested that religious practice tends to focus on mutual support and fulfilment within the religious group, distant from the public sphere; and that the Church has tended to provide individual Christians with a refuge from the discomfort of living in a world undergoing rapid social change, rather than equipping them to take an active part in it[280]. Similarly, some city congregations have been characterised as *"parodies of the consumerist culture around them"*, regarding the Church primarily as an institution which ought to cater for their religious needs and feelings[281].

However, the practice of many congregations of all denominations in urban areas represents a refutation of these views of the Christian function. A new spirituality has emerged, in which many urban congregations take for granted local, practical, social and community involvement. They have also developed new forms of liturgy and devotion, which both arise out of and meet the needs of their context[282].

The *Christians in Public Life programme* is an important attempt to counteract these tendencies. In so doing, it follows in an established tradition of encouraging active engagement by Christians in the political and public life of our cities, for example in Victorian times, as was explained in an earlier section of this Report. The support of many faith communities for the Citizen Organising Foundation (also referred to above) is an example of a similar initiative. The Foundation does not yet however, match similar bodies in the United States, in terms of influence: Church based 'civic education' groups have stimulated political awareness and supported grass-roots campaigning, in disadvantaged city districts throughout the West and South of the country.

The concept of 'Christian citizenship' has been evoked by some, to describe the responsibilities of individual Christians in their city[283]. Others have asserted the importance for individual Christians, of considering the 'option for the poor', and the Working Group supports this view. Father Austen Smith has written that, *"It is quite scandalous that such a term as 'fundamental option for the poor' should be a theologically debated topic: in terms of the hopefulness of the kingdom of God, there is no option of any kind, let alone a fundamental one."*[284] The starting point for all Christians has to be greater awareness of community needs and issues. One of the Church's responsibilities is to support and encourage this process.

The Church's role in supporting community provision

The Church has a well established role in supporting and delivering community provision in our cities. Many of these Church based schemes are run in partnership with voluntary organisations, Housing Associations and community groups. So far as the Working Group is aware, no serious effort has ever been made to quantify the Church's contribution to community life in this respect. If it was, the Working Group is in no doubt that it would be found to be very significant indeed, exceeding that of any other single provider.

Any number of illustrative examples could have been chosen, for the purposes of this Report. The services provided through Churches cover an enormous range, and include: community development, community cafes, drop-in centres for homeless people, advice and information, training and outreach, supported housing, youth work, Credit Unions, children's activities, health services, support for people with mental health problems, and drug and alcohol rehabilitation projects. The

Methodist Church and NCH Action For Children run a number of community based projects in partnership together, in disadvantaged city districts. Among the services offered are: help for women living with domestic violence, support for isolated lone parents, and housing and associated social work services for mothers who are recovering alcoholics, and their children.

One of the advantages of Church based schemes of these kinds are that they are often able to be very local to the needs which services are designed to meet, since churches are situated in most city neighbourhoods, including severely disadvantaged ones. These initiatives are therefore accessible to local people, and generally feel less intimidating than statutory services of a similar kind. They are also more likely to be flexible and adaptable to local needs, being closer to the 'grass roots'. Church based projects therefore have most of the advantages of other, community based services – a reminder of the fact that the Church is a dominant force in the voluntary sector in most cities.

Like other forms of community provision, Church based services need to be run professionally and efficiently. It may be, however, that the underlying Christian ethos of projects, comes through to influence the style and nature of the services which are offered. This is thoroughly welcome, especially if it results in a more caring, personalised form of service delivery than is sometimes found, for example, in the statutory sector. However, Church projects need to think carefully about their aims and objectives, and the extent to which an explicit Christian commitment fits in with these. This is not to say that such a commitment is misplaced, simply that projects should seek to ensure that local people are clear about the type of service they are receiving.

For example, *Pecan* is a successful training and educational outreach project in Peckham, a very disadvantaged district of South London. It is run as an ethical, community business, by a group of people who share a Christian commitment. Pecan's Christianity is, however, separate from the course work. One of the trainers found that religion kept cropping up with one group.

She steered the discussion back to job training, but arranged for those who were interested to meet occasionally at her home. There have been a few conversions, and a few lapsed Christians have started going back to church. The real impact of Pecan's Christianity, however, is seen in the motivation and mobilisation of the staff. They all receive the same (low) salary, regardless of their job title. One of the workers commented, *"Our Christianity lies in how we value people and in getting people to recognise their own unique worth. At the centre of what we're doing is that we're showing God's heart to people because we believe God is interested in the details of everyone's lives and all their daily struggles."* [285]

The Church is very well placed to facilitate dialogue between people in city neighbourhoods, and to bring service providers together to discuss issues of common concern. The Consultation Meeting which the Working Group held in Cardiff on the themes of housing and homelessness, was organised by the Cardiff Central Methodist Church. Staff at the Church brought together representatives from the statutory and voluntary sectors, and from tenants associations and Churches, across the city. The event was a great success, and at the end of the meeting, those attending commented on the fact that such a representative group had never before assembled in the city, to discuss their concerns. The same could probably have been said of most cities, and most issues. There is enormous scope for similar exercises elsewhere. It is often the case that only the Church has sufficient credibility and impartiality, to make a success of a meeting of this kind. Of course, the voluntary sector and local authorities frequently organise multi-agency meetings of this kind, but these often have a less open agenda, and can become frustrated by competing interests.

Church buildings: a problem or a resource?

One of the problems that besets all denominations in our cities, is deciding what to do about Church buildings that are under-used and very costly to run. These decisions are inherently difficult, and can become further complicated by deeply held feelings of tradition and attachment. Churches can evoke strong emotions, even in non-attenders, and it has been suggested that they remain important in the Church's missionary effort: *"dilapidated church buildings signal the decrepitude of faith with terrible eloquence"*.[286] Conversely, the beauty of our more distinguished Church buildings signals the continuing importance of spiritual values in the city. Churches are also a symbol of permanence, amidst so much change. Perhaps the best example of this is the fact that one of the most resonant images of London is the famous photograph of the dome of St. Paul's, wreathed in smoke, during the blitz. The Working Group is of the view that the Church is to be found primarily in its people, and not in ecclesiastical buildings, but at the same time, churches are clearly also more than merely disposable plant. The reality is however, that there are not enough resources to preserve everything.

When a church is no longer appropriately meeting the needs of a congregation, serious thought should be given to handing most, or all of the building, over to others who might be able to use it for the benefit of the local community. Some of the most vibrant community projects in British cities, began this way. In Bromley by Bow in the East End of London, for example, a dwindling congregation decided to offer their church to the local community, in November 1983. Today, it has become clear that their gesture has transformed the lives and aspirations of thousands of local people. In the same buildings, the Bromley by Bow Centre has gradually developed. They are now used for over 70 assorted social and creative activities. A variety of classes, offered in many different languages, provide places for 400 students. The Centre has recently been awarded a grant from the National Lottery to expand its activities still further.[287]

There is a growing and welcome tendency for small congregations which find their buildings beyond their need or maintenance capacity, not to close and move away or even amalgamate with other churches, but rather to relocate in more community-relevant local locations or buildings. Thus, the

Sheffield Inner City Ecumenical Mission has demolished or sold large, redundant churches and replaced them by more modest and accessible buildings in the same neighbourhood, or on the same sites. 'Churches' now take place in two shops, a large house, a housing association complex and most recently (1996) a public house[288].

Churches which are architecturally distinguished should be cared for and preserved. The interests of conservationists and those whose priority must be the gospel are not mutually exclusive. Indeed, the best allies of the conservationists are the communities of faithful people, who over the years, have preserved the fabric of many distinguished churches. It is partly through their efforts, that the churches remain, while so much else of architectural merit in our cities has been destroyed by insensitive, post-war redevelopment.

Encouraging greater community involvement

Churches can implement a number of practical measures, in pursuit of greater community involvement. They can, for example:

- First, conduct a 'situation analysis' or 'parish audit' of their neighbourhood, to discover who is there, and to start asking people about their feelings regarding their area[289]

- Take positive steps to find out whether local voluntary groups might be able to make use of any under-utilised buildings

- Make local alliances with a view to developing inter-faith work

- Set up or take part in local ecumenical networks, to exchange information about 'what works'

- Join local, voluntary sector information networks, and participate in grass-roots campaigning, where appropriate

- Consider the scope for developing active partnerships with local voluntary agencies, gather information, respond to unmet local needs

- Advertise their own facilities and activities, and take steps to advertise community events to their own congregations, perhaps using church noticeboards and circulars

- Consider setting up, or participating, in a local Credit Union or LETs scheme

• Seek young people's views directly, about how the Church can be made more attractive and accessible to them, and about their local issues and concerns.

The need for more strategic support for the Church in the city

The previous paragraphs give some insight into how much is already being done by the Church, to engage with local communities. However, just as with secular organisations in our cities, it seems that these successes are often due largely to the energy of particular individuals and of small groups of committed Church workers. It is important that these dynamic people are given sufficient autonomy to be creative, but there is the same requirement for a balance between support, supervision and accountability within the Church, as in secular institutions. 'Entrepreneurial' ministers and church workers also run similar risks of 'burn out' and isolation, to their secular counterparts. It is therefore important that the Church takes steps to support their activities.

Some of the achievements of the Church in the city, are probably more the product of fortunate accident and creative individualism, than of strategic design. This raises the wider question of what else the Church can do to encourage and support local churches' participation in the life of our cities. There is no doubt that the various Church of England initiatives which followed the publication of *Faith in the City*, have achieved a great deal in this respect. The development of methods for measuring the relative needs of urban districts has been important in helping to ensure that the resources which are available, are used in the most efficient way. These indices are very sensibly based on factors which reinforce social exclusion such as unemployment, rather than on the quality of an area's physical fabric[290]. However, despite all the achievements which have followed in the wake of *Faith in the City* and the establishment of the Church Urban Fund, it is also sometimes argued that much more could and should be done[291].

It is certainly important that the activities of denominations in our cities, are not hampered by the lack of an appropriate infrastructure to encourage and sustain them. Churches are clearly faced with a difficult balancing act in terms of freeing up local churches from the stifling effects of bureaucracy on the one hand, and the need for strategic management, on the other. However, if the full potential for Church participation in the city is to be maximised, the Working Group believes that the Methodist Church must find new ways of supporting city initiatives, and of disseminating the good practice which is taking place, throughout the country.

The Church could certainly do more to discourage apathy and celebrate success. A compendium of recent audits of Church based community initiatives which are under way, with an estimate of what has already been achieved, would be a good starting point[292]. National conferences and local seminars on 'what works', raise awareness and disseminate good ideas[293]. The production of briefing sheets for city churches, on the very practical steps they could take to increase their role in the local community often encourage some people to get started. Some churches may feel intimidated by the multi-faceted activities already under way in other neighbourhoods, but everyone has to start somewhere, and every little helps. Guidance on how to begin, is therefore particularly important.

Finally, the enthusiasm and skills of young people in the Church, must be tapped to the full. Within the Methodist Church for example, the Methodist Association of Youth Clubs is an invaluable resource. The recent MAYC campaign and publication, *Scandal*, on homelessness gives an indication of how much young people and youth groups can achieve, if provided with appropriate help and support.

Part 6

THEOLOGICAL REFLECTIONS ON CITY LIFE

1. A theology of the city

As the time came for Him to be taken up to heaven, He set his face resolutely towards Jerusalem, and sent messengers ahead. They set out and went to a Samaritan village to make arrangements for Him, but the villagers would not have Him, because He was making for Jerusalem. When the disciples James and John saw this they said "Lord, may we call down fire from heaven to destroy them?"
But He turned and rebuked them.

St Luke 9.51-55

An approach to the theology of the city seeks to combine at least two already complex fields. First is the human understanding of the city. Second is the Christian understanding of the faith. Above all, such an enterprise must take the Christian tradition seriously. The problems are considerable, not least because theological understanding is in a state of turmoil. Two particular issues arise.

First, a contemporary, theology will seek to be as inclusive as possible, an instinct that arises from the pressing need to live together in mass societies. On the other hand, the accounts that we find in Holy Scripture and in the tradition are often profoundly exclusive in character. A key theological concept that binds both Scripture and Tradition is that of **election**.

The Old Testament story is largely one of a people whom God elects by birth. *The New Testament* story is one in which God elects His people by baptism and by rebirth, by personal confession of the truth of God's love shown in Christ. This commitment to two sharply different doctrines of election has often confounded our desire to celebrate a common humanity; the conflicts between Christian and Jewish exclusive views of the world have been horrific and shaming.

Second, a theology of the city will seek to affirm the diversity of the city. But again, Jewish and Christian perceptions of the city have often been negative, again in sharply different ways. But many Christians are convinced that God is leading us to share in the life of an increasingly global society. In such a society, cherished traditions threaten to be dangerously sectarian. The first step towards an inclusive urban theology requires us to be candid about the exclusive nature of our former and current commitments, and risk the controversy that must arise. A vivid illustration of the question appears in Luke's story of Jesus and his disciples passing through a Samaritan village on the way to Jerusalem, and the conflict that breaks out between the Samaritans and the disciples. The patterns of conflict between Jews and Samaritans and between Jews and Christians are an integral part of our traditions. Those conflicts become critical when distinct communities seek to live together in peace. Do they allow their traditions to fuel their enmities? Or do they seek to interpret the received faith in ways that enable the tradition itself to transcend their enmities?

The city in history

Such a movement from an exclusive to an inclusive theological perception can be illustrated in five urban settings. First, Babylon in around 550 BCE, as the Jewish exiles take stock of their past. Second, Alexandria around 450 AD, as the Christians take possession of the Empire. Third, Florence, around 1450, from where it is possible to look back on half a millennium of distinctively and self-consciously Christian urban civilisation. Fourth, Amsterdam around 1650, from which point we appear to see in outline a post-Christian urban civilisation. Fifth, Manchester, an early urban industrial city, which continues trends set earlier, but which has its own surprising qualities.

Babylon 550BC

In around 550 BC, the Jewish exiles in Babylon compiled their reflections on who they were, and what God's purpose was for them. The first, great, decisive event for them is their creation as a distinctive people in the experience of the *Exodus*, a story so important that it is told a number of times in various versions. Each version tells of a people whom God has freed from urban slavery, a people made conscious of their sharp distinction from all the other peoples of the world; a people purged of disobedience, whom God seeks to create in the image of obedience to his will. They fight for a place in Palestine, their promised land. Their struggle is made the more ruthless because of the sharp difference that they perceive between themselves and the surrounding peoples. They engage in a Holy War against false gods and the ritual and moral pollution which such falsity brings in its wake.

This abomination is at its most evident in the sophisticated urban centres of the Levant, like Jericho, the Philistine cities and Damascus. There is clear conflict over the creation of the Hebrew monarchy, and over the establishment in Jerusalem of a royal court and the building of the Solomon's temple. The expansion of the Hebrews into Greater Israel makes them the rulers of new peoples; the commercial activity resulting from the construction of the temple and the city creates an uncomfortably diverse society. And like all the urban civilisations of the region, the short-lived Jerusalem theocracy comes to a bloody end, and to exile in Babylon.

Out of that experience spring two distinct theological perceptions. The first is a sharpening of the sense of radical distinction between the Jewish people and the rest of humanity. This perception entails the desire to return to Jerusalem and achieve the heroically impossible; to build a holy city, morally and ritually pure, at one of the world's busiest crossroads. This aim is doomed, and the despairing Jewish people feel themselves no longer merely caught up in the vagaries of history, but pitted against cosmic powers of pure evil. This apocalyptic sense of the universe as demonic evil focuses on the centres of urban civilisation. There is no possible remedy short of total divine retribution, followed by the descent from heaven of the New Jerusalem. The great example of this style is of course found in the *Book of Revelation*, an essentially Jewish text. These powerful apocalyptic texts bear little relation to current thinking in Judaism, but their clear meaning must be acknowledged.

The other strand is clear in the writings of the prophets. They look for the fulfilment of God's will not in the distinctiveness of the Jerusalem temple cult, but in the experience of a people, cast on the tide of history, but whose hearts are shaped by God wherever they are. They are to behave well, no matter what happens to them, for God is always with them. The theme is most splendidly developed by Jeremiah, as he tells his people how to endure, even enjoy, their exile in Babylon. The weakness of this strand, however, is a feature of its strength. The prophetic tradition was powerfully informed by an inspirational rhetoric rather than a written civic code, with important consequences for the concept and practice of justice.

The prophets were intent on proclaiming God's plan for a more just future state, but that future hope tends to be conditioned by the recollection of a simpler, more manageable past existence. That imagined past corresponded very little to reality. So future generations have sought to shape modern urban society on the basis of a not always accurate or useful nostalgia. The issues here are usefully discussed by Theodore Epsztein.[294] This tendency to romanticise the past applies to secular as to theological matters, as has been pointed out in a previous section of this book.

Alexandria 450CE

A millennium has passed. The impossible Jewish project, to create a holy city in the human world, is over. Towards the end of that time, a new Jewish sect arose in Palestine, claiming that God had spoken at last through the Messiah, through whose death and resurrection his followers are freed from the vagaries of history, and released into an eternal destiny. This sect has recast its beliefs in a way more consistent with gentile society, and has spread widely throughout the Empire. The Christian story is no longer one of liberation from Gentile society; it is a story of liberation into that society, for Christ's sake.

God has prospered the work. Christianity has become the official religion of the empire. Its new wealth and position is evident in Alexandria. It is the Empire's second city, and its most economically powerful. It is also the Empire's most Jewish city – a fifth of the population are Jews. Here in the Nile delta, the Passover is celebrated annually mere miles from the place of its institution.

For the Christians, the Exile in Babylon is now over; for the Jews, it continues, as the Christians overwhelm the Jewish claim to election. The great imperial cities from the Atlantic to the Persian Gulf, continue to thrive and change, supported on the revenues of the levantine grain trade– in this city more than anywhere. Sophisticated systems of banking credit make ambitious building plans possible. Ostentatious wealth is everywhere, but so is the notion that to give to charity is an essential feature of the Christian life. It is possible to claim that this double commitment to wealth and to welfare is a Christian innovation. This is a more humane society. Abortion, infanticide (through the custom of leaving babies to die of exposure) and divorce are forbidden. The old Christian concept of Koinonia, of shared fellowship, is hard to maintain in a mass society. But according to Robin Lane Fox, Christians do appear to love one another more, and a new kind of prosperous and humane society is developing.[295]

Two issues remain, however. The first is the obsession of this society with theological correctness. In sharp contrast to pagan society, it insists on close and exclusive definition of the truth about God. Unfortunately, these Christians are formidably rational, and the truth is very complicated; how can God be One if Jesus is truly God? One implication of this conundrum is the status of Mary. Is the Mother of Jesus thereby the Bearer of God, 'Theotokos'?[296] This is also the city for theological exactitude.

The truth about God is endlessly disputed, sometimes murderously so; in this city the Platonist philosopher Hypatia has just been lynched. The various Jewish and Christian factions of the Alexandrian mob rage against one another. The most successful contemporary theologian and manager of public tumults is Cyril, Bishop of Alexandria. But the truth about God and the politics of the city have become hopelessly entangled. These issues are presented in the most elementary works in Patristic theology, but they take on a new urgency when approached within the context of urban life.[297]

The second issue is an insistence on the wickedness of the fruits of prosperity. For this is the age when the most committed of Christian people retreat to the desert, seeking salvation in asceticism, imposing on the Church a sense that true Christianity can only be achieved by those who renounce the world, which means fleeing the city. A thousand miles to the West, Augustine, carried the recollection of the sack of Rome, and the sense that not even Christian civilisation was providentially guaranteed. He saw the politics of the city set in history, and having no special meaning in the purpose of God. In this he was deeply affected by the destruction of Rome, and he brings home to us the provisional nature of human affairs. He can see that there is a sharp difference between a good lawyer or trader and a bad one. But he can find no place in God's greater purpose for a constructive engagement of lawyers or traders in the workaday world. Real life is eternal life, and that is a matter of accepting the call of God to self-denial. Those who hear this call and follow it are, again, the Elect. Therefore, the ambivalence of Christianity in the workaday world is seen most clearly in the ascetic attitude to the city, and above all in Augustine's *City of God*.[298]

Florence 1480

This city is Catholic, at the heart of Christendom; no significant other influence exists. Islam is perceived as a distant, demonic threat, having swept over Alexandria eight centuries ago, the Great Simplifier of all questions about the nature of God and of social ethics. Here, remarkably, the bustling, prosperous, stylish

Tuscans defer somewhat to an ascetic, celibate sect–their own priesthood, whose presence dominates every corner of the city. Augustine clearly remains a powerful force, a thousand years on. The chief object of devotion in this celibate-led society appears on virtually every street corner; it is that of a woman caring for a child, Theotokos, the God-Bearer. St Cyril also casts a long shadow.

There is a thriving local and international trade, funded by credit. There are famous banks, for the Church has ambitious plans, and its own ambitions make credit essential. The competition for credit between Church, Empire and aristocracy keeps interest rates high, however, because these groups are a really bad risk; they can use force, or arguments against usury, to renege at any time. This was especially threatening for the Jews. All this makes borrowing difficult for normal transactions, and resorted to mainly by the desperate. But people lend at affordable rates to those whom they can trust, so limited growth occurs. Increasingly, as in the old empire, the most influential groups are self-selecting associations of traders and bankers who are held in check only by the threats and blandishments of the armed aristocracy.

The sense of election has diminished, for everyone is Catholic. This is a point of some importance. For nearly a thousand years the quarrels between pope and emperor, peasant, burgher and aristocrat have been conducted on agreed Christian grounds. Even the new learning of the Renaissance has been contained within the envelope of common belief. There is a new delight in creation, a rediscovery of the riches of thought and imagination contained in the urban cultures of antiquity. The ascetic call to exile continues, but this society prides itself on the Christian nature of its civilisation, and that civilisation is essentially urban.[299]

Nonetheless, the tensions between cathedral, palace and marketplace are becoming more destructive than creative, and they are beginning to envelop the whole Catholic world. The forces of modernity, in the form of the French and Spanish imperial nations, have little understanding of the commercial city but they generate deep convictions about the destiny of their nations.[300] Still united in faith, Western Christendom is divided by faction. A city like Florence can survive such conflict while Venice, a maritime empire in its own right, has the maturity to resist such factional in-fighting. But such restraint is not typical. The coming centuries will show that a civilisation and its cities, can come frequently near destruction if the claims of its most powerful interests cannot be harmonised, especially when they are endorsed by religious conviction.

Amsterdam 1650

Florence continues much as before, but getting poorer as the Empire squeezes the life out of the Mediterranean. The Catholic French and Spanish are perpetually at war, the later squandering the fortune in silver brought from the Americas.[301] Calvinist England and Holland are at war, but not so much as to interrupt business. Here there is strong competition for capital, but among people who trust one another's credit-rating so that interest rates are low. Holland is the world's first trading nation. It is the city of associations of strangers. It is essentially our modern world.

More than a century has passed since Christendom fractured into three sharply different reforming camps – Catholic, Lutheran, Calvinist. In Amsterdam a rather strict form of Christianity has been quite consistently applied to society for over a century, drawing its popular force from the long wars of liberation, fought against Catholic Spain in the name of the Calvinist God. The Reformation has expelled the professional ascetics, and now lay Christians are expected to discover their own capacity for God-fearing austerity. The Old Testament has been rediscovered, and the Calvinists who hold real power are proclaiming their vision of Babylon transformed into the New Jerusalem. There is widespread support for the notion of the moral society, but less practical effort made to help create it. The sheer uncontrollable dynamic of the global marketplace has created outbursts of huge wealth, and middling prosperity, and new masses of poverty. The Churches seek to maintain their charitable activity in the face of all this, but flounder.[302]

The certainties of faith are less sure still, despite the powerful Calvinist rhetoric of liberation. Observation and imagination are no longer exercised within the bounds of the Church. Human curiosity is focused on the future, on a clearly new world, in which religion is a varied phenomenon, and in which the nature of God is a problematic, not a matter of life and death, nor of eternal life and death. The sceptical Catholic Descartes is here; so is the sceptical Jew, Spinoza. Here too is the radical theologian Jacobus Arminius, who insists that God cannot be so cruel as to leave us in the shadow of an uncertain election; rather, the certainty of God's love for all humanity can be known by those who desire it.[303]

Here is a post-dogmatic city. Here no one thing has to be true. Here the doctrine of election seems to hold sway in a typically exclusive form, but the explosion of ideas is, in principle, established. For centuries yet, most people will live their lives in the conviction that their Christian commitment forms the only basis for social order; but increasingly a new class of intellectual explorers is ceasing to share this belief. Amsterdam is a reluctantly diverse society. In it are seen the first beginnings of a genuinely inclusive, plural society, in which difference is celebrated, and in which our most distinctive Christian commitment may be to the idea that no one thing has to be true.

Manchester 1850

In 1850 a suffragan bishop was appointed for Manchester. This move caused a national uproar, a debate which lasted a week in the Commons, and a bitter clash between Gladstone and Disraeli. Why the fuss? Because the Bishop was a Catholic. Liberal England prided itself on its tolerance, but Pius I X's plan to establish territorial sees was termed, officially, 'Papal Aggression'.[304]

In 1650, it seemed likely that the Dutch trend would extend to England to produce a revulsion against religious conflicts, and the accommodation of religion to exciting new philosophical and scientific visions – certainly for metropolitan urban life, no matter what happened in the provinces. Many related factors altered this expectation. Among them is the totally unexpected rise of two powerful new religious movements, each utterly different. They are the Catholics and the Methodists, and both are clearly evident in Manchester in 1850.[305]

By this time, a fifth of the population is Irish or of Irish descent. The huge expansion of the city had sucked in migrant labour from its nearest plentiful supply. In the meantime, Methodism has been born. One of the distinctive elements in its proclamation are those generously inclusive ideas of Arminius, now shaped in an English form. That proclamation speaks to an age that is fearful of the rapid social change of that period. In the midst of anxiety, assurance! And not just for a distant future, but now, in the immediate, intense experience of a loving community! This commitment to proclamation and organisation created the Methodist people, by 1850 a million strong in Britain, and fifty thousand of them in Manchester. In Alexandria, the age of primitive Christianity had long gone. In Manchester, nearly 1500 years later, that initial impulse has burst into spontaneous life, and something like the early church comes to life on a somewhat wider scale.

Indeed, it is in the North West that both Catholics and Methodists find a strong counterweight to the metropolis. The Catholics are much more urban, and much more representative of the life of the poor. They are also gathered in much greater numbers in each place. The differences between the two communities are profound, and their relationships those of mutual suspicion. On the one hand, the Catholics carry a clear ethnic identity, shaped by an ancient tradition. The Methodists, on the other hand, feel themselves to be created by the Holy Spirit in the image of the primitive Church. They are energetic, enthusiastic, and tend to share life rather intensely in small groups. They are also rather better off, and more upwardly mobile. The Methodist people had an early and important engagement with urban reality. However, the rather different Catholic story of engagement is an important historical element in the creation of the diversity and propensity for friction within the modern city.

Meanwhile, the Established Church is itself enjoying the expansion of enthusiastic factions – the Evangelicals who share something of the Methodist tradition; and the Anglo – Catholics who have their own vision of Gothic Christendom. This is personified by trends in city architecture: from the neo-classical and baroque of post-Christendom enlightenment, the Brave New World is actually being built in Gothic.

So the most striking thing about mid-century Manchester is its similarity to Alexandria – its vigorous, competitive, mutually-suspicious melee of organised religion, organised to a considerable degree for conflict. But the sharp difference with Alexandria is the extent to which there is general *indifference* to organised religion. For on the day of the 1851 census, only ten percent of the population of Manchester is in any place of worship at all. So, strangely, religion is much more a live issue in Victorian Manchester, but much less a live presence than is often thought today. True, three quarters of the city's children attend Sunday School, but the numerical trend is downwards, to be followed in the second half of the century by an accommodation to an increasingly secular view of society.

None of this appears so at the time, however; established religion is a life or death issue, although with deviations tolerated at the edges. When so alien a force as 'Irish Popery', as it was then termed, threatens serious competition with the status quo, fierce reactions ensue. The scene seems set for irresolvable conflict. But the case of Gladstone is instructive. In 1835 this high-minded, fiercely Anglo-Catholic young man believed that national salvation could stem only from the imposition of his kind of Anglicanism upon the nation. He is as intolerant of Catholics as he is of Dissenters. Fifty years later, he has a sufficient sense of the diversity of modern Europe to be able to imagine an independent, Catholic Ireland within it.[306] Here then, is a mind broad enough to contain both fierce Christian conviction and a far-reaching capacity for tolerance. In these broad ambiguities lies the possibility of life together in the modern city.

In 1850, questions of religious affiliation loomed at least as large as those of social justice. To our eyes today, Manchester in 1850 was a place of anarchic and terrifying poverty. To the contemporary observer, however, it appears to be a place of intensifying prosperity, whose terrible past was slowly being erased. Between the vast wealth of the cotton barons and the appalling poverty of the mill workers, there begins to grow up an intermediate class which greatly outnumbers the rich, and ranks in size with the poor.[307]

The problems of this city continue however, and they clearly cannot be addressed by charity alone. But how else? For a singular economic ideology envelops this city especially – 'Manchester Liberalism'. It claims a basis in irrefutable logic as much as St Cyril did. It is the practical wisdom to which theology must accommodate. It is a gloomy combination of Smith and Malthus. It suggests first that the market is the only efficient way to organise resources. It suggests, secondly, that any attempt to relieve poverty in any other way will simply provide more mouths to feed. Such a view of the world seemed one of irrefutable logic in the Liberal age, and to deny that logic threatened humanity, especially the poor.[308]

The great achievement of the Victorians was to risk the rebuttal of that dogma, because its implications for humanity were unacceptable. That leap of faith has proved immensely rewarding, but the problems of the late 20th Century probably require equally bold solutions. The 19th Century saw the cautious exploration of the limitations of the market; the notion that the State can solve every problem may perhaps have been the 20th century fallacy, and in each case theology has dragged along behind the driving force of contemporary wisdom.

2. A theology for today's city

Here, then, are elements for a theology of the city. Its first element is the logic of Election; that sense common to both Jewish and Christian traditions that one's people are not just better than others; they are The Chosen. This perception, at its worst, can be bigoted, paranoid and cruel. Christians can be very bad citizens.

The second element is the experience of Grace. Here is a tradition of spirituality rather than of theology. At its best, the tradition expresses an inward access to the love of God that illuminates the spirit and softens the heart. This generosity of spirit can transcend the logic that dogma imposes. It is possible to risk the notion that God invites us to celebrate a common humanity. Thus, John Wesley, himself impeccably orthodox wrote:

> *"I wish your zeal was better employed than in persuading men to be either dipped or sprinkled. I will employ mine, by the grace of God, in persuading them to love God with all their hearts, and their neighbours as themselves."*[309]

Such a robust and generous spirituality can thrive in the city, where the diversity of our humanity mocks our exclusive instincts on every street corner. The city is a teeming mass of difference, whose reality goes far beyond the pallid cliches that describe urban life as a 'multi-faith' or a 'multi-cultural' experience. There is a rich variety of experience of difference, which Alexandria failed to grasp, and which Manchester nearly failed to grasp. There is an apparent paradox here; the more distinctive is the Christian experience, the less exclusive does Christian behaviour towards others need to be. This experience of the love of God does create problems; but it does not solve them in an excluding way. Christians can be very good citizens.

It is the capacity to engage creatively with others that matters, rather than to rehearse continually the reasons why God has blessed his Elect. Some of the objective, historically-based theological realities have already been addressed. We have suggested that the pattern that has emerged over some centuries is one of movement from an exclusive to an inclusive pattern of theology and practice. This movement has become clear over half a millennium. The ferocity of the conflicts of that period are testimony to the difficulty of such a shift.

An attempt has been made here to sketch the ways in which the church has responded to urban life in the course of its existence. In this way we hope to avoid the temptation to take a given view of the world and simply to interweave some traditional theological terms. The tradition always illuminates contemporary concerns, particularly in the turmoil of urban experience.

We have seen the Jewish-Christian temptation to apocalyptic despair over the city. We have also seen the tendency in the tradition to seek its salvation outside the compromises of ordinary life in the pursuit of an ascetic way. A rather diminished form of this instinct is found in the relative austerity that informs much Christian behaviour, and which often makes it hard for us to accept the raucous vigour of much urban life. As a consequence we tend not to comprehend the degree to which sheer appetite and self-interest drives the city, and we fail to see the elements of trust and hope which inform such self-interested pursuit, and which generate the immense resources required to create and to renew the city. It takes some imagination to feel our mutuality and interdependence as a spirituality of love, when that interdependence is embodied in economic give and take. We find it easy to feel that it is blessed to give, and to receive; but it is generally more difficult to feel the same about buying and selling.

Our brief reflection on the past suggests that God is moving the Church to a more inclusive understanding of the divine purpose. That conviction shapes the following theological observations on the contemporary city. The four theological themes that we wish to raise are:

Creation
Incarnation
Cross and Resurrection
Pilgrimage

Creation

In the earlier Jewish tradition, creation formed a minor theme in comparison with the choosing of the people of God; in classical Christianity, the theme of creation often serves to introduce that of the Fall. By contrast, contemporary theology speaks of a continuing engagement between the Holy Spirit and the created order, and the city is clearly where that process is seen at its most dynamic and challenging.

Until very recently, the created order was seen as hostile to human purposes. At its hands, humanity generally, and women and children in particular, experienced disease, pain and premature death. Humanity has asserted itself within creation, gained the upper hand for the present, and has wrought great harm upon it. The modern city has also proved hostile to human flourishing, although it is a human creation. Its complexity renders it difficult to plan and to control, without inducing a kind of stagnation and decline that results in the next wave of urban growth moving elsewhere. The process of creative destruction is nowhere more evident than in the city, and it is the great and exhilarating task of Christians to seek to manage that process for the benefit of all its people.

Our historical reflection has drawn attention to the commercial nature of the city. The city requires immense resources to come into being. The simplest city still draws to it that variety of people who build it, service it, profit from it. The city is not just a mass of people living together, nor is it a failed monastery. It is inextricably linked with money and power, and those elements will always be found in great concentration within its walls. Many Christians appreciate that these forces may foster good, but are equally suspicious of the glitter and falsity that sometimes accompany them, and challenge the inhumanity that they frequently mask.

It is hard to be comfortable with the city. It demonstrates in a spatially small area, the depths of poverty and the pinnacles of wealth. Yet the clearest impression given in most cities of the industrial world, certainly in the 1950s and 1960s, has been one of widespread middling prosperity and contentment. Nonetheless, even in the most favourable circumstances it can seem almost impossible for all a city's inhabitants to work together in pursuit of a common good. Self-interest is so evident in the city that commonality seems continually threatened by selfishness.

The city can be so sophisticated, impersonal and inhuman that it is difficult to see it as a place of blessing and creativity. But God gives us the example of the Body of Christ, of Koinonia in the early Church. Our own experience of alienation, homelessness, youth unemployment, and street crime indicate that it is in our shared interest to challenge these injustices. As we have seen, the early Church found it difficult to maintain such a commitment to Canine once it embraced the whole of Roman society, but the challenge remains.

Laurie Green has written well of the particular spirituality of the city.

> *I sense the majesty, energy and power of God in heavy industry and in that a sense of belonging with God in a solidarity with God's creativity. I feel delighted by a sense of wonder in industry that we have been given gifts to work with such complexity and find comradeship, worth and identity in the endeavour. In the service industries too I find sacraments of God's presence – hospitals, shops, sewers and dustbin collection – all gifts in their fascinating urban complexity. And with every such gift I sense too the challenge and anguish when we get in wrong. When industry becomes unjust; when political groups seek their own aggrandisement; when social services are badly resourced; I still feel God within it all, but now yearning and suffering with his children.*[310]

Incarnation

The second key concept is that of Incarnation. An exclusive theology of the Incarnation makes our sharing in Christ's humanity a possibility only for believers. A bolder doctrine sees Jesus come among us all, as one of us, participating in the common life around him, rejoicing that in him all things hold together, and that the created order serves a recognisably human purpose.

One of the most exciting features of contemporary theology is the exploration of Christian doctrine that now occurs outside the constraints of the classical tradition. Much of this work expands the meaning of those few words in the Epistle to the Colossians:

> *Christ exists before all things, and everything is held together in him. He is, moreover, the head of the body, the church.*
> (Col 1.17-18)

What does it mean for God to have created his relationship with humanity, in the form of Christ, from the beginning of creation? Current reflection on the doctrines of the Trinity and of the Incarnation must inform our thinking about God's relation to the whole of humanity, and especially in its most problematic form, the city. But a spirituality of the city must precede an elaborated theology; it is only when we are moved by the sheer diversity of the city that we feel deeply the experience of God's grace unconditionally among us. That experience creates a new kind of spirituality, which in turn seeks a new kind of theological understanding. If the universe has a human face, then so must the city. It is this conviction that has so powerfully influenced the calling of those who might otherwise have fled the city.

John Vincent has written of a spirituality of incarnation which introduces disciples to a contemporary, secular, identification with Christ:

> *First, there is the level of incarnation. We need to confirm ourselves in the areas of need. If we are not there, a few of us need to move there. Second, there is the level of healing. We*

need people on the ground who will express love and compassion in the face of obvious injustice and victimization. Third, there is the level of parables. We need people, preferably locals, who will take up the gut-level happenings of an area, and hold them up for others to see. Fourth, there is the level of acted parables. We need visible examples, prophetic signs, acted parables, proleptic instances, of what we want, set up for all to see. Fifth, there is the level of disciple-group. We need people really committed to each other, to the place and to the disciplines necessary for significant acting. Sixth, there is the level of crucifixion. We need to be at the places where the oppression of the powers is really encountered and felt, so that we can be borne down by it, as others are borne down by it. Seventh, there is the level of resurrection. We need to be around when old things are raised up, when old things get started again, when the commitments crucified by the enemies are brought to life again. Eighth, there is the level of the new city. We need to be backyard visionaries; plucking from the future the things that all humanity seeks, and digging in bits of them in city backyards.[311]

It is in the city that so many poor, excluded and stigmatised people have discovered their true humanity and their Christian vocation. The Church has a duty to tell their stories and to celebrate them. It is also in the city that many have identified with the poor and excluded and have thereby found their own calling alongside them. That too is a valid and empowering form of discipleship, and it too calls for rejoicing.

Cross and resurrection

In the tradition, the death and resurrection of Christ have been the means by which we are released from the vagaries of history into an eternal order. We have seen the tendency within the tradition to retreat from the crudities of temporal life, not least in the flight from the city. By contrast, it is tempting to adopt a glib incarnational theology that implies that co-operation between all people of good will must surely prevail.

On the contrary, God's creation is marked by such profound

desolation that the ordinary processes of renewal, and hope for change, are rendered thoroughly inadequate. The family growing up in squalid housing, knowing that its experience of social exclusion is likely to work out relentlessly through growing children. In the city, the old and frail often eke out the long, final periods of their lives in a system of Community Care that functions badly enough in prosperous areas; elsewhere it can be a kind of continual crucifixion endured in cold, pain and misery. Again, it is a commonplace that in the robust urban marketplace there are both winners and losers. But the slow death of a business can blight the lives of a whole family as it fragments in despair. Added to these are the stories of young people whose lives have been early blighted by hopelessness, and who experience a long decline into homelessness and destitution.

It is easy in each of these cases to produce a glib prescription for future social renewal through better application of existing resources. But such a response fails to embrace the pain of unbearable personal suffering, felt now. In such affliction, each day's dawn brings the prospect of the cross. But each day also brings the promise of that suffering shared with God, and, by his grace, with others during the course of that day. In this way, each day become both cross and resurrection, but only if Christians are able to share that suffering with one another, and so be blessed with the experience of resurrection. Of course, the experience of desolation shared with God and others is not exclusively urban, but the multiplicity of such suffering in our impersonal cities is especially intense.

The Cross stands among those who endure inconsolable pain. So too, the Cross stands in judgement over the whole of human endeavour, revealing the flaw at the heart of even the most heroically faithful followers of Christ. Pharisees, disciples, even reflective Christian community workers, have fallen short of the glory of God. In concrete terms, it is important to recognise the sinfulness of all humanity, and to resist the temptation to complacent self-righteousness. The good news of the re-surrection is that faithfulness is taken up into God's greater purposes – the dead are raised!

Pilgrimage

A spirituality of Pilgrimage arises in many urban contexts today, not so much the middle class notion of personal 'journeys', as the trials of the aliens, the dispossessed, the migrant. So Andrew Davey describes his Peckham parish:

Themes of migration, the search for 'home' and of being the outsider feature regularly in our experience and discussions.

Most of us were brought up with Bible maps which plotted in huge squiggles, Abraham's wanderings through the ancient near east. On one occasion, a group plot alongside such a map their own journeys, from the Caribbean to the Southern States at the height of segregation, from London to Nigeria and back again, from rural Ulster to urban Belfast and then on to London, from the Caribbean to Southport to Balham to Peckham. All roads somehow lead to Peckham at least in these stories!

Within those stories, we heard of the search for Christian community, of risks taken, of expectations raised and misunderstandings. The community which Abraham and Sarah drew around them seems a paradigm of our experience and aspirations, a place where blessings are shared, strangers are welcomed, faith is passed on, hope takes root, alongside faith being tested to the extreme. A community where people are drawn from traditional cultures has many hazards and pitfalls. It can also have the feeling of a counter culture apparent particularly when welcoming and hospitality are discussed. Our reflection has also helped with a partnership being created with an evangelical agency working with refugees and speakers of other languages based on our premises.[312]

Cities themselves are on a journey. They evolve over time, parts decay and others regenerate. But they do persist over long periods of time, an issue that we are particularly aware of with the approaching millennium. It is encouraging to see so many Christian people committed to more than simply the current needs of cities. They also have a pride in the past, and a desire to imagine the future. In every journey of pilgrimage it is important to acknowledge the past, and realise its impact on the present. There is much in the past and the present to celebrate, and there is hope for the future of cities. Like Jeremiah, we have a vision of making our home in Babylon, a world not made according to our wish, but created to serve the divine purpose. It is our calling to work and pray for the good of the city, even if it is the place of our exile.

The descriptions in this book of the consultations and the questionnaire results are evidence of such a pilgrimage. The Working Group has been shown a wide range of Christian location and experience. There is, for example, the thriving suburban church, whose members take on a variety of very significant roles in the urban society around them. Yet such a church is likely not to celebrate that diverse vocation, and still less likely to use that material to create a searching critique of the church, the city and the Christian vocation within the city. In sharp contrast, a struggling inner-urban church may have few members who exercise any decisive role in the city, yet theirs may be a sharply critical voice in the midst of a largely powerless community. And simply because it is so remote from even the lower levers of power, such a church is likely to define its task in terms of the community alliances it is able to forge, with little access to the influence that suburban Christians exercise daily. All city churches, in the inner city, the outer estates and the suburbs are part of the same body, so it is fitting that we should all share the same pilgrimage.

As we have seen, the Biblical understanding of the city is very diverse ranging from horror to delight. In the Bible the city is depicted as the heavenly New Jerusalem, possible only after the total destruction of the corrupt imperial city. It is similarly seen as Nineveh and Babylon, the cities of pagan gods, harbouring the ritually unclean and morally evil. But Babylon is also seen as the place where the exiled Jewish people can make their homes in hope, and from Jerusalem to Rome the city is the place where the Gospel is hopefully and joyfully proclaimed. The city is both an image of God's presence in creation and also the epitome of human ambition, vanity and greed. It is the product of human creativeness and also the result of an abuse of resources, people and relationships. There are constant tensions between what the city could be and what it is, between the dream and the reality.

While Christians may sometimes feel that they do not fully belong to the city, both Scripture and Tradition challenge us to live with this tension. We should wholeheartedly devote ourselves to promoting the welfare of the city in all its parts, despite our discomfort about some of its activities. Christians are always to some extent exiles.

To reiterate a point made at the start of this discussion, theology is not about simple solutions and grand schemes for change, it is about wrestling with insights from inside and outside the church. It is about a pilgrimage through daily life in which Christians seek to respond openly to the whole of human experience. That commitment is to a just and compassionate God, who has revealed in Christ an equal concern for us all; there is no male or female, Jew nor Greek, slave nor free. God places equal value on the lives of each human being and asks of us that we do the same.

Part 7

CONCLUSION AND RECOMMENDATIONS

1. Conclusion

This Report has tried to cover a wide range of complex issues, affecting all aspects of city life and all city dwellers. For this reason, readers are advised to consult the individual sections within Part Five, for detailed conclusions on the major policy areas which the Working Group have sought to address. The paragraphs which follow aim to draw out a number of key points, and to provide the context within which the Working Group's recommendations may be understood.

The introduction to *Faith in the City* (1985), contains the following words, *"Nothing in this report should be interpreted as evidence against our firm belief in an urban future of which all citizens may be proud."* Twelve years later, this Working Group on the Cities would have liked wholeheartedly to endorse this view, but based on the evidence before us, we find it impossible to be entirely confident about the future of Britain's cities. The Working Group's reservations derive from two main factors: first, an awareness of the sheer scale of the economic forces now affecting Britain's cities; and second, a doubt, based on past experience, as to whether any Central Government will have the political will to create the necessary framework of policies and resources, to enable our cities to move confidently into the future, as prosperous, socially just, sustainable and safe places within which to live and work.

Perhaps the most significant urban development since the publication of *Faith in the City*, has been the increasing impact of globalisation and technological innovation, on the economic fortunes of our cities. Views differ about whether their overall effect will be to strengthen or undermine urban economies. It is clear, however, that these forces are accelerating; that we are only at the beginning of a period of instability and adjustment; and that there will be winners and losers among Britain's cities. Meanwhile, the populations of many of our cities are continuing to decline, or at best, stabilise.

The city authorities which the Working Group have met with, seem to be fully aware of the economic context within which they are now operating, and need no persuasion about the importance of fostering economic development. They know that prosperity cannot be taken for granted and that they are engaged in the fiercest of competitions, regionally, nationally and internationally. There is an accepted prescription for economic success for European cities, which depends on them reinventing themselves and focusing their economies around 'people-oriented' activities such as information exchange, culture, creativity, tourism and education. This Report has described the ways in which Salford and Glasgow, for example, are striving to regenerate themselves by putting these ideas into practice. They are doing so, as all cities must, by identifying and maximising their own competitive advantages, and by attracting inward investment and helping small and medium sized businesses to grow.

Economic prosperity is a necessary, but not sufficient, ingredient for a successful city. It is one of the six characteristics of the desired city which emerged from the Working Group's survey of city dwellers. This Vision of the City is not a utopian dream, but rather, a more humane and civilised version of what we already have. Its characteristics are:

- Greater economic prosperity and vitality
- A more socially just society
- A safer city
- A more sustainable city
- A city with a stronger sense of community
- The Church enhancing its role in community life.

This Vision is not unattainable, but if cities are to move closer towards its realisation, public policy will have to change fundamentally, in several important respects. Although individual citizens, business, the Church and local organisations have a vital role to play as partners in this process, central Government alone is in a position to provide the framework to foster and support the necessary changes.

For example, in the years to come, all cities will be compelled to face up to the adverse impact of environmental degradation on economic viability and the quality of life. Projections suggest that technological advances will not be enough to counteract this problem, and the need for significant lifestyle changes seems unavoidable, especially those to diminish car use. This Report shows that British cities lag behind some of their competitors in Europe, in terms of the measures being taken to encourage greater sustainability. Many city dwellers are concerned about environmental issues, but lack a thorough understanding of why sustainability matters and what 'sustainable citizenship' means. Much more needs to be done by Government to raise public awareness, and to provide the leadership for the changes that we must all make in our lifestyles.

In the Working Group's survey, a 'greater sense of community' was the development which most city dwellers thought would make most difference to the quality of city life. Richard Sennett has persuasively argued that there has been a conflict within our cities since at least mediaeval times, between *"on the one hand, the desire to cut free of communal bonds in the name of individual liberty; on the other side, the desire to find a place in which people care about each other"*.[313] All the evidence suggests that we are still struggling with this dichotomy today, and that many people feel that the balance is too firmly in favour of individualism, rather than community. The Working Group believes that local democracy must be reinvigorated, if this situation is to change. This Report has also set out the important role of the Church, in encouraging tolerance and mutual respect, and in diminishing social fragmentation; and of community based organisations, in rebuilding a sense of confidence in particularly disadvantaged city districts.

The Working Group has found however, that the factor which

beyond all others is preventing British cities from moving towards a greater sense of community, and indeed, towards the broader Vision of the balanced, modern city, is 'social exclusion', especially when it is concentrated in disadvantaged neighbourhoods in the inner city and on the periphery. Despite the best efforts of local authorities and community groups, and the investment of substantial Central Government resources through urban regeneration programmes, inequality and social exclusion have increased significantly within our cities over the last decade.

The Working Group believes that in the new sort of economy which is developing, cities will no longer be able to afford social exclusion on the current scale, because this erodes their competitive advantages in many damaging ways. Social exclusion for example, militates against a sense of community and diminishes the feeling of well-being in a city. Social exclusion is also generally associated with high levels of crime, although the exact nature of the relationship is complex, as this Report has shown. In an internationally competitive environment, companies will increasingly decide where to locate on the basis of factors such as these, and severely disadvantaged areas are unlikely to be able to foster the growth of small and medium sized businesses.

These considerations reinforce the fact that policies which encourage social inclusion in our cities are not only morally right, but also make sound economic sense.

This Report shows however, that the potential benefit of urban regeneration programmes will not be realised unless coherent policies are developed and implemented to address the structural factors which adversely affect these places. This means, in particular, measures to alleviate poverty, tackle racism, restructure the housing market, and remove barriers to employment. Government sponsored research emphasises that it has been the failure of governments of all political persuasions to do this in the past, that largely explains the failure of regeneration programmes to turn round these neighbourhoods, and reintegrate their socially excluded inhabitants. The same research also makes clear that unless this happens in the future, inequality and social exclusion are set to increase within our cities, with potentially disastrous effects on the social and economic well-being of all city dwellers. If our cities are to be successful in the future, there is a pressing need to invest more resources in children and young people, particularly but not exclusively, through high quality education and training programmes.

Urban regeneration programmes cannot achieve the necessary transformation in our cities, on their own. Yet they do have a crucial role to play, and in this respect, the Working Group is deeply concerned about the decline in the funding allocated to the most disadvantaged city areas, and about some other features of current regeneration regimes.

At present, regeneration funding is allocated competitively, on the basis of the potential of individual bids to maximise their economic and more socially oriented outputs, by attracting matching funding from the private sector and from other funding sources. The enhanced awareness in these programmes, compared with their predecessors, of the importance of capacity building in disadvantaged city districts, is welcome. However, the Working Group is not persuaded that the current system is necessarily the best, or the most efficient way of allocating scarce resources. The most disadvantaged areas of our cities are in greatest need of regeneration, yet they often (but not always) have less potential than other places, according to these criteria, and therefore lose out in the competition for funds. This is a particular risk for isolated, peripheral housing estates.

The fact that the competitive bidding system is much less efficient than at first appears, can be illustrated by two features: first, local authorities, community groups and others may waste significant amounts of time in devising bids which then fail to attract funding; and second, competition militates against competing bidders sharing good ideas, and can mean that they individually 'reinvent the wheel'. These costs are 'real', are borne by local authorities and communities, and ought to be set against the benefits of competition, when evaluating the overall success of the design of urban regeneration programmes. They are currently ignored in these computations, so are easily forgotten.

The limited way in which the costs and benefits of public policy interventions in our cities are officially measured is a significant barrier to policy reform, because it tends to reflect and reinforce the assumptions which underpin current policies. For example, the costs of social exclusion in British cities, are masked by the separate budget headings under which they fall. Social exclusion is strongly associated with ill health, but the total sum of the increased health costs in disadvantaged districts (eg. extra demand on GP surgeries and hospitals, loss of productivity for workers and of education for school children), is not usually computed. If it was, the cost of social exclusion would become more visible, and the case for change would be strengthened. Similarly, the adverse impact of development on the city environment is often concealed by the lack of an official system of measurement. In contrast, this Report has shown how Sweden, for example, has calculated its environmental debt. This makes visible the cost of failing to repair environmental damage, and emphasises that every adverse factor impacting on the environment carries a cost, which will either have to be paid now, or by future generations.

New systems for measuring the impact of policies and developments on our cities, must therefore be devised and implemented – systems which take into account and actively encourage the transformation which our cities must make, in social, economic and environmental terms, if they are to be successful in the years to come.

Some may argue that Britain cannot afford to address the structural disadvantage of the worst hit neighbourhoods in our cities, but on the basis of the evidence before it, the Working Group would assert that we cannot afford not to do so. Political will to affect policy change at central Government level, is however, the necessary pre-condition for the transformation of our cities. Some trends are moving in support of this. The Working Group's survey of city dwellers shows that there is a widespread desire for our cities to become more humane, better balanced places. Numerous examples of community action in this Report suggest that any Government which manages to persuade city populations that it is determined to improve the quality of city life, and puts in place policies to achieve this, will find that there is a great deal of untapped, local enthusiasm on which to draw. This is particularly true of young city dwellers. Public opinion research shows that young people are increasingly disillusioned with traditional politics, and that the issues about which they feel most strongly include homelessness, unemployment, racism and the environment – all of which this Report has shown to be of crucial importance to the future of our cities.

Britain's cities face enormous challenges in the years ahead, but it would be wrong to assume that this is a new experience. The older British cities in particular have survived many reverses of fortune. London for example, has renewed itself after every crisis it has suffered during nearly two thousand years of development: after the Roman withdrawal, following the disasters of the Plague of 1665 and the Great Fire a year later, and after the Blitz. Cities are therefore resilient, adaptable entities. The Working Group believes that these capacities will be of crucial importance in the years to come, because it is quite clear that Britain's cities must change, if they are to succeed and prosper in the third millennium.

2. Recommendations
Church practice

1. General principles

1.1 The Church affirms the importance of the City as a central part of God's creation, in which all people have the right to share.

1.2 In an increasingly urban society such as Britain today, the City must be central to the Church's concerns, and the Church as a whole must learn to listen to its disciples in cities.

1.3 The Church must develop an expanding and inclusive theology of and for the City, which arises out of the discipleship of its members.

1.4 All Christians who live or work in our cities have a part to play in God's mission. The Church has a responsibility to help them to determine how best they can contribute to this.

1.5 The Church must exercise its leadership and set clear policies to help people to cross the boundaries between Church life and the Church in the City. These should always be designed to make the most efficient use of available resources, in response to emerging opportunities, not out-moded, or unduly defensive priorities. This requires a process of constant review and assessment, reflecting the rapidly changing nature of need in our cities today.

1.6 City churches should identify their wealth of human resources and be willing to share these skills and talents with the wider community.

2. Building bridges within and between communities

2.1 Churches in cities rejoice in the pluralism of their contexts and offer important resources in terms of people and properties.

2.2 Local churches can form alliances and networks with other denominations and communities of other faiths, and take positive steps to develop relationships of mutual trust and respect in their areas.

2.3 Hearings are an excellent way of ensuring that local people's voices are heard, helping churches to increase their understanding of local concerns, and providing opportunities for co-operation and neighbourhood action.

2.4 Minority ethnic groups are making positive contributions in cities, yet the continuing existence and effects of racism and racial harassment require constant vigilance and resistance. Local congregations should take positive steps to eliminate racial injustice within the church, church structures, and the wider community.

2.5 Local churches should reflect theologically upon, and publicise the realities of life in cities, the problems, struggles and achievements, to policy makers and the wider public. At national level, this can be encouraged by active participation in bodies such as the Inner Cities Religious Council, and support for campaigns and ecumenical groups such as Church Action on Poverty and the Churches National Housing Coalition.

2.6 There have been many successful examples of the 'twinning' of Churches in very disadvantaged areas with others in more affluent districts in mutually beneficial ways. The concept of 'twinning' therefore merits consideration and exploration by congregations.

3. Christian vocation

3.1 Many Christians exercise their vocations in city contexts, and need greater encouragement and support from churches in sustaining these.

3.2 The development of the concept of 'Christian citizenship', which is not new to Methodism, may help some Christians to decide how best they can contribute to mission and ministry in cities today.

3.3 Churches should encourage Christians to consider the 'option for the poor', as a response to the Gospel. This includes the challenge for Christians to take their presence, skills and openness to live and work alongside those who are disadvantaged.

3.4 The involvement of young people in Christian mission in cities is often through volunteering schemes, and would benefit from encouragement and recognition.

3.5 Churches should keep the need for new initiatives in mission constantly before them. They should also give greater encouragement to centres with courses that provide resources and utilise city contexts for theology and training for mission and ministry - eg. those already run by the Urban Theology Unit in Sheffield, the Evangelical Coalition for Urban

Mission and others, using the skills and experiences of practitioners in city settings.

4. Involvement in communities

4.1 City churches should consider the scope for increasing their involvement in local community provision, through engaging in partnerships with other local voluntary agencies and joining regeneration networks.

4.2 Churches could take steps to encourage greater involvement by congregations in community provision through, for example, the production of a handbook on 'how to get started', and/or the holding of conferences which celebrate achievements and disseminate good ideas.

4.3 Possible developments to make churches more accessible and welcoming to local people include: longer opening hours, outreach work, and better advertising of events.

4.4 When churches respond to needs and provide services to local people, it is important that these are organised with appropriate management, supervision and support in place.

4.5 Particular attention should be given nationally and locally, to involving young people in the work of churches and to ensuring that their views are actively sought, heard and incorporated within community activities.

4.6 Nationally and locally, the Church is in an excellent position to bring together policy makers and service providers to discuss issues of common concern, and should take every opportunity to do so.

5. Church Life

5.1 Congregations are often charged with the care of buildings that are no longer appropriate, and left with the difficult task of deciding how these resources can be of greatest use to local communities. They may sell or hand over buildings to other local organisations, and relocate themselves to a more suitable site nearby. These situations need to be handled in ways that are sensitive to the deep attachment of some people to particular buildings.

5.2 Architecturally and historically distinguished city churches should be cared for and preserved wherever practical, or altered in ways that preserve the most important features of buildings.

5.3 Appropriate church buildings in cities can be adapted to provide suitable residential accommodation, alongside a worship centre.

5.4 Churches should encourage different styles of Christian presence in city districts, including those which comprise very small numbers of people. In many places, city congregations survive or thrive in very diverse locations, such as community centres, houses, shops, public houses and schools.

5.5 City churches are providing Christians everywhere with opportunities for new forms of devotion and prayer, worship, hymnody and meditation. Churches should encourage, and provide support for, such expressions of indigenous and rooted spirituality from and for the city.

5.6 City contexts are witnessing the developing of new forms of theology that reflect the many cultures represented there, such as Black Theology. Local churches can embrace such developments and so enrich their life.

5.7 Affluent congregations and individual Christians should support the needs of under-resourced congregations in disadvantaged city districts. Finding ways of sharing common wealth is a way of expressing membership of one Body of Christ.

5.8 Much of the Church's work in the City depends on the activities of dynamic individuals and small groups, who are carrying out God's mission in response to the call of Christ. The Church has a responsibility to identify, train, support and sustain these people; and to ensure their accountability to the wider Church.

5.9 New ways in which Churches can relate to each other in urban areas, should be explored. These include ecumenical alliances and the renewal of Methodist interdependency relationships.

Public policy recommendations

If Britain's cities are to develop so as to come closer to the Vision of the balanced, modern city which emerged from the survey carried out among city dwellers for this Report, significant public policy changes are required. The Working Group recognises that Governments cannot insulate cities from many of the forces bearing down on them such as technological innovation and globalisation, but believes that they can help foster the conditions in which city dwellers are better able to take advantage of the opportunities which these forces bring, to the benefit of us all. The Working Group believes that it is also Government's responsibility to safeguard the welfare of particularly vulnerable city dwellers. If Government is to succeed in these tasks, it must work in partnership with the local authorities in our cities, and affirm and support all those who deliver public services to city dwellers.

1. Government's role in providing strategic leadership
   for the regeneration of Britain's cities

> 1.1 Current economic trends suggest that some British cities are likely to fare better than others, in the years to come. It is Government's responsibility to ensure that the quality of life does not deteriorate to an unacceptable degree in any of Britain's cities, as a result.
>
> 1.2 The Department of the Environment should work in partnership with local authorities to ensure the widest possible dissemination of the best regeneration practice. This could be achieved through more support for seminars and conferences, and the publication of reports and briefing papers.
>
> 1.3 New mechanisms must be developed by Central Government, to assess the full social, economic and environmental costs and benefits of proposed public policy interventions in Britain's cities.
>
> 1.4 A high priority should be placed on ensuring that all children and young people, especially those in disadvantaged districts, receive an education which equips them to succeed in the new economy which is evolving in our cities. This means an emphasis on literacy and numeracy, computer skills, flexibility, problem solving and team working.

Supplementary education programmes such as Saturday schools, mentoring schemes and voluntary 'Universities' for school children during the holidays, should be expanded.

2. Regenerating the most disadvantaged city districts

2.1 The current decline in the funding invested in regenerating the most disadvantaged city districts, must be reversed.

2.2 The allocation of urban regeneration funding should not depend exclusively on a system of competitive bidding. Further elements must be introduced, to ensure that very disadvantaged city districts which repeatedly fail to secure funding according to competitive criteria, receive resources too.

2.3 Urban regeneration programmes must be restructured to ensure that there is sustained investment in the most disadvantaged areas, to help them recover from the effects of long term decline.

2.4 Set amounts of funding should be ring-fenced within regeneration programmes, to ensure that an agreed proportion of the available resources is directed specifically at meeting the needs of black communities, and at regenerating very run-down housing estates.

2.5 The costs incurred by voluntary sector organisations in helping to put together and deliver bids, should be recognised and compensated by a system of grants. Funding should also be available to encourage and sustain the local networks which are vital to the long term success of regeneration programmes.

2.6 The increased emphasis on 'capacity building' within regeneration funding programmes is welcome, but more Government support is needed to encourage the further expansion of innovative, community based schemes, such as Credit Unions, LETs schemes and community businesses.

3. Tackling social exclusion

3.1 Government must take steps to restructure the housing market and address more effectively and strategically than at present, the changing housing needs of city populations.

3.2 Housing policy in our cities should focus on: increasing the availability of homes at affordable rents through new building and rehabilitation programmes and the development of measures to stimulate and support the private rented sector; planning transport, employment, shopping and recreation facilities alongside the development of new housing; providing more grants and subsidies to improve owner occupied and rented housing conditions, especially in disadvantaged districts; and developing a strategic programme to prevent and alleviate single homelessness in British cities, especially young single homelessness.

3.3 Government funded programmes to help relieve unemployment in city districts should concentrate on: reconnecting unemployed city dwellers with recruitment channels and labour markets, especially young and long term unemployed people; developing their application skills and self-esteem; and radically improving the quality of vocational education and training.

3.4 Concerted measures are needed to alleviate poverty in city districts. These should include reforms to the benefits system to remove 'benefits traps' and so help unemployed people back into work, including part-time and casual employment; policies to increase the supply of affordable child care for mothers who would like to return to the labour market; and raising the levels of benefits and reviewing their eligibility criteria.

3.5 Racism in our cities will only be combated through the adoption of a strategic, multi-agency approach towards the law, public attitudes and behaviour. Key aims should be to address the serious discrimination currently experienced by many black people in the housing and labour markets.

4. Creating safer cities

4.1 Cost effective, long term crime prevention programmes should be developed in all Britain's cities. These should include schemes to prevent vulnerable adolescents from drifting into crime, such as: mentoring projects; the development of innovative ways of delivering a full-time education to persistent truants and young people who have been excluded from school; much increased investment in the Youth Service; and support for projects in disadvantaged city areas such as family centres, which help keep families together. Local people, including young people, should be involved in the development and running of these services.

4.2 A concerted drug education strategy must be developed by local agencies, including schools, the voluntary sector and the Police, in partnership with local communities, and delivered to children and young people throughout our cities.

4.3 There should be more support for public education initiatives such as 'Zero Tolerance campaigns', which seek to discourage domestic violence; and more local advice and support programmes to help women and children living in violent situations.

4.4 Community based, crime prevention schemes in disadvantaged districts should be expanded, in accordance with local needs and priorities. These might include the upgrading of home security measures; steps to 'design out' the potential for crime; and neighbourhood security schemes for small businesses.

4.5 Mediation projects should be established to help resolve neighbourhood disputes, and tougher measures implemented in more serious cases. To be effective, these must entail more than simply moving 'problem families' from one disadvantaged estate to another. Where appropriate, longer term support and supervision should be available. Those who break the criminal law should be prosecuted by the police.

4.6 The development of an effective prevention strategy in cities, and of more determined responses to racist attacks should be high priorities. Local people must be involved in planning and implementing these programmes.

4.7 City councils should work in partnership with other agencies to develop schemes which encourage more people to go out at night for their leisure, so preventing neighbourhoods from becoming hostile, empty places once darkness falls. Such developments have been shown to increase community self-confidence and so deter crime.

5. Towards more sustainable cities

5.1 Government must do much more to educate city dwellers about what sustainability means, and why it matters, at school and through public education campaigns. Carrying out Environmental Audits and computing the Environmental Debt in British cities would help make clear the cost of failing to improve the city environment.

5.2 Government should encourage the widest possible dissemination of good practice in terms of sustainability, by providing more support for projects being developed under Local Agenda 21.

5.3 Improving air quality in our cities by discouraging car use, ought to be a high priority. Among the policies which should be pursued are ones which: support stricter, EU wide atmospheric pollution measures; significantly enhance public transport systems; encourage the development of 'green cars'; enforce the cleaning up of heavily polluting vehicles; penalise through excise duties and taxation, company cars, non-residential, city centre car parking spaces and heavily polluting vehicles; encourage cycling through more cycle lanes; lead to the pedestrianisation of more city streets and the further development of effective traffic calming measures, in response to local needs.

5.4 A less wasteful approach towards the use of energy and other resources in our cities is required and could be encouraged by, for example: investing more money in energy conservation measures; promoting recycling, by for example, increasing the provision of local facilities, and piloting waste sorting in some areas.

5.5 The creation of 'greener' environments in Britain's cities would greatly improve the quality of city life and could be encouraged by: cleaning up and restoring city parks, squares and open spaces; providing more safe, accessible, playspaces for city children, especially in disadvantaged areas; promoting high quality public architecture, which enhances city districts; promoting 'urban forests, 'wildflower projects' and allotments; and supporting Groundwork Trusts, which improve commercial and industrial environments in British cities.

6. Creating a greater sense of community

6.1 Policies which address social exclusion such as those recommended above, are vital if a greater sense of community is to be generated in Britain's cities.

6.2 Local authorities must take steps to work in partnership with local people, in developing and implementing policy. Consultation exercises must be real rather than 'tokenistic', and should avoid raising unrealistic expectations in the local population. Councils should explore ways of gaining more consumer feedback on policy development and service delivery through for example, local surveys and meetings.

6.3 Local authorities should identify and support, the networks of groups and individuals operating at grass roots level. The ability to foster and promote this activity is likely to be crucial for cities' long term, economic and social success.

6.4 It is important to make good the current deficit in local democracy. This could be achieved by: increasing the proportion of local expenditure which is locally determined; restoring to local authorities, some of the responsibilities which have been removed from them during recent years; and considering the benefits of developing more active, local democratic mechanisms, such as citizens' juries, local referenda and neighbourhood councils.

6.5 City governments should be strengthened by: giving London a city-wide government; considering the role which a mayoral system might play in all our cities; and encouraging the development of 'City Pride' prospectuses and City Vision or Mission Statements.

APPENDICES

1. Motion accepted by Methodist Conference, 1995, setting out aims

2. Survey questionnaire to Methodists in cities

3. Proposals for study and action

Appendix 1

"Proposed Commission on the Cities

The Methodist Conference of 1994 approved the following
Notice of Motion:

A Methodist Commission on the Cities

"The Conference again draws attention to the continually
deteriorating situation in the cities, characterised by poverty,
deprivation, reduction of services and increases in community
problems, especially in inner cities, housing estates and other
poor areas.

The Conference in 1992 and 1993 drew attention to these
problems and requested HM Government to set up a Royal
Commission on the cities. The request gained the support of 80
Members of Parliament, who signed an Early Day Motion
urging the Royal Commission.

The Conference now expresses its great disappointment that
the hoped for Commission has not been set up. However, the
Conference remains convinced of the vital importance of
furthering the concerns of the Petition of Distress from the
Cities and of seeking to work towards a new Vision for the
Cities.

The Conference therefore believes it appropriate to set up a
Methodist Commission on the Cities to consult as widely as
possible on the issues involved. The Conference requests the
Home Mission Division Committee on Urban Mission, NCH
Action For Children, the Division for Social Responsibility and
the Urban Theology Unit to give consideration to this project
and to bring firm proposals, including estimates of cost, to the
Conference of 1995."

In pursuance of this, a Working Party was set up which presented the following report to the Conference of 1995.

The Working Party has met 3 times and submits the following, unanimous Report.

1. Reasons for the Commission

The Working Party considers that the task should be undertaken for several reasons:

i) The time is ripe for people to work together towards a new Vision for the Cities.

ii) There are Biblical and theological perspectives, and spiritualities of the people which have contributions to make towards this vision

iii) The significant changes in government policies and their implications for good and ill for all parts of our contemporary cities.

iv) The opportunities to learn from places where achievements have been registered in the cities.

v) The fact that the needs of different cities vary so greatly.

vi) The increasing divide between most citizens and the poorest 20%; and the redistribution of wealth from poor to rich, eg. by taxes.

vii) Contemporary questions in relation to law and order, health, education, care in the community, employment, housing and economic viability.

viii) The implications of new current concerns over conservation, environment and the quality of life, as these impact on the cities.

ix) The difficulty of looking at all relevant issues together, and the need for seeking the good of the city in all its parts.

2. The Aim of the Commission shall be:

To prepare and present to the Churches and the Nation a Report which shall be:

i) A testimony to the realities of life in the cities today, based on the contemporary experiences of people living there.

ii)   A survey of past and present government and other
      policies and attitudes towards the cities.
iii) A critique of the effects of current government, local
      authority and private and voluntary sector policies on
      the cities.
iv)   Recommendations regarding models for the structure
      and life of cities in the future - Visions of the Cities.
v)   Proposals for action by individuals, churches, local and
      national government, and the private and voluntary
      sectors.
vi)   Some reflections and questions about an appropriate
      spirituality for the church in the city. (Added at
      Conference 1995).

3. Method of Working

The Working Party proposes:

a)   That the term "Working Group" be used, following some
     adverse comment regarding the use of the word
     "Commission."
b)   That the work be conducted within the context of
     existing urban ecumenical relationships and other
     partnerships, utilising the present wide connections of
     the four agencies involved.
c)   The appointment of a small Working Group which
     would operate as a Core Group, on the basis of utilising
     the staffs, memberships and wider constituencies of the
     four agencies.
d)   That the Working Group arrange consultations with
     specific persons from relevant sectors, such as:
     • residents in all sectors of city life
     • policy makers
     • service providers and service users
     • urban, environmental, health and social researchers.
e)   The Working Group would be serviced by a
     researcher/writer.
f)   That the Working Group presents its findings to
     Conference 1996. Subject to being received by
     Conference, the report and other media and study
     material will be made more widely available for an
     Action Programme for the Connexional Year 1996-7

Appendix 2

Survey questionnaire to Methodists in cities

 The Methodist Church

Clare Sparks
Working Group on the Cities
c/o NCH Action For Children
85 Highbury Park
London N5 1UD.

Telephone: 0171-226 2033.
Fax: 0171-226 2537.

October 1995

Dear Friend,

We are inviting you to take part in what could be one of the largest surveys carried out by the Methodist Church. The Working Group on the Cities, which was established at Conference this year, wants you to tell us what living in Britain's cities is really like.

What are the issues that concern you about living in your city? What are your worries for your children? Are there adequate resources for older people in your community? What does your church contribute to community life? What other things do you think the Church should be doing?

The questionnaire that is attached is being sent to churches throughout England, Wales and Scotland. The questionnaires are anonymous, but are coded so we know which town or city you live in. The results will form a vital part of the report of the Working Group that will be brought to Conference in 1996.

Please fill in the questionnaire and encourage as many people as you can from your church to do the same. Please fill out one questionnaire per person. If there are other things you would like us to know, for example if you have information about a local community project that you would like to send us, please attach all that information and send it to us at the address above.

We need all the questionnaires back by the 21st November at the very latest. Your Minister has a Freepost envelope that all the questionnaires from your church can be sent back in, or you can send it back direct to us.

Thanks so much for taking the time to do this,

Clare Sparks.

Clare Sparks
Researcher/Writer
Working Group on the Cities

Cities questionnaire.

Life in the cities.

1. Please tick the three things that you like best about living in the city:

- ☐ Access to jobs
- ☐ Architecture
- ☐ Art galleries
- ☐ Arts (dance/drama/theatres/music)
- ☐ Business opportunities
- ☐ The "buzz" of city life
- ☐ Cinemas
- ☐ Close to family
- ☐ Colleges and universities
- ☐ Eating out
- ☐ Festivals and carnivals
- ☐ Fast food places
- ☐ Friendliness
- ☐ Health services
- ☐ Historic buildings
- ☐ Leisure facilities
- ☐ Libraries
- ☐ Local community groups

- ☐ Local government
- ☐ Multi-faith society
- ☐ Multi-racial society
- ☐ Museums
- ☐ Music venues
- ☐ Neighbourhood community life
- ☐ Nightlife
- ☐ Parks and open spaces
- ☐ People
- ☐ Places of worship
- ☐ Public transport
- ☐ Pubs
- ☐ Schools
- ☐ Shopping
- ☐ Sport/sporting venues
- ☐ Street markets

Other - Please specify _____

2. What do you not like about living in the city? (e.g. crime, noise, traffic)

_____

_____

_____

3. What do you think would improve the quality of life in the cities for:

a) the general community?

_____

_____

b) children?

_____

_____

c) young people?

_____

_____

d) people with disabilities?

_____

_____

e) older people?

_____

_____

4. How do you think your church contributes to the life of your local community?

_____

_____

_____

5. In what other ways do you think your church could improve the quality of life for the people in your local community?

_____

_____

_____

6. Looking ahead into the future, how would you like to see life in the cities developing?

_____

_____

_____

_____

About you

7. How old are you? (please tick the appropriate box)

☐ Up to 13   ☐ 14-17   ☐ 18-29   ☐ 30-49   ☐ 50-64   ☐ 65 or over

8. What sex are you? (please tick)

☐ Male   ☐ Female

9. Please tick the category that you consider best describes your ethnic or racial origin:

☐ White
☐ Black - Caribbean
☐ Black - African
☐ Black Other - Please specify _____
☐ Indian
☐ Pakistani
☐ Bangladeshi
☐ Chinese
☐ Other - Please specify _____

10. Would you say you live in: (please tick)

☐ an inner city area of a large city?
☐ the suburbs or outskirts of a large city?
☐ a small city/large town?

11. Do you live in a multicultural area?

☐ Yes   ☐ No

12. Roughly how long have you lived in a city? (please tick)

☐ Under 1 year   ☐ 1 to 5 years   ☐ 6 to 10 years
☐ Over 10 years   ☐ All your life

13. Could you please tick the box that best describes your current situation.

☐ In education
☐ Retired
☐ Employed
☐ Unemployed and dependent upon benefits
☐ At home
☐ Other - Please specify _____

Appendix 3

Proposals for study and action

"For study and action"

The Methodist Conference of June 1996 directed that "specific proposals for action by the Methodist Church" be brought to the Conference of June 1997.

These specific proposals will be the Proposals in Part Seven, plus some of their implications.

These will be published separately, together with a Study Guide for Churches and Members, to assist the process started by this Report.

Please address enquiries regarding Booklets and Study Materials to one of the following:

Rev. John Kennedy
The Methodist Church
Unit 1
Central Buildings
London SW1H 4NH

Rev. Bill Lynn
NCH Action For Children
85 Highbury Park
London N5 1UD

Rev. Inderjit Bhogal
Urban Theology Unit
210 Abbeyfield Road
Sheffield S4 7AZ"

NOTES

1   *Staying in the city*, A report by the Bishops Advisory Group
     on Urban Priority Areas, Church House Publishing,1995.p31.
2   *Civilisation*, by K. Clark, BBC Books, 1969. p4.
3   *Victorian cities* by A. Briggs, Penguin 1968. p72.
4   G.M. Young, quoted in Briggs, supra
5   *Poverty in the United Kingdom* by P. Townsend, 1979 Penguin,
     quoted p45, *Socio-demographic change and the inner city*,
     DOE 1995, HMSO
6   p45 *Socio-demographic change and the inner city*, supra
7   p93,   "   "   "
8   *The Inquiry into income and wealth*, Joseph Rowntree
     Foundation, 1995
9   Note vii, pp. 53-8.
10   *The Economy of cities*, J. Jacobs, 1969
11   *Medieval economy and society*, by M.M. Postan,
     Penguin, 1972. pp9-10.
12   Note ix, p239.
13   *Tudor England*, by S.T. Bindoff, Penguin, 1950. p30.
14   Note xiii, p293.
15   *Docklands* by S. Williams, Phaidon, 1993, p10.
16   Note 3, p59.
17   Note 3, p184.
18   *Cities of tomorrow*, by P. Hall, Blackwell, 1988, p48.
19   Quoted p109, supra
20   *The containment of urban England* (2 vols) by Hall, Thomas,
     Gracey and Drewett, Allen and Unwin, 1973,
     Quoted p306, Hall supra
21   *An anarchist approach to housing*, by C. Ward,
     Freedom Press, 1976, p51.
22   *Cities of tomorrow*, supra, p225.
23   *Race, urban policy and urban problems: a critique on current
     UK Practice*, by Ian Munt in Urban Studies,
     Vol. 28, No.2, 183-203, 1991
24   *Unequal city*: final report of the Birmingham inner city study;
     Inner London: proposals for dispersal and balance: final report
     of the Lambeth inner city study; and *Change or decay*:
     final report of the Liverpool inner area study. All HMSO, 1977
25   *Urban economic development: new roles and relationships*,
     by Young and Mason, Macmillan, 1983

26   Social regeneration: directions for urban policy in the 1990s,
      by Colenutt, Centre for Local Economic Strategies, 1992

27   London: the emerging Docklands city by R. Ward in Built
      Environment, Volume 12, 1986,
      quoted in Cities of Tomorrow by Hall, supra

28   As pointed out in Docklands, by Williams, supra

29   Urban regeneration and economic development: the local
      government dimension, by the Audit Commission, HMSO, 1989

30   Rethinking urban policy: city strategies for the global economy,
      M. Ward, Centre for Local Economic Strategies, 1994, p38.

31   Citizens and cities: urban policy in the 1990s, by D. Hill,
      Harvester, 1994, p108-9.

32   1981: The Brixton Disorders, 10-12 April 1981:
      Report of an Inquiry by the Rt.Hon the Lord Scarman OBE,
      HMSO, 1982

33   Urban regeneration and the voluntary sector: a report on the
      new cities 1994 conference, NCVO, 1994

34   Community involvement in city challenge, a policy report,
      NCVO, 1993

35   Assessing the impact of urban policy
      by B. Robson et al, 1994, HMSO

36   in Behind the chimera of urban funding by Nevin and Shiner,
      in Local Work No.52, June 1994,
      Centre for Local Economic Strategies

37   The SRB: taking stock, by S. Hall, in Planning Week, 27/4/1995

38   The SRB: urban funding and the future for distressed
      communities by Nevin and Shiner, in Local Work No. 58,
      Centre for Local Economic Strategies, January 1995

39   See footnote 36 supra

40   "   "   "   "

41   Invisible partners, the impact of the SRB on black communities,
      by J. Crook, NCVO, 1995

42   See footnote 35

43   See footnote 36

44   SRB, First report of the Environment Select Committee,
      House of Commons, HMSO, 1995

45   See footnote 35

46   "   "   "

47   Further to go: an assessment of the 1996/7 SRB approvals and
      their impact on voluntary and community organisations,
      by the Urban Forum, NCVO, 1996

48   This has been the conclusion of some academic evaluations, eg.
      Urban Trends 1, PSI, 1992, p81 .

49   See footnote 36

50   from *Letters to the clergy on the Lord's prayer and the Church*, by John Ruskin, 1880

51   *Reuniting the cities* by Hilary Russell, in *Keeping faith with the cities*, Christian Socialist Movement, 1995, p8.

52   *England in the eighteenth century*, by J.H. Plumb, Penguin, 1950, pp42-44.

53   *Public Interiors* ed. by M. Kloos, Arcam Press, Amsterdam, 1993, p19.

54   *Faith in the city*, the Report of the Archbishop of Canterbury's Commission on Urban Priority areas, Church House Publishing, 1985, p63. footnote 3; p31.

55   p210, footnote 3.

56   *Faith in the City*, supra, p27ff.

57   p93, footnot e23

58   *In the streets of every city*, by T. Holden, 1988

59   *Two nations, one Gospel?* 1981; *What churches can do*, ed. G. Rogers, 1982; *Gospel from the poor,* ed. J. Vincent, 1984, Urban Theology Unit (UTU), Methodist Home Mission Division. *A Petition of Distress from the Cities* (ed. J. Vincent, 1993 UTU/Methodist Home Mission Division) was presented on 21st April 1993 on behalf of Methodist inner city and housing estate ministers and community workers, by Kathleen Richardson, Tony Holden and John Vincent

60   *The Church on the housing estate* by T. Lockwood, 1993

61   *Policy and priorities*, by the Methodist Church Urban Mission Committee 1995

62   quoted in *Staying in the city*, supra

63   *The 1991 Census*, HMSO

64   *Report on the state of world population*, United Nations 1996

65   Except that is some cities, such as Glasgow and Cardiff, a significant proportion of the population is concentrated on peripheral estates. The sample of people who responded to our questionnaire under represented this group in these cities.

66   Unfortunately, a small number of Ministers of churches not situated within cities were also sent questionnaires by mistake. This was a result of the erroneous self-classification of churches on the Methodist Church database from which the sample was selected.

67   *The Blue Guide to England*, A & C Black Ltd, 1995, p690.

68   *Socio-demographic change and the inner city*, DOE 1995, p21.

69   see earlier section on the history of British cities

70   The Housing Act 1996 gives successful homeless applicants
     the right to only temporary accommodation, rather than a
     permanent home
71   An additional meeting was held in Glasgow at a later date with
     representatives of the Methodist Church in Scotland, that
     discussion informing some of the later Sections in this Report
72   Glasgow's health: old problems, new opportunities,
     Greater Glasgow Health Board, 1993, p16.
73   Working together for Glasgow's health: Glasgow City health
     plan 1995, Glasgow City Council, p11.
74   Civic Guide, Salford City Council, 1990
75   Blue Guide to England, supra, p571.
76   quoted in The Classic Slum: Salford life in the first quarter
     of the century, by R. Roberts, Penguin, 1971
77   p49, supra
78   p238, supra
79   Figures from Salford: the city of opportunity,
     Salford City Council Economic Development Unit
80   See footnote 75
81   For information about the City Pride initiative see
     section on Urban Policy
82   A list presented in a lecture on the future of urban regeneration
     by Brian Robson, Professor of Geography and Vice Chancellor
     of Manchester University, at the annual conference of BASSAC
     in Manchester, Autumn 1995
83   Manchester City Pride: a focus for the future
84   The Lowry Centre, a project for the millennium,
     Salford City Council
85   See footnote 80
86   The argument set out over the following paragraphs is heavily
     based on Between Sheffield and Stuttgart: Amsterdam in an
     integrated Europe and a competitive world economy,
     by J. O'Loughlin, in Understanding Amsterdam:
     essays on economic vitality, city life and urban form, ed.
     by L. Deben, W. Heinemeijer, and D. van der Vaart,
     Het Spinhuis, 1993
87   European cities, the informational society and the global
     economy, by M. Castells, in Understanding Amsterdam etc..
     1993, supra, p10.
88   Rethinking urban policy: city strategies for the global economy,
     by M. Ward, CLES, 1994, p9.
89   Turn up the lights: a survey of cities in the Economist magazine,
     1995, p7.

90   *Urban Economics*, by A. Evans, Blackwell, 1994, p112.
91   See footnote 86
92   See footnote 87, and Robson, supra
93   Castells, p12-13, supra, also *The Empty Raincoat*,
      by C. Handy, p251.
94   *The stimulus of a little confusion*, by E. Soja, in
      Understanding Amsterdam, supra
95   by O'Loughlin, see footnote 85, supra
96   *Islands of renewal in seas of decay*, by B. Berry, in *The new
      urban reality*, ed. by P. Petersen, The Brookings Institute, 1985;
      Gentrification of the city, by N. Smith and P. Williams,
      Allen and Unwin, 1986
97   O'Loughlin, supra
98   *Socio-demographic change and the inner city*, supra, para. 6.1 ff.
99   para. 6.30-6.43, supra
100 *Cities of tomorrow*, P. Hall, supra, p400.
101 Households below average income statistics, cited in
      Poverty: the facts, by C.Oppenheim, CPAG, 1996
102 *Losing ground*, by C. Murray, Basic Books, 1984
103 *The emerging British underclass*, Institute of Economic Affairs,
      1990
104 *Socio-demographic change and the inner city*, supra, pp96-7.
105 See footnote 99, supra
106 *Homeownership: differentiation and fragmentation*,
      by Forrest, Murie and Williams, Unwin Hyman, 1990
107 *Cities and housing after the welfare state*, by A. Murie,
      Amsterdam Study Centre for the Metropolitan
      Environment, 1994
108 *Social Trends* 1995, HMSO, Chart 10.1, p173.
109 *Cities and housing after the welfare state*, supra, p19.
110 by Murie, in *Cities and housing* etc. supra
111 *Social Trends*, 1995, HMSO, Chart 10.2, p175.
112 *Social Trends* 1995, HMSO, Table 10.17, p181.
113 *Socio-demographic change and the inner city*, supra, p76.
114 Research carried out by Coventry City Council, 1990,
      and the Spitalfields Skills Audit, cited p76
      Socio-demographic change, supra
115 *A new geography of centers and margins*, by S. Sassen in
      Cities in a world economy, Pine Forge Press California, 1994

116 *Explaining persistent inner-city unemployment*: a case study in Nottingham, by Green, Maguire, Roberts & Wray, in *Local Economy*, 1991; *Recruitment in local labour markets: employer and employee perspectives*, by Elias and White, Research Paper 86, Department of Employment, 1991

117 *Bridging the gap: skills, training and barriers to employment in Bristol*, by J. Lovering, SAUS, Bristol University, 1991

118 *Socio-demographic change and the inner city*, supra, p83.

119 *The beneficiaries of employment growth: an analysis of the experience of disadvantaged groups in an expanding labour market*, by Buck & Gordon, in *Critical issues in urban economic development*, Vol. II, ed. by Hausner, Clarendon, 1987

120 *Local authority aid to industry: an evaluation*, by Cameron et al, DoE, 1982; *Economic development policies: an evaluation study in the Newcastle Metropolitan region*, by Robinson et al, 1987, Clarendon

121 We have already seen that by this definition, about a quarter of Britain's population is currently living in poverty, see page.....

122 *Socio-demographic change* etc., supra, reported pp54-5.

123 *The Poor are poorer*, by P. Townsend, Statistical Monitoring Unit, Bristol University, 1991

124 *Family spending 1990*, OPCS, 1992

125 *Socio-demographic change*, supra, Figures from CIPFA, reported Table 5.2, p51.

126 *Low income statistics*: Households below average income tables, HMSO, 1991

127 Review of the economy and employment, by the Institute for Employment Research, University of Warwick, 1994

128 *Work and welfare: tackling the jobs deficit*, by Balls and Gregg, Commission on Social Justice, IPPR, 1994

129 *Poverty close to home*, by H. Russell, Mowbray, 1995, p58.

130 *Work force restructuring, social insurance coverage & the black economy*, by C. Hakim, Journal of Social Policy, 18.4, 1989

131 *Explaining persistent inner-city unemployment*, by Green et al, Local Economy 1991

132 *Some remarks on informal work, polarisation and the social structure*, by R. Pahl, *International journal of urban and regional research*, 12, 1988

133 *Social Trends 1995*, HMSO, Table 2.11, p34.

134 *Moving off Income Support: barriers and bridges*, DSS, 1996

135 *Report of the Inquiry into income and wealth*, Joseph Rowntree Foundation, 1995

136 *Report of the Inquiry into Income and Wealth*, JRF, 1995, supra

137   *The Health of the Nation: variations in health*, DoH, 1995

138   See for example, *Low Income, food, nutrition and health: strategies for improvement*, Nutrition Task Force, DoH; *Poverty and Nutrition*, NCH Action For Children, 1992

139   *A lost generation?* (1991), *Poor expectations* (1995) and *Unequal opportunities* (1994), all NCH Action For Children.

140   *Credit and debt in Britain*, by Berthoud and Kempson, PSI, 1990

141   *Patterns of Afro-Caribbean migration and settlement in Great Britain: 1945-1981*, by C. Peach, in *The Caribbean in Europe*, ed. by C. Brock, Frank Cass publishers, 1986; also, *Transients, settlers and refugees. Asians in Britain*, by V. Robinson, Clarendon Press, 1986

142   *The Politics of race and residence*, by S. Smith, Polity Press, 1989

143   *Ethnic minorities and council housing in Glasgow*, by Bowes, McCluskey and Sim, in New Community 16 (4), July 1990

144   DoE figures, reported p35 *Socio-demographic change and the inner city*, supra

145   *Ethnic minorities and council housing in Glasgow*, supra

146   *Socio-demographic change and the inner city*, supra, p31.

147   *Social Trends 1994*, Chart 4.29, p78.

148   *Britain's ethnic minorities*, by T. Jones, PSI, 1993; *Positive action employment and training: developing local initiatives*, by M. Boddy, in Local Economy 7.1, 1992

149   *The beneficiaries of employment growth: an analysis of the experience of disadvantaged groups in the expanding labour market*, by N. Buck and I. Gordon, in *Critical issues in urban economic development*, Volume II, ed. by V. Hausner, Clarendon, 1987

150   *Report of the Inquiry into Income and Wealth*, JRF, 1995, supra

151   *Socio-demographic change and the inner city*, supra, p99.

152   *Staying the course: the role and structure of community regeneration organisations*, by S. Thake, JRF, 1995

153   Reported in *A bit of cheer. But only for some*, by B. Hughill, the *Observer* , 11/8/1996

154   Reported in *Money...who needs it?* by D. Sandler, in the *Independent on Sunday*, 1/9/1996

155   *Community networks in urban regeneration: 'it all depends who you know'*, by C. Skelcher, A. McCabe, V. Lowndes and P. Nanton (University of Birmingham), Policy Press, 1996. (in association with the Joseph Rowntree Foundation

156   *Staying the course*, supra

157 *British Crime Survey*, Home Office, 1994 HMSO;
Anxiety about crime, findings from the British Crime Survey,
Home Office Research and Planning Unit, 1996
158 *Social Trends, 1995*, HMSO, Tables 9.2 and 9.3, p155.
159 *Social Trends*, supra, Table 9.8, p157.
160 *Racial attacks and harassment, first report of the Home Affairs Committee session 1989-90*, HC/17, Cm 1058
161 Reported in *Citizens and cities - urban policy in the 1990s*,
by D. Hill, Harvester, 1994, p149.
162 *One in ten non-white households suffer racial harassment*,
by M. Braid, in the Independent newspaper, 11/3/1993
163 *Racial attacks: a survey in eight areas of Britain*, CRE, 1987;
Multiple victimisation: racial attacks on an east London estate,
Crime Prevention Unit paper 36, Home Office, 1992. Both
reported in *Citizens and cities* etc. by D. Hill, supra
164 Reported in *Now and then: an index of childhood*, by
D. Holder, in the *Independent on Sunday* 8/9/1996
165 *More sinned against than sinning*, by Hartless et al,
British Journal of Criminology, January 1995
166 *Children and young people: drug misuse services*,
NHS Advisory Services, 1996; *Young people in 1992*,
Schools Health Education Unit, University of Exeter, 1993
167 *Young people and crime*, by J. Graham and B. Bowling,
Home Office, 1995
168 *Reclaiming the streets, Nursery World*, 16/11/1996
169 *Rethinking urban policy*, by M. Ward, CLES, 1994, supra, p27.
170 *Social Trends 1995*. Based on a survey of 54,000 shops carried
out by the British Retail Consortium in 1993, Table 9.5, p156, .
171 See for example, *Young people and crime*, by J. Graham and
B. Bowling, Home Office, supra
172 *Social Trends, 1995*, Table 9.14, p160.
173 *Aspects of crime: young offenders 1994*,
Home Office Research and Statistics department, 1995
174 *Setting the record straight: juvenile crime in perspective*,
by S. Ruxton, NCH Action For Children, 1993
175 *Crime and the Family*, by D. Utting, FPSC, 1993
176 *Community safety, crime prevention and the local authority*,
by J. Bright, in *Policing and the community*, ed. by P. Wilmott,
PSI, 1987
177 *The Politics of the police*, by R. Reiner, Wheatsheaf, 1985
178 *National Prison Survey*, OPCS, 1991

179 Research carried out, for example, by D. Dickinson, University of Cambridge, reported in *Poverty close to home*, by H. Russell, supra

180 *Prison Statistics*, Home Office, 1992; National Prison Survey, 1991, OPCS

181 *Poverty close to home*, by H. Russell, supra, p150.

182 For example, *Unhealthy societies* by R. Wilkinson, 1996, Routledge

183 *The emerging British underclass*, by C. Murray, 1990, IEA

184 *The demoralisation of society*, by G. Himmelfarb, 1995, IEA

185 *The drop out society: young people on the margin*, by C. Wilkinson, Youth Work Press, 1995

186 Youthaid estimates, based on analysis of Labour Force Survey statistics, reported in *A lost generation?* NCH Action For Children, 1993

187 *A lost generation?* NCH Action For Children, 1993, supra

188 *Young people and crime*, by J. Graham and B. Bowling, supra

189 *Families, children and crime*, ed. by A. Coote, IPPR, 1994

190, 191 Labour Force Survey, CSO, reported *Social Trends* 1996

192 *Young people and crime*, by J. Graham and B. Bowling,1996

193, 194 *Setting the record straight*, by S. Ruxton, NCH Action For Children, 1993

195 *Rethinking urban policy*, supra, p24.

196 *Safer communities, safer Britain*, Labour Party, 1995, p13.

197 Reported in *Peace on the street where you live*, by D. Donnison, *Guardian* 25/10/1995

198 by M. Ward, in *Rethinking urban policy*, supra

199 Consumer Association survey of 1000 civilians and 400 police officers, reported in the *Independent* 30/7/1996

200 *Social Trends, 1995, supra*, Table 9.12, p159.

201 *Partnerships in practice*, DoE 1993, p114.

202 This summary is based on one produced by the Local Government Management Board (which services the Local Agenda 21 initiative in the UK), *Greening economic development*, reported in *Rethinking urban policy*, by M. Ward, supra

203 Reported in *How we can clear the air*, by N. Schoon and D. Osborn, in the *Independent* 22/9/1996

204 Figures from the European Environment Agency, reported in *How we can clear the air*, supra

205 *Social Trends 1995*, supra, p192.

206 Reported in *How we can clear the air*, supra

207 *Rethinking urban policy*, by K. Smyth, in Local Work, March 1995, CLES

208, 209 *One False move – a study of children's independent mobility*, by Hillman et al, PSI, 1990

210 *Independent mobility and children's physical development*, by N.Armstrong, in *Children, Transport and Quality of Life*, ed. Hillman, PSI, 1995

211 *Independent mobility and children's mental and emotional development*, by S. Kegerreis, in *Children, Transport* etc, supra

212 In *How We Can Clear the Air*, supra

213 *Rethinking Urban Policy*, by M. Ward, CLES, 1994, supra, p29.

214 *Social Trends, 1995*, supra, Table 11.5, p189.

215 *Architecture: a modern view*, by Sir Richard Rogers, Thames & Hudson, 1990, p60.

216 Reported in *Manchester gears up for facelift*, by M. Halsall, in the *Guardian* 5/9/1996

217 *The death and life of great American cities*, by J. Jacobs, Jonathan Cape, 1962

218 *Man about town: Frank Lloyd Wright in New York city*, by H. Muschamp, MIT Press, 1983

219 The Lambeth Community Care Centre was built by Edward Cullinan architects during 1980-85. See *London: a guide to recent architecture*, by S. Hardingham, Artemis, 1994, p106.

220 ESRC funded research study by L. Martens, reported in *Waiting on the Cafe Rouge revolution*, by G. Cooper, in the *Independent* 31/71/1996

221 In *Variations on a theme park*, by D. Sudjic, *Guardian* 5/9/1996

222 *Greening the city*, by K. Chambers, in *Prospect*, (the Journal of the Royal Incorporation of Architects in Scotland) 96 58, 1995

223 *Creating a sustainable London*, Sustainable London Trust, 1996; *Growing food in cities*, T.Garnett, National Food Alliance, 1996

224 In Greening the city, supra

225, 226 *Partnerships in practice*, supra; *Independent mobility and children's rights*, by M.Rosenbaum, in *Children, transport and the quality of life*, ed. Hillman, PSI 1995

227,228,229,230 *The ecological city*, Report to the OECD, Swedish National Board of Housing, Building & Planning,1995

231 *Social Trends, 1995*, supra, Table 11.2, p188.

232 *Creating a sustainable London*, supra, p20.

233,234 *Partnerships in practice, partnerships in change*, DoE, 1994, supra, p114ff, p116.

235 Reported in *Pool of fears*, by D. Carlisle, *Guardian* 7/8/1996

236   The following list is based heavily on one proposed by
     N. Schoon in his article, *How We Can Clear the Air*, supra

237   *Ruling Britannia*, by A. Marr, Michael Joseph, 1995

238   *Social Trends, 1995*, supra, Table 13.3, p216.

239   *The strange death of civic America*, by R. Putnam,
     Prospect magazine, March 1996

240   *The Classic slum*, by R. Roberts, Penguin, 1971, supra

241   *Social Trends, 1995*, supra, pp220-221.

242   A point made in *Powerful whispers*, by the Bradford
     Metropolitan Faith in the City Forum, 1995, on p35.

243   *Cities within cities*, by A. Anderson, in *New Scientist*,
     The future supplement, 15/10/1994, quoted in *The creative city*,
     by C. Landry and F. Bianchini, supra, p15.

244   *The philosopher in the city*, by H. Arkes, Princeton
     University Press, 1981; quoted in *Citizens and cities*,
     by D. Hill, supra, p.3.

245   *Subversive language of citizenship*, by D. Marquand,
     Guardian 2/1/1989

246   *Cities and citizenship*, by D. Hill, supra, pp1-8.

247   From the *ADT Fourth World Journal*, Spring 1994. by J. Penet,
     quoted in *Poverty close to home*, by H. Russell, supra, on p259.

248   It is important to acknowledge that this view of community
     would not be universally accepted. Right wing, libertarian
     thinkers tend to see community in a more limited way, in terms,
     for example, of small groups which people may choose to
     contract into, or not. The emphasis of these thinkers is
     essentially on the individual, acting within a market context.
     See for example, *Social justice, Labour and the New Right*,
     by R. Plant, *Fabian pamphlet 556*, Fabian Society, 1993

249,250   *The rise of do-it-yourself democracy*, by A. Marr,
     Independent 18/1/1996

251   *The creative city*, by C. Landry and F. Bianchini,
     Paper 12, Demos,1995, pp5-7.

252   Royal Commission on local government in Greater London,
     1857-60 (*The Herbert Report*), Cmd 1164, HMSO, 1960;
     Committee of Inquiry into the conduct of local authority
     business (*the Widdicombe Report*); Cmd 9797, HMSO, 1986

253   *Rethinking urban policy*, by M. Ward, supra, p38.

254   *The road to serfdom*, by F. von Hayek, Routledge, 1944

255   *Democracy in America*, by A. de Tocqueville, ed. H. Heffner,
     Mentor Books, 1956, Part 2, Book 2, Section 28t.

256   *Accountable to none*, by S. Jenkins, Penguin, 1995, p256ff.

257   *National rot, patent remedy*, by Sir C. Patten,
      Independent 15/9/1995

258   See for example, *Power to the people of London town*,
      by A. Whittam Smith, the *Independent* 15/7/1996

259   *Citizens juries*, by J. Stewart et al, IPPR, 1994

260   *The Citizen's charter: raising the standard*,
      Cmd 1559, HMSO, 1991

261   *Citizens and cities*, by D. Hill, supra, P220.

262   *Accountable to none*, supra, p261.

263   quoted in *Gloom will bring us together*, by A. Marr,
      in the *Independent* 9/9/1995

264   In an article on Communitarianism by A. Coote,
      in the *Independent* 3/7/1995

265   *Social Trends, 1995*, supra, Table 13.14, p222.. The 'Trinitarian
      Churches' comprise the Anglican, Presbyterian, Methodist,
      Baptist, Roman Catholic, Orthodox and Other Free Churches.

266   *MAPP guide*, by T.Holden, 1995, *Monitoring of projects*
      by M.Mackley, 1994, both Methodist Home Mission Division;
      also MAPP monitoring group, *Agenda of the Methodist
      Conference*, 1996, pp 223-237.

267   *The unsecular city: the revival of religion in east London*,
      by G. Smith in *Rising in the East: the regeneration of East
      London*, ed. T. Butler & M. Rustin, Lawrence & Wishart, 1996

268   by A. Mawson, in *Community regeneration*, p147,*Church for
      the city*, ed. E. Blakebrough, Darton, Longman & Todd, 1995

269   *Church ministry in London*, by R. Chartres, in *Church for the
      city*, supra, p29.

270   *Faith in the City*, The Report of the Archbishop of Canterbury's
      Commission on urban priority areas, supra;
      the *Petition of distress from the cities*, supra

271   *Race for the millenium*, by D. Haslam, CCBI, 1996

272   This was substantially, the conclusion reached during the
      meeting of representatives of Methodism in Scotland which the
      Working Group convened

273   *London's racial crisis*, by K. Leech, in *Church for the city*, supra

274   See *Called to love and praise - the nature of the Christian Church
      in Methodist experience and practice*, Methodist Conference
      paper 1995, section 3.2.12

275   *London's racial crisis*, by Leech, supra, pp71-2. This also
      substantially reflects the views expressed by the theologian,
      Robert Beckford, who teaches at Queen's College, Birmingham,
      and whose opinions the Working Group sought as part of the
      process of preparing this Report.

276 A point made in *Poverty close to home*, by H. Russell, p124.
277 *Powerful Whispers*, the report of the Bradford urban hearings, produced by the Bradford Metropolitan Faith in the City Forum
278 *Faith from the city*, ed. by C.Rowland and J. Vincent, Vol. 2 of *British Liberation Theology* series, UTU, 1996
279 *Faith in the city*, supra, para. 3.7, p49.
280 *Clericalism, church and laity*, by A. Dyson, in *All are called: Towards a theology of the laity: essays from a working party of the General Synod Board of Education under the Chairmanship of the Bishop of Oxford*, CIO, 1985, pp13-16.
281 *Church ministry in London*, by R. Chartres in *Church for the city*, supra, p40.
282 *Hymns of the city*, ed. J. Vincent, UTU 1996; *City prayers*, ed. M. Wallace, Norwich - Canterbury Press, 1994
283 by R. Chartres, supra
284 *Journeying with God: paradigms of power and powerlessness*, by A. Smith, Sheed and Ward, 1990, p108.
285 From *Biblical sense of self-esteem*, by M. Bunting, in the *Guardian* 7/2/1996
286 *Church ministry in London*, by R. Chartres, in *Church for the city*, p46-7.
287 Reported in *Fresh script for east-enders*, by M. Simmons, in the *Guardian* 14/8/1996
288 *Into the city*, by J. Vincent, Epworth Press, 1982; *A public house of God*, *Methodist Recorder*, 11/4/1996; *The Outside Church*, by D. Calvert, Methodist Division of Property, 1993
289 *Situation analysis*, by J. Vincent, UTU 1976; *Faith in the City* (supra), pp367-370
290 *Index of Deprivation, Urban Priority Areas*, Church House, London, 1995
291 eg. by R. Chartres, in *Church ministry in London*, supra
292 For Anglican *Faith in the City* projects see *Staying in the city*, Church House Publishing 1995, *Hope in the city? The local impact of the Church Urban Fund*, CRESR, Sheffield Hallam University, 1994; for MAPP projects, see *Monitoring of projects* by M.Mackley, 1994, both Methodist Home Mission Division; also MAPP monitoring group, pp 223-237 *Agenda of the Methodist Conference*, 1996

293   The bi-annual Urban Mission Congresses arranged by the
       Evangelical Coalition for Urban Mission are notable. The first,
       Jesus in the City, was held in Liverpool, November 1995.
       Details from ECUM. The annual Urban Mission May
       Consultation at UTU in Sheffield, organised by UTU and the
       Methodist Urban Mission Committee, is a more concentrated
       seminar on specific themes. Details from UTU. There are now
       also four-yearly International Congresses on Urban Ministry,
       the first being in Nairobi, November 1996. Details from IUMN.
294   *Social Justice in the Ancient Near East and the People of the
       Bible*, by L.Epsztein, SCM Press, 1986
295   *Pagans and Christians*, by R. Lane Fox, Viking, 1991
296   *Fathers and Heretics*, by Prestige, SPCK, 1940
297   op.cit
298   *The political writings of St. Augustine*, by H:Prolocki,
       Gateway, 1982
299   *Florence and the Medici*, by J.Hale, Thames and Hudson, 1977
300   *The City in history*, by L. Mumford, Secker and Warburg, 1961
301   *The Thirty Years War*, by G.Parker, Routledge, 1987
302   *The Embarassment of Riches*, by S. Schama, Fontana, 1987
303   *The Reformation*, by O. Chadwick, Penguin, 1964
304   *Religion and Political Culture in Britain and Ireland*,
       by D. Hempton, Cambridge University Press, 1966
305   op.cit
306   *Gladstone*, by R.Jenkins, Macmillan, 1995
307   *Victorian Cities*, by A. Briggs, Penguin 1963
308   *The idea of Poverty* by G. Himmelfarb, Faber, 1985
309   *History of the Methodist Church*, (vol.4)
       ed. by G.Davis and G. Rupp, Epworth, 1964
310   *God in the inner city*, by L.Green, Urban Theology Unit, 1993
311   *Into the City*, by J.Vincent,Epworth Press, 1982
312   *Being Church as Political Practice*, by A.Davey, in C.Rowland
       and J.Vincent (eds) *Liberation Theology UK vol.1*, of British
       Liberation Theology, Urban Theology Unit, 1995, pp55-74,
313   *Flesh and Stone: the body and the city in Western Civilisation*,
       by R. Sennett, Faber & Faber, 1994, p.159.